CITIES
OF
INDIA
PAST & PRESENT

CITIES OF INDIA
PAST & PRESENT

G.W. FORREST

English Edition

PUBLISHERS AND DISTRIBUTERS
404, Ravi Building, 189/191 D.N. Road, Fort, Mumbai 400001

Publisher's Note

A S somebody sagaciously once observed: "History never goes out of fashion". One may well add that "nostalgia also never goes out of fashion". Consequently, we, as publishers, felt that we should project history (and the accompanying nostalgia) through a different perspective, i.e., through the birth, evolution and growth of certain cities which have attained prominence for one reason or the other. The result is this captivating volume, which seeks to transport the reader back in time when the Raj, played a very influential role in the subcontinent. The old, if somewhat peculiar, spellings of cities and monuments have been retained, chiefly in order to evoke the flavour and the authenticity of the bygone era. Also, a volume like this serves another significant purpose in that it provides valuable source material for historians and other researchers.

We hope that this book will keep the reader enthralled and stimulate his or her curiosity and interest to delve further into the subject.

Preface

THE sketches which are here collected and reprinted were some of the records of many journeys at the time the writer's avocations led him to travel almost yearly across the continent of India. They were labours of love, written during the intervals of graver occupations, and the author trusts that the work may reflect some of his own keen enjoyment in these cities, and some of their serene charm and Oriental enchantment. He has endeavoured, both by conversation and reading, to enter into the spirit of the times in which each temple or mosque or palace was produced, and into the manners and customs of those who erected it. By selections from the ancient records and old books of travels, and the great Anglo-Indian classics, he has endeavoured to give life to old scenes, and to reproduce sentiments unfamiliar to the present generation. After giving an account of the story of each city, he has referred to the prominent objects of interest in it, and he has borrowed freely from the inquirers of other days whatsoever he considered important, as illustrating their architecture or antiquity. He has endeavoured to acknowledge in all cases the sources of his information, but as some of the papers were written twenty years ago it has not always been easy to trace them. He has also borrowed from the Introductions to the volumes of State Papers edited by him, on the old principle that a man may once say a thing as he would have it said—he cannot say it twice.

These papers have been selected and arranged so that the volume might adapt itself to the traveller. The visitor, if he starts from Bombay and stays a few days at the cities in the order in which they are given in this book, will see a great deal that is best worth seeing on the continent of India, within moderate compass of time. All he can never see, and there is subject enough for twenty quartos. As a large number of people who must remain at home take an interest and feel a pride in our Indian Empire, it is hoped that these papers may offer them some pleasure and some information. Of their omissions and imperfections, no one can be more conscious than the author.

The papers headed Bombay, Delhi, and Calcutta appeared in the *Pall Mall Magazine*, and the permission to reprint and use the illustrations is hereby gratefully acknowledged.

It remains to thank those from whom the writer has had the privilege of receiving advice, and who have assisted him in the dull task of proof reading and correction. The spelling of Indian words is bound to cause great difficulty; but in a book of this kind it would be out of place to follow always too closely the somewhat pedantic official system of transliteration, which has proved a stumbling-block to ordinary English people, and a great non-conductor of interest.

Contents

CONTENTS

Illustrations

BOMBAY

THE last week in October we left Victoria Station to join the P. & O. mail steamer at Brindisi. The air was chill and damp, and the fog lay thick over city and river. At dawn, fourteen days after, we were anchored in the harbour of beautiful, sun-girt Bombay, and the air was sultry with the heat of summer. A rosy mist was hanging over the blue mountains in the distance, and the fishing boats, with their large brown lateen sails, were gliding away before the bright morning breeze. Steamers and brigs, and Arab dhows, with their broad, raised poops—like the poops of the vessels that sailed the Spanish Main—are anchored before us; and not far from the dhows are two turret ships of ugly, but imposing presence, meant to protect the gate of our Indian Empire. In the far distance rises into sight a well-wooded hill, and between it and a long spit of land lies the city of Bombay, whose towers and domes soar clear in the serene and transparent air. Immediately in front of the deck are the grey walls of the old castle, which has been ours for two centuries and a quarter.

When in the year 1663 Mr. Humphrey Cook and his men took possession of Bombay in the King's name, they found —" a pretty well Seated, but ill Fortified House, four Brass Guns being the whole Defence of the Island." " About the House was a delicate Garden, voiced to be the pleasantest in *India*, intended rather for wanton Dalliance,

Love's Artillery, than to make resistance against an invading Foe." Ten years after, " Bombay opened itself " to John Fryer, M.D. Cantabrig., and Fellow of the Royal Society, and during that time a great change had been wrought " in this Garden of *Eden*, or Place of Terrestrial Happiness. The Walks, which before were covered with Nature's verdent awning and lightly pressed by soft Delights, are now open to the Sun, and loaded with the hardy Cannon : the Bowers dedicated to Rest and Ease are turned into bold Rampires for the watchful Centinel to look out on ; every Tree that the Airy Choristers made their Charming Choir, trembles, and is extirpated at the rebounding Echo of the alarming Drum ; and those slender Fences only designed to oppose the *Sylvian* Herd, are thrown down to erect others of a more War-like Force." Captain Alexander Hamilton, who was in Bombay within twenty years of its occupation, informs us in *A New Account of the East Indies* that " No sooner had Mr. Cook acquired the Island than he forthwith began to fortify regularly, and to save Charges of building an House for the Governor, built a Fort round an old square House, which served the *Portuguese* for a Place of Retreat, when they were disturbed by their Enemies, till Forces could be sent from other Places to relieve them." In erecting the Fort in its present situation Hamilton considered " Mr. Cook showed his want of skill in *Architecture*, when a proper and convenient Situation ought to be well considered " ; but " As for the Magnitude, Figure and Materials of the Fort, there is no fault to be found in them, for it is a regular Tetragon, whose outward Polygon is about 500 Paces, and it is built of a good hard Stone, and it can mount above 100 Piece of Cannon ; and that is all that is commendable in it. But had it been built about 500 Paces more to the Southward on a more acute Point of Rocks, called *Mendham's* Point, it had been much better on several Accounts." A French traveller, who visited **Bombay** the same year as Fryer, describes the Castle as "a very fine Fort in which the English President commonly keeps residence"; and the Fellow of the Royal Society tells us that even at that early date the Governor of Bombay held considerable state. "The President," he writes, "has a large Commission, and is *Vice-Regis*; he has a Council here also, and a Guard when he walks or rides abroad, accompanied with a Party of Horse, which are constantly kept in the Stables, either for Pleasure or Service. He has his Chaplains, Physician, Chyrurgeons, and Domesticks; his Linguist and Mint-Master. At Meals he has his Trumpets usher in his Courses, and Soft Musick at the Table. If he move out of his Chamber, the Silver Staves wait on him; if down Stairs, the Guard receive him; if he go abroad, the *Bandarines* and *Moors* under two Standards march before him: He goes sometimes in his Coach, drawn by large Milk-White Oxen, sometimes on Horseback, other times in Palenkeens, carried by *Cohors*, *Musslemen* Porters: Always having a *Sumbrero* of State carried over him: And those of the *English* inferior to him, have a suitable Train."

Sir Gerald Aungier, President of the East India Company's factories and trade, was, at the time of Fryer's visit, the ruler over Bombay, "for the King, finding that the Charge of keeping Bombay in his own Hands, would not turn to account, the Revenues being so very inconsiderable," had made the island over to the Company. It was to be held by them of the King "in free and common Soccage as that of the Manore of East Greenwich on payment of the annual rent of £10 in gold on the 30th September in each year." Gerald Aungier was one of the men who make empires and bind them together. During his three years' stay at Bombay he so improved the fortifications of the place that, finding "Bombaim" fort as "stark as de Deel," the Dutch retreated to their boats without any booty. Aungier quelled a formidable mutiny, and by strict discipline pre-

3

pared the troops for action, and formed the inhabitants into a militia to act with the garrison. He laid out a town on the site of a few fishermen's huts, and erected houses for the factors' warehouses to store his masters' goods, a granary, mint-house, and a court of judicature. He organized the administration, and made his famous convention with the inhabitants—a wise and statesmanlike measure which has done much to promote the welfare of the island. His Imperial policy, however, did not meet with the approval of his masters at home. They blamed him " for the great charges expended, and the grandeur he used on their island Bombay." But Aungier replied that " Fame hath aggrandized the expenses of Bombay more than really it is." " The moneys expended in public appearance were, by serious debate in Council, made suitable to the decency and advantage of your affairs free from vanity or superfluity, and ever ended with the same reasons that also produced them." As for the buildings, they were judged " absolutely necessary and such as you cannot be without," " yet if you shall not approve thereof your President offers to take them to his own account provided you will please to allow him reasonable rent for the time they have been employed in your service and give him leave hereafter to improve them to his best advantage."

For twenty years Gerald Aungier conducted the government of Bombay and Surat with great skill and judgment. Then, in a letter dated " Surat, ye 30th June 1677," we read, " It hath pleased God to our great sorrow after a tedious sickness to take out of this life our worthy Presidt Gerald Aungier, who decd this morning between four and five of ye clock, of wch wee thought good to give you this timely notice, yt you might prevent all innovations or disturbances upon ye island." The Bombay Council, in acknowledging the receipt of this sad intelligence, remark : " Wee cannot rightly express ye reallity of our grief wee conceived at ye perusal of ye deplorable news of the death of our late noble Presidt. Multiplicity of words may multiply ye sense of our loss, but cannot depaint its greatness." Forty years after Aungier's death, Hamilton wrote : " The name of Mr. *Aungier* is much reverenced by the ancient People of *Surat* and *Bombay* to this day. His Justice and Dexterity in managing Affairs got him such Esteem that the Natives of these Places made him the Common Arbitrator of the *Differences* in Point of Traffick. Nor was it ever known that any Party receded ever from his Award." Three centuries have passed since Gerald Aungier threw up the bastions between Bombay Castle and the sea, and the " old square house " which we took over from the Portuguese, and in which he lived and did his great work, still stands. Here should be placed a tablet to the memory of the man who was the first—and not the least noble—of the long and illustrious line of administrators who have made our Indian Empire. On his foundation they have built. He " brought the face of Justice to be unveiled."

Facing Bombay Castle, on the land side, in the days long done, there was a wide tract of common land, about fifty acres in extent. James Forbes, in his *Oriental Memoirs*, one of the most charming works ever written about the East, has given us a view of Bombay Green as it was in the year (1763) when Lord Bute resigned and proceedings were begun against Wilkes for No. 45 of the *North Briton*. A company of soldiers is drawn up before the church. A gentleman with cocked hat, knee-breeches, and a long stick, with a native servant holding an umbrella over his head, is gazing at them. A coach, drawn by four horses, preceded by a company of sepoys, is being driven by the church. It may be the coach of His Excellency the Governor. A humble factor is being carried in an open palanquin, with two sepoys with drawn swords preceding him. There is a gentleman riding in a chaise and pair, as a native bullock-

carriage was then styled. When Admiral Watson, the brave
old sailor whose name is so closely linked with that of Robert
Clive, came to Bombay in 1774 with his squadron, " palanquins," writes the surgeon of the ship, " were placed at the
disposal of his sick by Government, whilst the Admiral had
a chaise and pair of these oxen allowed him also by the
Company. They are commonly white, have a large pair of
perpendicular horns, and black noses. The Admiral often-
times went in the chaise for an afternoon outing to Malabar
Hill, and to the end of Old Woman's Island, to Marmulia
and many other places. In England, if these creatures are
forced out of their usual pace, it is too well known that they
will faint or lie under their burthen ; but at Bombay they
trot and gallop as naturally as horses, and are equally serviceable in every respect—except that they sometimes
incommode by the filth thrown upon you by their tails."
An admiral in uniform driving about in a small bullock-cart,
with his knees close to his chin, must have been a quaint and
interesting sight.

Twelve years after the visit of Admiral Watson, James
Forbes reached Bombay as a writer in the Company's
service, and he gives us a graphic account of the daily life
in the settlement, at the beginning of the last century.
Early rising prevailed throughout the Presidency. " The
morning was then dedicated to business ; everybody dined
at one o'clock ; on breaking up, the Company went to their
respective houses to enjoy a siesta, and return after a walk
or ride in the country to pass the remainder of the evening
and sup where they had dined." Forbes pays a handsome
tribute to the character of his countrymen in exile. " In
private life they are generous, kind, and hospitable ; in their
public situations, when called forth to arduous enterprise,
they conduct themselves with skill and management ; and
whether presiding at the helm of the political and commercial department, or spreading the glory of the British arms

BOMBAY: VIEW FROM THE UNIVERSITY TOWER.

7

with courage, moderation, and clemency, the annals of Hindustan will transmit to future ages names dear to fame and deserving the applause of Europe." When Forbes landed at Bombay, "comfort, hospitality, and urbanity," he states, characterized the settlement ; and all who have had the privilege of visiting the island will bear willing testimony that in one respect Bombay has not altered.

A commanding feature in the view of Bombay Green presented in the *Oriental Memoirs* is the church. On the arrival of Richard Cobbe as chaplain to the island, he found that services were held in a room in the fort ; and, in a sermon preached on the First Sunday after Trinity, he impressed on his congregation the necessity of a suitable church.

"Well, Doctor," said the Governor after the service, "you have been very zealous for the church this morning."

"Please, yr Honour," he replied, "I think there was occasion for it, and I hope without offence."

"Well, then," said the Governor, "if we must have a church, we must have a church. Do you see and get a book made, and see what every one will contribute towards it, and I will do first."

Cobbe himself gave Rs. 1,427 ; Cornelius Toddington gave "For my wife when I have her," Rs. 20 ; and Mr. Richard Walters, Rs. 11, paid him for doing the service in absence of the chaplain. A commutation from penance corporal at Surat was Rs. 150. A substantial sum was collected, and on November 18, 1718, the foundation stone of the church was laid. Three years after, on Christmas Day, it was opened. The Governor went in procession, and was met at the entrance by the chaplain in his canonical dress. During the service a child was baptized, the Governor, Mrs. Parker (the Deputy-Governor's wife) and Mrs. Crommelin "standing Gossips." When the service was concluded the Governor, his Council, and the ladies repaired to the vestry, where they drank success to the new church in a glass of sack. The church was prosperous under the vigorous ministration of Cobbe, but the man whose strong will and inflexible purpose established it, could not move in the regular official routine and keep the waters smooth. Mr. Braddyll, Member of Council, complained that Mr. Cobbe had "affronted him at the Communion Table, when he was going to receive the Holy Sacrament, and he had likewise affronted him publicly several times before." From the letter which Mr. Braddyll wrote to the President and Governor of Bombay and Council it can be gathered that Mr. Cobbe had frequently complained about his employing workmen on Sunday, and that the Member of Council had advanced the plea of necessity. The quarrel culminated in the following occurrence :—

"After the congregation, of which I happened to be one, had placed themselves at the altar in a posture for receiving the Communion, Mr. Cobbe having consecrated the elements, turned himself towards me and spoke with a loud voice, and said, ' Mr. Braddyll ' ; to which I made no answer, thinking him to be out of his senses ; but he repeated it a second time, and said, ' Mr. Braddyll, have you done working on Sundays ? unless yt, I cannot administer you this Sacrament.' To the best of my remembrance I told him I had. He went still further, and said he would not give me Communion unless I would promise him and the congregation then present that I would work no more on Sundays. I told him I would not unless necessity obliged me, upon which he condescended to treat me like ye rest of the community." The Board demanded an explanation of his conduct from the Chaplain, and he replied " that he was sorry to find that a person in Mr. Braddyll's station should, instead of being ashamed, make it a matter of complaint for a reproof of a sin so exceeding sinfull, but is God Almighty less in India than He is in England ? Or has He given any man license to sin ? Is the violation of this holy day become the less enormous, because it is so frequently and irreligiously profaned, or must it out of good manners be past by unobserved, connived and winked at, especially when it comes from so eminent a quarter ? " The Board came to the conclusion " that the second Rubric," from which the Chaplain based his defence, did not apply to the case, as it referred only to " an open and notorious evil liver," and they " ordered Mr. Richard Cobbe to ask Mr. Braddyll pardon publickly in the church on Sunday morning next immediately after in the following words : ' Whereas, on Sunday the 3rd instant, through mistake, I did affront Mr. Braddyll at the Communion Table, I do hereby notify to this congregation here present, that on more mature consideration I find myself to be in the wrong, and do hereby beg Mr. Braddyll's pardon for the injury done him and the offence given him and to the other communicants.' "

Mr. Cobbe refused compliance with the Council's order for two reasons : firstly, because according to the rubric after the Nicene Creed nothing is to be proclaimed during the time of Divine service " but what is prescribed in the rules of the Book of Common Prayer or enjoined by the Queen or by the ordinary of the place " ; and secondly, because such compliance " would not only give encouragement to them by lessening too much the credit of reproof, but inevitably draw contempt upon the clergy, and wound even religion through the sides of the ministry." He concluded the letter with these words : " For this, therefore, I hope, gentlemen, you will pardon your servant in that I cannot, I dare not, yield my assent without declining that duty, without betraying that trust, for which I am accountable to a more awfull tribunal." Mr. Cobbe, however, offered to give Mr. Braddyll any satisfaction he could, except what the Board had ordered. But the Board refused to listen to any compromise, and proceeded to review his past conduct. Notice was taken of a sermon that he had preached at the members of the Government from the text, " Though hand joyn in hand, yet the wicked shall not go unpunished," and the Board declared that it was " but too notorious and usual with him to draw odious characters in the sermons and apply them to such persons with whom he has any difference. . . . In order, therefore, to secure this Government against the evils which such seditious sermons and discord may possibly have on the minds of some people, especially at this time of actual warr with one enemy, and an apprehension of a rupture with our neighbours the Portuguese, when there is all the need imaginable of union and firm resolution, it was resolved that Mr. Richard Cobbe, Chaplain, be suspended from the Right Honble Company's service and from officiating as their chaplain, receiving no further salary or other allowances of the Right Honble Company from this day." Cobbe returned to England, and lived to a ripe old age, and in the decline of life wrote an account of the church which he founded, now the cathedral of a vast diocese.

Near the Cathedral, about the centre of the old Green, is situated Elphinstone Circle, a block of commercial buildings which would do credit to any European capital. They surround a small garden which has the glory of colour that nature lavishes on shrub and flower in the East. Here is a statue to the Marquis Cornwallis, who, as the inscription informs us, died at Ghazipur, on October 5, 1805. The Indian climate proved too much for a constitution already shattered by the anxieties and vexations of his Irish administration, and the difficult and delicate task of conducting the negotiations which led to the peace of Amiens. "A peace that will not dishonour the country," wrote Cornwallis ; an expression afterwards happily converted into " peace with honour " by one who knew how to borrow. Cornwallis had not the genius of Hastings, or of Wellesley ; but he was a man of sterling integrity, and his death was regarded in India as a public misfortune, on account of his whole previous administration having been imbued with the spirit of justice and moderation. At a public meeting of the British inhabitants of Bombay it was resolved to erect a statue to the late Marquis. James Mackintosh, the " Man of Promise," at the time Recorder of Bombay, wrote to

Flaxman :—" As one of the committee appointed for that purpose, I naturally turned my thoughts towards you, for reasons which it might be indelicate to mention to you, and which it must be unnecessary to state to any one else. It is enough to say that I feel very great solicitude to leave to our most distant successors, whoever they may be, not only a memorial of the honour in which we hold virtue, but an example of the progress of Art in England in the beginning of the nineteenth century. The neighbouring subterranean temples of Elephanta, Canari, and Carli contain, perhaps, the most ancient sculptures in the world. Twenty or thirty centuries hence, some native, whose name is now unknown, may compare these works of barbaric toil with the finished productions of the genius and taste of an English artist. Without your help I do not think that the comparison would be fair or the contrast complete."

After this delicate flattery, Mackintosh proceeds to state that the statue is to be of the natural size, or larger than life, with such basso-relievos and subordinate figures as the artist might judge most characteristic and ornamental. " I need not tell you that the character of Marquis Cornwallis was more respectable than dazzling. I am persuaded that you will find pleasure in employing an art, too often the flatterer of tyranny, to give lustre to the virtues most useful to mankind. Prudence, moderation, integrity, pacific spirit, clemency, were very remarkable qualities in Marquis Cornwallis's character. Perhaps his establishment of a system of secure landed property in Bengal—and extended over India—might furnish some hints to your genius. It was a noble measure of paternal legislation, though I know not whether it could be represented in marble."

The Permanent Settlement in Bengal is hardly a theme to fire an artist's imagination, or a subject capable of being represented in marble except in the form of boundary pillars. Flaxman, however, refused to undertake the work, and the statue was executed by Bacon. In the garden there is another statue by the same sculptor, erected by the merchants of Bombay to the honour of the Pro-Consul whose intrepid intellect and lofty ambition consolidated the Empire which the daring genius of Hastings founded ; of whom his illustrious brother said :—" Had he been but a younger son he would have been the greatest man in Europe." The clean-cut and decisive features of the Marquis of Wellesley are rendered with considerable skill. His slight and wiry figure rests on a massive marble pedestal, with finely modelled male and female figures in front, and a life-sized lion and tiger behind. The merchants of the East India Company could not appreciate Wellesley's vigorous and far-seeing policy, and they recalled him. Thirty years after, when his despatches, which combine comprehensive and elevated views with so much circumspection and dignity, were published, the Court of Directors assured him, by a unanimous resolution, " that in their judgment he had been animated throughout his administration by an ardent zeal to promote the well-being of India, and to uphold the interest and honour of the British Empire ; and that they looked back to the eventful and brilliant period of his administration with feelings common to their countrymen." They also voted him a grant of £20,000, and ordered his statue to be placed in the India Office. But this tardy recognition of his services did not satisfy the great Marquis, and his closing years were embittered because the Ministry would not create him Duke of Hindustan, the only title which would gratify his Imperial soul.

Leaving the garden, we come to a stately flight of steps leading to the Town Hall, which mainly owes its existence to the enthusiasm and exertion of James Mackintosh. He was anxious that a building should be erected " for the reception of the statues of Marquis Cornwallis and Mr. Pitt, and of any future monuments of British Art which public gratitude may bring to Bombay," and " for the accommodation of the Literary Society, and the reception of their valuable and increasing library." Soon after his arrival James Mackintosh held, under his own roof, the first meeting of the Literary Society of Bombay. Jonathan Duncan was present, not as a Governor of Bombay, but as a scholar who had made his mark by contributing some important papers to the Bengal Asiatic Society ; General Nicolls, the Commander-in-chief, a man of science, who had devoted much time to the meteorology of the island ; Boden, the Quartermaster-General, and subsequent founder of the Boden Professorship at Oxford ; and Edward Moore, the author of *The Hindu Pantheon*, a work of considerable research. The President, in an eloquent address, stated the subjects which he trusted the members would pursue in India, because so much could be found in the land which could be got in no other country : metallurgy, mineralogy, botany and economics were the subjects which he specially brought forward to the notice of the members. The history of the Bombay Asiatic Society is a record of brilliant success. It has done the work for which it was founded— —" the investigation and encouragement of Oriental Arts, Science, and Literature." In 1827 the Society adopted the proposal of the Royal Asiatic Society of Great Britain and Ireland for a union between the two Institutions, and the Literary Society of Bombay became the Bombay branch of the Royal Asiatic Society of Great Britain and Ireland.

One of the first objects that engaged the attention of the Society was the foundation of a Public Library. Early in 1805 a bargain was concluded for the purchase of an extensive collection of books which had been gathered together by several medical gentlemen of Bombay. Under the wise administration of Sir James Mackintosh, the library grew, and when he returned to England he sent out, at the request of the Society, a collection of the standard books of the day, and the principal publications as they appeared. It is due to the wide reading and sound literary taste of the author of *Vindiciæ Gallicæ* that the library of the Bombay Asiatic Society is so rich in the literature of the eighteenth century. The Society has also had frequent gifts of rare and valuable Oriental publications from the Bombay Government and the Government of India, and the library has grown up to be a goodly collection of thirty thousand volumes. Savants who visit India will receive at Bombay a warm and generous welcome from a learned Society, devoted to spreading through the land a spirit of philosophical inquiry and literary research, and owning a library rich in books of solid worth.

Retracing our steps from the Town Hall, we pass the Cathedral, and driving through Church Street we come to a spacious Platz, with a handsome fountain. The name commemorates the services of a great ruler, who, during his five years' tenure of office, changed an Indian city into one of the finest capitals of the Empire. Bartle Frere was appointed Governor of Bombay at the comparatively early age of forty-seven. " God grant you," wrote Lord Canning, " health and strength to do your work in your own noble spirit ! " He did it, in spite of much opposition, in his own imperial spirit ; and no Governor, except Mountstuart Elphinstone, did more to improve the condition of the people, or to increase the prosperity of the great Presidency entrusted to his charge. He won the respect of those he ruled by his courageous temperament, and their affection by his strong human sympathies. Man that is born of woman hath his faults ; but with all his minor blemishes and infirmities, a high rank must be assigned to Bartle Frere among the great statesmen who served the East India Company.

At the corner of the Platz, where two roads meet, is a fine statue of the Queen-Empress, which stands as a monument

of the loyal attachment and admiration of the great Feudatories for the first Sovereign who has, since the dawn of
history, ruled over all India. The statue was given to
Bombay by the munificent Khandi Rao Guicowar, the ruler
of the Baroda state. Her Gracious and Imperial Majesty
is represented seated on an elaborately carved state chair,
which is placed on a lofty marble platform led up to by steps.
In the centre of the canopy is the Star of India, and above
it the Rose of England is united with the Lotus of India,
and around them are England's old motto " God and my
right," and India's watchword " Heaven's light our guide."
Leaning against the handsome rails which encircle the statue
are a group of rustics. There is the old father and his spouse,
a matronly dame, two stalwart sons, black, wiry men from
the coast, and their spouses—light-hearted, merry young
women, whose crimson, blue, and orange robes fall in graceful folds over their supple figures. They are showing a
little girl and a couple of half-naked boys, wearing gorgeous
caps embroidered with tinsel, the beauties of the statue,
and they are discussing with considerable volubility the
Royal lady beyond the sea. Queen Victoria is in India
no mythological personage, the wife of " John Company."
Three of her sons have visited the land. The Prince of Wales
by his gracious tact caused the great chiefs to feel that
they are not merely important factors in a vast administrative system, but Royal Feudatories of a great sovereign.
The Duke of Connaught has commanded a division in
Bengal and the Bombay army ; and in many a distant home,
seated of an evening around the village fire, the sepoy on
furlough has told his companions about the great Queen's
son, who could address them in their own language. The
private and personal virtues of the Queen long ago became
known, and enthroned Her Majesty in the hearts of many
millions of her distant subjects. In a remote village in the
north of India a peasant had a grievance, and he called the

village schoolmaster to his aid, and they wrote a letter stating the case, and they addressed it "To the Good Lady in England," and the letter reached Balmoral. To be

STATUE OF THE QUEEN-EMPRESS.

known to distant subject races as "The Good Lady in England" was an achievement of which any monarch might well have been proud.

17   C

From the Queen's statue to the statue of His Majesty as Prince of Wales runs a broad road known as Rampart Row, lined by lofty offices and splendid shops, which would do credit to Paris or London. The equestrian statue of the Prince, a good example of Boehm's best work, was the gift of the late Sir A. Sassoon, and commemorates the Heir-apparent's visit to the city. On each side of the granite base are two well executed castings, one representing the historic scene of the landing of the Prince at the dockyard, and the other depicting the picturesque episode which lives in the memory of those who took part in it—the presentation of flowers to His Royal Highness by the Parsee children at the great children's *fête* held in his honour.

Not far from the Prince of Wales' statue is the Wellington fountain, a meretricious structure unworthy of the great name it bears. Colonel Wellesley came to Bombay in 1803, and during the hot months of March and April worked with his wonted ardour in getting ready the transports to convey the forces under General Baird to Egypt. It was intended that they should co-operate in the important object of expelling the French from that land, and Colonel Wellesley had been appointed second in command. A severe attack of fever, however, prevented him from accompanying the expedition. He was much disappointed at having lost what seemed a splendid opportunity for active service, but he remained behind to win the decisive battle of Assaye, while the vessel in which he was to sail was lost. On October 2, 1803, Jonathan Duncan, Governor of Bombay, received a letter from General Wellesley announcing in a few simple words the hard-won contest which made us masters of India.

After his great and decisive victory General Wellesley visited Poona, and descended the Ghauts to Bombay, and the capital received him with due honour. " I was feasted out of Bombay as I was feasted into it," he wrote to a friend. The victor of Assaye was glad to escape from steamy Bombay to the cooler Deccan, where he employed himself in writing State papers, urging a policy of conciliation and moderation. " The Governor-General may write what he pleases at Calcutta, we must conciliate the natives, or we shall not be able to do his business ; and all his treatment, without conciliation and an endeavour to convince the Native Powers that we have views besides our own interests, is so much waste paper."

A short distance from the Wellington fountain is a splendid testimony of the wisdom of the soldier-statesman's policy in dealing with the native powers. The palatial Home for Sailors, whose foundation stone was laid by H.R.H. the Duke of Edinburgh, was the gift of the same great loyal Feudatory who caused to be erected the statue of the late Queen. Near to the Sailors' Home is the Royal Bombay Yacht Club, to which ladies accompanied by members are freely admitted, and where the traveller who has the privilege of honorary membership will find every comfort, and from the deep verandah overlooking the harbour will enjoy one of the most beautiful views in the world.

Returning from the Yacht Club, and bearing to the left, we come to a shallow expanse of water, bounded by two tongues of land—Colaba and Malabar Hill. Facing the bay is a line of buildings, imposing as a whole, but too suggestive of modern English taste and conventionalism. The Secretariat, where the offices of the Secretaries to Government are located, is a massive pile whose main features have been brought from Venice, but all the beauty has vanished in transhipment. It is as lacking in sentiment as the work conducted in it, and is the complete expression in stone of the spirit of an official architect. The University Hall, erected from designs by Sir Gilbert Scott, seems to have been meant for a western College Chapel, and is as exotic as the system of education which we have introduced into the land. A few yards from the Senate Hall is the University Library, designed by the same architect, which seems a little too small for the lofty clock tower, built after the form of the campanile of Giotto at Florence, that adjoins it. The High Court is a large, imposing, ugly Gothic construction, out of character with the climate ; but the building is probably not more out of character with the climate than the mode of administering justice within its walls is out of character with the habits of the people.

Not far from the University, the home of modern science and culture, there rises a long black wall, from above which dense volumes of noisome smoke drift over the road, and many bright sparks float in the air. This is the Hindu burning ground, and the smoke and sparks arise from the funeral fires.

> "The Trojan king and Tuscan chief command,
> To raise the piles along the winding strand ;
> Thence friends convey the dead to fun'ral fires,
> Black smould'ring smoke from the green wood expires,
> The light of Heaven is cloaked, and the new day retires."

From a low and narrow door comes forth a procession of priests in saffron robes, carrying small bundles in their hands : behind them follow a crowd of men and women wailing and beating their breasts. They cross the railway which runs parallel to the beach, and repair to the sea, where, after various oblations and ceremonies are performed, the priests open the little bundles and cast their contents into the waters. They are the ashes of the dead. The mourners sit on the turf by the seashore, and refraining from vain tears they alleviate their grief by reciting after the priests verses culled from the Puranas. "Foolish ashes, who seeks permanence in the human state, unsolid like the stem of the plantain tree, transient like the foam of the sea. All that is low must finally perish ; all that is elevated must ultimately fall ; all compound bodies must end in dissolution ; and life is concluded with death. Unwilling do the manes of the deceased taste the tears and rheum shed by their kinsmen :

BOMBAY: UNIVERSITY BUILDINGS.

then do not wail, but diligently perform the obsequies of the dead." Under the shadow of the University tower the Hindu diligently performs the obsequies of the dead as they were performed on the winding shore, when " the wood was heaped for funeral," and " apart Achilles stood."

Bombay is the common meeting ground of many different creeds and nationalities. A short distance beyond the burning yard is a long upper-storied building, which a charitable Muhammadan gentleman has built to accommodate the pilgrims proceeding to Mecca ; and facing a sweep of the bay rises Wilson College, which bears the name of its founder, the great Scotch missionary, who made Bombay his home, and devoted a life of strenuous labour to her advancement. A man of most varied acquirements and excellent judgment, Dr. Wilson became a considerable force in the land, and Viceroys and Governors sought his advice on delicate problems of State. Endowed with an unusually attractive and winning character, he won the hearts of all classes, English, Parsee, Muhammadan, and Hindu. The land and its people interested him. He was versed in their ancient literature and philosophy ; he spoke and wrote some of their living languages, and without a tinge of sentimentalism he appreciated their many fine qualities. He freely criticized Hinduism, Muhammadanism, and Zoroastrianism ; but his plain speaking did not impair the affection with which he was regarded, for no man has a keener appreciation of chivalrous honesty than the Oriental.

Beyond the Wilson College the road begins to rise to Malabar Hill, and at intervals along the base of the beetling rocks are patches of trees and groves of lofty palms. On the top of the hill two roads meet ; one follows the crest, and the other leads to Malabar Point, " where the Governor," writes Lady Falkland, " has a residence consisting of several good-sized bungalows." Lady Falkland, who was one of the first to prove, by her bright book *Chow Chow*, that India

VIEW OF THE BACK BAY FROM MALABAR HILL.

23

is not hopelessly dull, was fond of staying at Malabar Point during the time her husband ruled the island. Mountstuart Elphinstone, when Governor, built a bungalow at Malabar Point, on the site of an old temple ; but a residence of some kind had existed before his day, for we read of Malabar Point being, in 1789, " the Governor's occasional retreat." Maria Graham, better known as Lady Caldecott, and the author of *Little Arthur's History of England*, has the following in her *Journal of a Residence in India* :—

" *August* 5, 1809.—After walking nearly two miles through gardens, or rather fields of vegetables, we came to a small *bungalo*, or garden-house, at the point of the hill, from which there is, I think, the finest view I ever saw. The whole island lay to the north and east, beautifully green with the young rice, varied with hills and woods, and only separated from Salsette and the Mahratta shore by narrow arms of the sea, while the bay and harbour to the south, scattered with beautiful woody islands, reflected the grand monsoon clouds, which, as they rolled along, now hid and now discovered the majestic forms of the ghauts on the mainland. Within a few yards of the bungalo is a ruined temple ; from what remains, it must have been a fine specimen of Hindoo architecture ; almost every stone is curiously carved with groups of figures, animals, and other ornaments. Tradition says that the Portugueze, in their zeal for conversion, pointed cannon against this temple, and destroyed it with its gods ; its widely scattered remains seem to countenance the report. Close to the ruin there is a cleft in a rock, so narrow, that one would wonder how a child could get through it ; nevertheless there are multitudes of pilgrims who annually come to force themselves through, as a certain method of getting rid of their sins."

Moore, in *The Hindoo Pantheon*, writes : " At the very extremity of a promontory on the island of *Bombay*, called *Malabar* Point, is a cleft rock, a fancied resemblance of the *Yoni*, to which numerous pilgrims and persons resort for the purpose of regeneration, by the efficacy of a passage through this sacred type. This *Yoni*, or hole, is of considerable elevation, situated among the rocks, of no easy access, and in the

stormy season incessantly buffeted by the surf of the ocean."
Moore goes on to relate that the famous Brahman Ragoba,
the father of the last of the Peshwas, was, when he resided
at Bombay, in the habit of passing through the cleft ; and
that Shivaji, the daring founder of the Mahratta State, had
been known to venture secretly on the island of Bombay,
" at a time when discovery was ruin, to avail himself of
the benefit of this efficacious transit."

About half a mile from Malabar Point is the village of
Walkeshwar, one of the most sacred spots in Western India.
The name implies Lord of Sand, for legend states that the
great god Rama—whose history is familiar to every village
child—came to Malabar Point in the course of his travels,
tired and thirsty, and found no water, so he shot an arrow
into the sand on the seashore, and water immediately appeared. Passing through narrow streets, lined with tall,
quaint houses, painted all colours, the sacred pool is reached.
It is situated in the centre of a vast square, entirely surrounded by temples of all sizes and forms—temples shaped
like a sugar-loaf, temples with domes, temples with pinnacles
and turrets, whose niches are filled with small images.
Under the trees are small shrines with pointed roofs ; and
what Jeremiah the prophet saw and denounced we see
around us everywhere : " And they set them up images
and groves on every high hill, and under every green tree."
Around the tank are tall white obelisk-shaped pillars, painted
`n parts red and green, and numerous little altars containing
the Tulsi plant. Before the temples are placed—carved in
black stone—the Sacred Bull, or Nandi. All proclaim the
foul worship against which the Old Testament is one long
protest, and whose symbols were the grove, the golden calf,
and the brazen serpent. Long flights of steps lead down
to the water's edge, which is some yards below the level of
the road. Men and women in clothes of various colours
press round the brink of the silent pool : some plunge into,

or besprinkle themselves with the sacred liquid; others kneeling on the steps remain in a state of blessed contemplation; all are praying with the utmost fervour. Around the tank on worn and ragged mattresses lie a multitude of impotent folk, of blind, halt, withered. A scene rises before us: "Sir, I have no man, when the water is troubled, to put me into the pool; but while I am coming, another steppeth down before me. Jesus said unto him, Rise, take up thy bed and walk; and immediately the man was made whole, and took up his bed and walked." Read in the light of the East, the sacred volume recovers its native colour, and glows with the vigour of new life.

A short walk brings us again to the broad road which runs along the crest of the hill. It is lined with handsome bungalows, with green lawns, and small gardens well kept, with oleander, hibiscus and palms of all varieties. About the end of the ridge, along the brow of a precipitous cliff, are the beautiful grounds of the Ladies' Gymkhana. Sir Henry Yule, in that most delightful work *Hobson-Jobson*, writes as follows about the word Gymkhana, fast becoming naturalized in England :—

"This word is quite modern, and was unknown twenty-five years ago. It is a fictitious word, invented, we believe, in the Bombay Presidency, and probably based upon "Gend-khana" —ball-house; the name usually given, in Hindu, to an English racket-court. It is applied to a place of public resort at a station, where the needful facilities for athletics and games of all sorts are provided, including—when that was in fashion—a skating-rink, a lawn-tennis ground, and so forth. The 'gymn' may be simply a corruption of 'geno' shaped by 'gymnastics.' The word is also applied to a meeting for such sports; and in this sense it has already travelled to Malta."

A short distance beyond the Ladies' Gymkhana are the Tulsi Reservoirs and Waterworks, and their situation is exceedingly beautiful. Beneath is a forest of palms, with white houses gleaming among them; and immediately be-

yond is an azure bay, with a narrow strip of land running
into it covered with massive and lofty buildings. In the
far distance rise the high peaks and ridges of the volcanic
hills of Mahratta land, and rocks and islets of fantastic
nature stud the great inlet of the sea known as Bombay
Harbour. On one side lies this calm, fairy scene ; on the
other stands out the dull, ugly wall which surrounds the
Towers of Silence, where the Parsees deposit their dead, to
be devoured by vultures. On the trees and on the walls
scores of these hideous birds can be seen. Suddenly they
rise in the air : a bier is being brought up the long flight of
steps which leads to the hills on which the Towers are
situated. Close by the bier are two bearded men, and
behind them follow a train of Parsees, dressed in white robes
with their clothes linked. At the door of the Towers the
relatives leave the body, and it is taken within by the two
priests. Inside the large roofless tower are stages, or stories
of stone pavement, slanting down to a well, covered with
a grating, and on the upper tier are placed, stark naked,
the bodies of men ; on the second those of women, and on
the third those of children. The moment the priests leave
the body the vultures swoop down and strip it of every
particle of flesh. The skeleton is left for a few days to
bleach in the sun and wind till it becomes perfectly dry ;
then the carriers of the dead, who are a separate class and
not allowed to have any social intercourse with other
Parsees, come gloved, and with tongs (for a dead body is
regarded as an unclean thing) remove the bones and cast
them into the well. This mode of disposing of the dead
the Parsees have practised from time immemorial. In
Grose's *Voyage to the East Indies*, printed in 1772, we have
a sensational picture of "The Parsee repository for the
Dead," and the following description :—

"Eastward of the middle of Malabar Hill stands a stone
building, used by the Parsees for depositing their dead, it being

contrary to their religion to bury them. This building is circular,
25 feet in diameter and 12 high, open at the top ; in its centre
is a well in part grated over, round which is a stone platform,
sloping from the sides to the centre. On this platform the dead
bodies are exposed to the birds of prey, such as kites and vultures,
which are here in great numbers. These immediately seize
on the corpse, commonly beginning with the eyes ; a man is
kept on purpose to observe carefully which eye the bird picks out,
and on this they form their conjecture of the state of the soul
of the defunct, the right being that which denotes happiness.

" The Parsees believe that any one looking into this building,
except the person whose immediate business it is, will in consequence thereof shortly die. I once went up to examine it : a
Parsee, in a friendly manner, begged me to desist ; assuring me
that I should not long survive the gratification of this idle
curiosity."

Leaving the Towers of Silence, we descend a steep hill,
and a short drive brings us to Breach Candy. At the end
of the Breach, or beach—" from the breach of the sea was
our sister drowned"—are the temples of Mahaluxmee,
almost as sacred as those of Walkeshwar ; and beyond
them is situated the Vallard, or rampart, built to
protect the flat land between the ridges from being
flooded at high tide. From Mahaluxmee a road runs along
the dreary flats, now being covered with mills and lodging-
houses, to the Governor's house at Parelle, which was
originally a Portuguese monastery. Fryer mentions, " Parell, where they [the Portuguese] have another Church and
Demesnes belonging to the Jesuits." Grose writes : " There
are two very pleasant gardens belonging to the Company,
cultivated after the European manner ; the one a little way
out of the gates open to any of the English gentlemen who
like to walk there ; the other much larger and finer, at about
five miles distant from the town, at a place called Parell,
where the Governor has a very agreeable country house,
which was originally a Roman Chapel belonging to the
Jesuits, but confiscated about the year 1719, for some prac-

THE "TOWERS OF SILENCE."

29

tices against the English interest. It is now converted into a pleasant mansion-house, and what with the additional buildings and improvements of the garden, affords a spacious and commodious habitation."

Jonathan Duncan, who was a bachelor, lent Parell to James Mackintosh. "We have," writes Mackintosh to a friend in England, "about five miles of excellent road over a flat from our capital. We inhabit, by the Governor's kindness, his official country house, a noble building with some magnificent apartments, and with two delightful rooms for my library (overlooking a garden and parkish ground) in which I am now writing." Seven years Mackintosh loitered away in the magnificent apartments at Parell, reading for the composition of the great works which he never wrote. He read Tiedemann's *Spirit of Speculative Philosophy*, and Richardson's Correspondence, "which contains important materials for literary history." He was delighted with Cooper's third volume more than with either of the former. "His mixture of playfulness and tenderness is very bewitching ; he is always smiling through his tears." Thus the weeks and years sped away. He was always sighing for the literary society he had left in London and the " King of Clubs," and for him, as for Macaulay, neither the land nor the people possessed any real interest. After Mackintosh there came to Parell a man just the reverse of him. Mountstuart Elphinstone was, like Mackintosh, a man of great powers of reasoning, of accomplished learning, but he had what the latter lacked—sustained energies. When engrossed in the multifarious duties attendant on governing a vast province, Mountstuart Elphinstone found time to read Cicero *De Claris Oratoribus*. "It is not the most brilliant of his works, but still I read it with great pleasure, and discover to myself evident signs of that proficiency which he has attained to *cui Cicero valde placebit*." He greatly admires what he has read of Bentham, including half the whole *Traités* ; and he had " finished Clarendon's History, and am going to begin his Life." The study of *Manfred* led him to *Prometheus* : " both have sublime passages. I am most struck with those in Æschylus, though, perhaps, the calm grandeur and majesty of Lord Byron's mountains may equal the storms and tempests, the thunders and earthquakes of his rival." Twenty years after Mountstuart Elphinstone left Bombay, Lady Falkland, who had all the brightness of her mother, Mrs. Jordan, the famous actress, came to reside at Parell ; and, being a close observer of nature, she enjoyed the beauty of its grounds. " Near me," she writes, " was the Asoka, which in spring bears beautiful red blossoms ; many casuarinas, with their light and graceful foliage, being intermixed and contrasted with the broad leaves of various kinds of palms." A poetic Hindu legend states that the contact of the stem of the asoka with the foot of a beautiful woman makes it blossom.

About two miles from Parell are the Victoria Gardens, which owe their existence to the genius and energy of Sir George Birdwood. He found a swamp, and he drained it, made broad paths and smooth lawns, laid out a garden, and with lavish hand filled it with botanical treasures. Palms of all variety and tropical plants of every kind are, of course, growing there in the greatest luxuriance, but also trees and shrubs gathered from every quarter of the globe seem at home and happy : there is a fine tree with long pinnate foliage covered with yellow and scarlet flowers that came from Africa, its seeds having been found in the Indian Ocean by a sailor who brought them to the Gardens ; a bush from Australia, whose leaves glow like gold ; and a plant from Brazil, a blaze of crimson blossoms. Around the stem of a stunted palm trails a creeper, a convolvulus, with long blue flowers, very similar to the English flower, which was introduced into Bombay from the Canarese country.

Brighter than the flowers are the Parsee women, with their

brilliant-coloured silk robes, which suit their slim, lissom figures. They are talking, gesticulating, and laughing, with olive-complexioned mites with large black eyes and long eyelashes. Hindu women in white robes, and the marigold in their great coils of shiny black hair, are showing the animals to intelligent, bright-looking children, with little, soft, round faces. Men, women, and children all seem amused and happy. It is a pleasure to stroll about the grounds, all fragrance and flowers, and note the gentleness, the attention, and polished behaviour which marks a people whose manners are some thousand years old.

Life in India is a life of startling contrasts. A broad, dusty road leads us from the Victoria Gardens to the Byculla Club, one of the most famous and comfortable clubs in the East, and we are transplanted into London life. A group of men are sitting in the large and airy verandah, discussing the last news from England, the infinite sins of Mr. Gladstone, and then, naturally, modern democracy. There is not unanimity, however. An ex-Cabinet Minister who, like Ulysses, " has been in many cities, and knows the thoughts of many men," warmly defends his old chief, and he vigorously tilts against the pet prejudices of the Anglo-Indian official. He has studied Indian problems in bluebooks, and the men around him have devoted their lives to solving them. They have the advantage of experience ; he has the advantage of regarding them from the wider and more intellectual atmosphere of European statesmanship.

But we must not loiter long at Byculla, for we have to dine in the Fort. We leave London club life, and plunge into the native city, a paradise of luxury and splendour, stench and squalor. The richness and variety of the outlines of the narrow and curving, but not crooked streets, take hold of the imagination. The many-tinted houses, the colours white, yellow, and red, the luxurious or wild carving lavished on the pillars of wood, the balconies, rosettes

VICTORIA RAILWAY STATION.

D

of the windows, and the architraves of the roofs, give an air of refinement, of subtle grace which defies description or criticism. The Hindu temple with its gaudy-coloured mythological subjects, and the Mussulmans' simple white mosque, are vividly contrasted. It is a world of wonder. Here all races have met : Persians in huge shaggy hats, and British sailors in white ; the strong, lithe, coal-black Afreedee seaman, tall martial Rajpoots, peaceful Parsees in cherry-coloured silk trousers, Chinamen with the traditional pig-tail, swaggering Mussulmans in turbans of green, sleek Marwarees with high-fitting parti-coloured turbans of red and yellow. This tide of human life rolls down the centre of the street, unruffled by the vehicles from all quarters of the earth ploughing their way through it. There is the tramcar from New York drawn by walers from Australia, with pith helmets to protect them from the rays of the sun ; the phaeton from Long Acre drawn by high-stepping Arabs ; the rude vehicle of the land, innocent of springs, with a single square seat, drawn by handsome sleek bullocks. With much trouble and much shouting the driver works his way through the enchanted street, and we see the im-mortal eunuch, the porter, and the veiled lady standing near a shop filled with gold and silver stuff. Each trade has its own *locale*, as it was in the days when " Zedekiah the king commanded that they should commit Jeremiah into the court of the prison, and that *they should give him daily a piece of bread out of the bakers' street*." There are rows of bakers' shops, with large ovens, and vast round loaves of unleavened bread. There are long lines of confectioners', in which the sweetmeats are piled up in all sorts of fantastic shapes, and behind his pile sits the fat, greasy, half-naked confectioner. Then come the shops of the *bunias*, which are crowded with baskets filled with pulse and grain ; and the Oriental grocer kindly chatters to three or four women as he weighs their flour in a pair of primitive scales, and after much bargaining

A STREET IN GIRGAUM.

35

they purchase for a farthing a lump of salt and two green
chillies, which are their sole luxuries in life. Long and sharp
is the ting-ting that proceeds from the shops where Javan,
Tubal, and Meshech trade " their vessels of brass in thy
market." They are filled from floor to roof with large pots
and small pots ; for as the Hindu eats and drinks only from
vessels made of brass, the brazier's art is an important one
in the land. There are the shops of the money-changers,
who are seated square-legged on their carpet, with heaps of
rupees and shells before them. In a small hovel is a lean old
man who, with a blowpipe and small hammer and a pair
of pincers, is manufacturing "the chains and the bracelets,
the ear-rings, the rings and the nose jewels." Sable eve
spreads swiftly, and the great brass lamps hanging from the
roof are lighted, and the earthenware cressets before the
dark shrines are illuminated. As we lift up our faces to the
richly carved balconies, one blaze of light, we see what
Jehu saw as he entered in at the gate—" Jezebel, who
painted her face and tired her hair, and looked out of a
window."

The dawn had hardly broken in the East when we went
on board a small yacht to sail to Elephanta. After a couple
of hours' sail the landing-place at Elephanta is reached.
Here, in the days of old, there used to be a colossal stone
elephant, from which the Portuguese named the place.
After ascending the steep path, and a steeper flight of stairs,
we find ourselves on a small plateau, and before us opens a
wide cavern. We enter, and when the eye becomes accustomed to the darkness we see before us a gigantic *trimurti*, or three-formed god. The expression of the first face
is one of far-off, deep contemplation, and is grand and noble
in its calm serenity. It represents Shiv in the character of
Brahma, the creator ; in his left hand he holds a citron, an
emblem of the womb. The right hand is broken. The

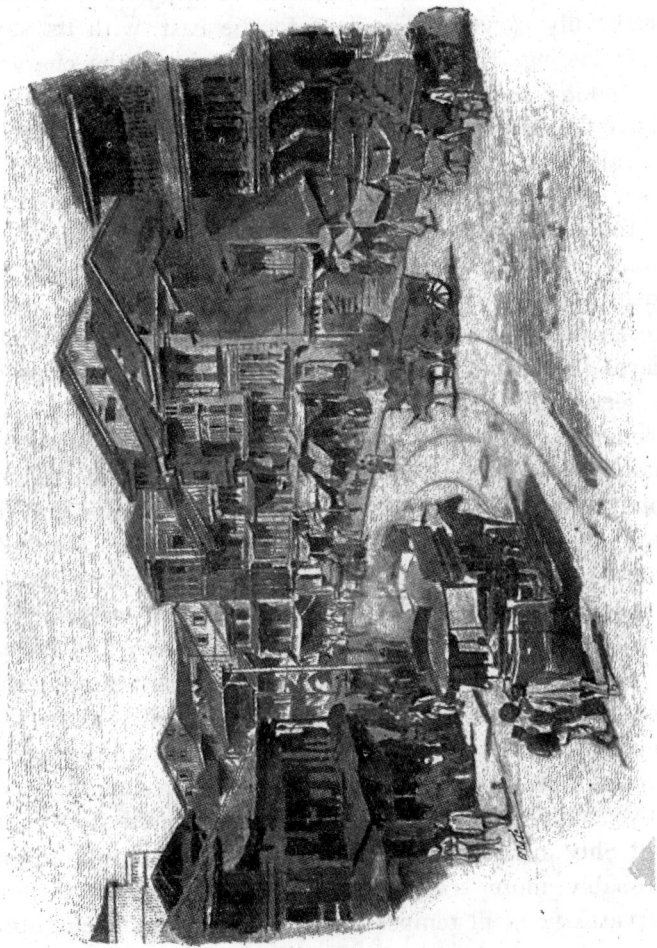

STREET IN THE NATIVE BAZAAR.

breast is adorned with a necklace of pearls, and below it is a deep, richly-wrought heart ornament. The head-dress consists of the hair raised and crowned by a royal tiara most beautifully carved. The face to the east, with its stern, commanding, Roman expression, is Shiv in the character of Buddha, the destroyer, and the brow has an oval swelling above the nose, representing a third eye. He is smiling at a cobra, which is twisted round his arms, and w th stretched hood looks him in the face. Among his ornaments are some of the peculiar symbols of Shiv—a human skull over the temple, a leaf of the *Gloriosa superba*, a branch of the milk bush, twisted snakes instead of hair, and high up a cobra erect with outstretched hood. To the west there is a gentle, placid face, which is Shiv in the character of Vishnu the preserver, and he holds a lotus flower in his hand. The Trimurti is the main object of interest in the cavern, but many hours can be profitably spent in examining the different compartments, with their sculptures full of power and life, representing the gods and goddesses of the Hindu Pantheon, and the stories of their lives. Shiv, with his consort Parvati, is a favourite subject. In one compartment we have Shiv and Parvati seated on the holy hill of Kailas ; and Parvati being in a pet, or *mana*, has her head slightly turned away. Legend says that the demon Ravan chanced to pass by at the time, and being angry at the hill stopping his progress, took it in his arms and shook it. Parvati, feeling the hill to move, ran for protection to Shiv's arms. One story states that Shiv in his rage stamped Ravan under foot ; another (probably more true) that he blessed him for stopping Parvati's fit of ill temper. Behind Parvati is the figure of a nurse executed with great spirit, and she carries a child astraddle on her left hip, as carried in India at the present hour. These sculptures illustrate how unbroken in the East are the links between the past and the present ; they are an epitome of the religious and social life that makes the continent of India so deeply interesting. The gross and passionate effigies of Hindu Mythology completely express the Oriental mind—" humorous, amorous, obscene, subtle, and refined."

II

SURAT

FOR all travellers who take an interest in the history of the rise of British dominion in India, their first point of stoppage after leaving Bombay should be Surat. It was at the port of Surat that English enterprise, after roaming over the Indian seas, first furled its wandering sail and there established a small factory which proved to be the foundation by an English trading company of a great Oriental Empire. The province of Gujarat, of which Surat is one of the chief towns, has, on account of its natural advantages for both agriculture and commerce, from the earliest times occupied an important position in the history of Hindustan. "Goozerat," says a renowned Italian traveller, "is a great kingdom. The people are idolaters, and have a peculiar language and a king of their own, and are tributary to no one." According to the permanent boundaries indicated by natural formation and the language of the people, Gujarat is about equal to Great Britain in extent, and somewhat resembles a horseshoe in shape. The Gulf of Cambay forms its inner boundary, and Surat is one of its most ancient ports in that part of the coast; how ancient it is impossible to decide, for on that point the historians are not in accord. Local traditions, however, are agreed in fixing the establishment of Surat as a modern city in the last year of the fifteenth century, and in 1514 the Portuguese traveller, Barbosa,

THE CASTLE, SURAT.
From an old Print.)

41

describes it as "a city of very great trade in all classes of merchandize, a very important seaport, yielding a large revenue to the king, and frequented by many ships from Malabar and all parts." Barbosa's own countrymen were, however, for many years the greatest enemies to the growth of the prosperity of the town. Two years before his visit they had burnt it, and subsequently in 1530 and 1531 they again laid waste the city. In order to protect it from their frequent attacks, the King of Ahmedabad commanded the present castle to be built, and, in spite of the efforts of the Portuguese, who tried by force and bribery to prevent its construction, the fortress was finished about 1546.

In 1572 the fertile fields and park-like lands of Gujarat attracted the attention of the great Akbar, and he appeared with overwhelming forces and received the submission of the province. For nearly two centuries after this, Gujarat continued to be one of the provinces subject to the house of Tamerlane, and Surat was ruled by Governors appointed by the Emperors of Delhi. Akbar, always willing to encourage foreign enterprise, concluded a treaty with the Portuguese, which made them virtual masters of the Surat seas. The example set by Portugal was not lost upon the other nations of Europe. The Dutch began to turn their attention to the Eastern trade, and rapidly to supplant the merchants of Lisbon. The great Elizabethan mariners took up the tale, and the first Charter of the "Governor and Company of Merchants of London trading with the East Indies," which, after various renewals, amalgamations, and changes of title, retained through all its vicissitudes a traditional identity, was granted on December 31, 1600. In 1608, or just about a century after the arrival of the Portuguese, Captain Hawkins of the good ship *Hector* brought to anchor the first English vessel in Gujarát waters. He tells us that he was kindly received by the natives "after their own barbarous manner," but was much harassed by the Portuguese. At this time, Surat is described as of considerable size, "with many good houses belonging to merchants," and "a pleasant Green having a Maypole in the middle on which at high festivals were hung lights and other decorations." The city was very populous and full of merchants. The people were "tall, neat, and well clothed in garments of white calico and silk, and very grave and judicious in their behaviour."

Before the English could trade a reference had to be made to the Viceroy of Gujarat (then at Cambay) and upon a favourable reply goods were sold and purchased. Hawkins, who had a letter from James I to the Emperor Jehangir, set out for the Moghul Court, and William Finch, with three or four English domestics, was left at Surat "to sell the remainder of the goods that had been landed." Hawkins met the Emperor, and married "a whyte mayden out of his palace," but he could succeed only in obtaining the verbal assurance of Jehangir that his countrymen would find protection, but no formal engagement. The Portuguese continued to harass them, and the coast in the neighbourhood witnessed many hard-contested struggles before the English were permitted to share in the lucrative trade of the city.

In September, 1611, Sir Henry Middleton arrived with his three ships at Surat. The local authorities however refused to allow him to trade, and Middleton, leaving the port, retaliated upon the Surat traders in the Red Sea. He captured "the great Pilgrim ship, the *Rehemy*, of Surat." She was of 1,500 tons, had on board, it is said, 1,500 souls, and belonged to the Moghul's mother, whose devotion had built and maintained this ship for the accommodation of pilgrims to Mecca, most of whom, as in all the other ships, "carried adventures of traders." In September, 1612, that goodly seaman, Captain Best, reached the coast with his two ships, the *Dragon* and *Hosander*, and the local authorities, having the fear of God instilled into them by Middleton, concluded with him a trading agreement. On November 29, the Portuguese fleet, consisting of four galleons and more than twenty frigates, appeared off the bar of Surat to drive the two English ships away. Three stubborn fights ensued. Then Best determined to fight them in an opener sea, and, crossing the gulf, anchored at a bay where the Moghul troops were besieging a fort. On December 22 the four Portuguese galleons appeared, and at night anchored within shot. "Early in the morning Captain Best stood towards them, who weighed and put before the wind, cannonaded until out of reach, for they sailed better. The next morning, at sunrise, he stood to them again, and maintained the fight until noon, when both sides weary (such is the phrase) parted." [1] On the 27th Best's two ships, "no longer dogged by the Portuguese, anchored at Swally and resumed the intercourse with their factors at Surat, where the event of their fights raised the English reputation even in the opinion of ill-will." The trading agreement had been confirmed by an Imperial Firman or decree. The Governor sent it to Swally as a common letter of business, but Best refused to receive it unless delivered with the usual solemnities. "This spirit brought the Governor and his son-in-law, the custom-master, to Swally, who presented it in state and congratulated : but were very curious to know whether the English ships had not suffered more than was said, in the late engagement." From this Firman dates the foundation of our power in India. And " this spirit " has made it extend from Surat to Attock.

Two years later that stern and experienced seaman,

[1] *Historical Fragments of the Mogul Empire, of the Morattoes, and of the English Concerns in Indostan, from the year MDCLIX*, by Robert Orme, F.A.S., p. 330.

Nicholas Downton, with a fleet of fine ships—the *Merchant's Hope* (200 tons), *Hector* (300 tons), *The New Year's Gift* (600 tons), and *Solomon* (of 500 tons), came to anchor in South Swally—" God be thanked, in safety, having lost in the ship the *Solomon*, till then since our departure from England, only one man." Downton learnt the next day that the Great Moghul had debarred the Portuguese from trade in any of his dominions " by reason of a ship they took at the bar's foot of Surratt of very great value pertaining to his subjects, as also had besieged a town possessed by them some twelve leagues to the southward of Surratt called Damon [Daman] which siege as yet continueth, though with little hope of prevailing." The Governor pressed him that he should go and aid them in the siege of Daman, but Downton refused. However, having " somewhat (as we thought) mollified the Governor," they began to discharge their goods about the primes of November. In December Downton heard that the Viceroy of Goa was equipping a great force against him. On January 18 " came to the bar of Surrat the Viceroy of Portugal—with six galleons from 800 to 1,000 tons, three smaller ships from 150 to 300 tons, two galleys and some 60 frigates." [1] Don Jeronimo de Azevedo, the Viceroy, hoisted his flag as Admiral on board the *Todos Santos*, of 800 tons. The Portuguese fleet carried two hundred and thirty-five guns. The European soldiers and sailors amounted to two thousand six hundred, the native sailors to six thousand. The four English ships carried only eighty guns of inferior calibre, and their soldiers and sailors amounted to four hundred men. But Downton was an excellent bold seaman. On the 20th three of the smaller Portuguese vessels with many of their frigates came within the sands at Swally. Downton weighed from " our usual road," and going near the entrance " the General

[1] *Letters Received by the East India Company from its Servants in the East*, vol. ii., 1613-1615. William Foster.

sent the *Hope* a distance from us to give an edge to their courage whereby to have some rash attempt practised by them, which fell out accordingly." [1]   The three smaller vessels and most of their frigates attacked the *Hope* " and with great resolution came aboard her and once or twice entered her."   The other English ships went to her rescue and were attacked by the rest of the frigates.   But they repulsed them and so galled the three ships with their fire that those on board had to forsake them " and enter their frigates for quicker speed to be gone."   " But their haste was to their ruin, and their speed their overthrow, for we let fly at them with our great ordnance and small shot, so that by them many of their frigates were sunk and their inhabitants lost their lives.   Till sunset we continually battered one against the other."   In the meantime the *Hope* cleared herself " and doubting what traitors might be left aboard the Portugal ships thought it the best course to fire them, which accordingly they did."   The English loss was five men slain and divers wounded, " which number (thanks be to God) was far inferior to the enemy's loss."   The Shahbandar, or Marine Superintendent of the Surat port, stated that the Portuguese carried to Daman to be buried 360, " besides divers that we saw daily floating on the water and lying on the sand."   The mainmast of the *Hope* had been burnt, and Downton was unable to break the blockade and attack the Portuguese outside the bar.   But each morning and evening he fired across the strip of sand a volley at the enemy, aiming his best cannon at the Viceroy's prow— " which I did to try his best temper."

The Portuguese, having lost three ships, got within ten days three more from their settlements at Daman and Diu— " after whose arrival, to weary our men and keep them in action, they made many shows and proffers to come in

---

[1] *Letters Received by the East India Company from its Servants in the East*, vol. ii., 1613–1615.   William Foster.

with their ships, but never effected it." In the hour of his trial and of his triumph there fell a blow on Nicholas Downton, which broke his stout old heart. " On February 3," he writes, " it pleased God, this day, at night, where I had least leisure to mourn, to call to His mercy my only son." The volleys aforesaid, appointed to try the temper of the Viceroy, he adds, " served also to honour his burial." On February 9, at 10 o'clock, the enemy at night sent two fire boats chained and stuffed with powder, wildfire, and other combustible matters down on the English ships. " One whereof came aboard the *Hope*, but, God be thanked, cleared herself without hurt and so burning drave by her." The next night at the same time they exercisedt he like with two very dangerous fires. The first contained two boats and the next four, which were all chained together, fired and let drive amongst us; but putting our ships under sail we cleared us of them, which drove ashore and there burnt out." The Viceroy, seeing that their force and stratagems took no better effect, "the next day, with his whole fleet, set sail and went and rode at the bar, from whence the day following they all departed, but whither not yet certainly known ; we daily expected their return hither again or encounter at sea, where it may be they lie in wait for us, wherein God's will be done."

In August 1615 Sir Thomas Roe, sent by James I as Ambassador to the Court of the Moghul, arrived at Surat. It was a critical moment. He found his countrymen oppressed and treated with severity. As he relates in his diary :

" Soe base are our Conditions in this Port and subject to soe many slaueryes, such as noe free hart can endure, that I doe resolue eyther to establish a trade on free Conditions or to doe my best to dissolue yt. For noe profitt can be a good Pennywoorth at soe much dishonor ; the person of euery man landing loccked vp and searched like a theefe ; sometymes two

47

dayes before leaue can be had for any man to passe the riuer; a poore bottle of wyne sent to the sick deteyned; and euery trifle ransacked and taken away, with unsufferable insolencyes."

Roe held a high estimate of the nature of his appointment. When the Surat authorities suggested that his company might be searched "according to the custome of the country," we find him protesting

"that I was the Ambassador of a mightie and free Prince: that I would neuer dishonnor my Master so much, whose Person I bare, as to subject myselfe to so much slauery."

Roe's tact, dignity and energy won the day, and three years later he succeeded in obtaining certain further privileges for his countrymen. He also made a separate treaty with the Moghul Emperor's third son, Prince Kharram, afterwards the famous Shah Jehan, to whom had been assigned by his father the Government of Surat. By this treaty the English gained the rights of building a house, bearing arms, exercising their own religion freely, and settling their own disputes among themselves. The modest house at Surat was the first permanent connexion of the English with India, and the growth of the Surat Factory forms an important and interesting chapter in the history of our Indian Empire.

Twelve years after the English got permission to build a house; the President received the high-sounding title of Chief of the Honourable Company of English Merchants trading in the East. The Portuguese did their utmost to use their influence with the Moghul to expel the Dutch and English from his dominions. In a letter dated October 25, 1630, we have a graphic description of a stubborn engagement with the Portuguese. After a sketch of the formation of the troops we are informed :—

"But such was the undauntednes of our English, being stirred up to a high measure of furie by the hourly vexations and braveings of the enemy, as being now come within shot with a generall resolution rejoycing att the occasion, after a shot or two received first from the Portuigalls pushed on in the verye face and mouth of all their ffriggats and perceaveing that but 3 of them could use the advantage of their prowes against them, and that some of the rest were brought aground, and had only their Harquibuses acrooke to gall them advanced forwards still plying their small shot with very good discipline, and the Portuigalls noe lesse valliently replying with their double forces, as well from their ffriggats at sea, as the squadrone on shore, but not able it seems to endure the obstinate rage of our people they began to give grounds, and our most fiercely following, entered pellmell amongst them, even into the water, within lesse then pistoll shot of their ffriggats ; in which intrim the Vice Kings sonne was conveyed aboard but soe narrowly escaped that the party who provided for his safety was himselfe taken prisoner in the accon [action] : many of the English not feareing to runn up to the chin in water, even to the very sides of their ffriggats pursueing the victory with great slaughter both at shoare and at sea, and at length returned with 27 Portuigalls prisoners taken alive, without the losse of any more than one ancient man (a corporall), not wounded but suffocated only with heate, and the wounding of 7 more of our people. This they happily performed in sight of Meirza Baker, and divers of these country people to their great admiration and our nations greater honour, to that good God that led them by the hand be the glorye." [1]

To revenge his defeat the Portuguese Admiral made an effort to destroy the English ships, which proved disastrous to his own fleet. The President writes in the postscript to his letter :

" At this very instant is come newes from ye Commanders below that the last night (being Sunday againe) about 8 of the clock, the Portuigalls put in execution their maine stratagem soe much depended on by them, and not without cause much feared by us, in fireing of their 4 prepared vessells chained together for the intended destruction of our fleet, but the vigi-

---

[1] *Selections from the Letters, Despatches, and other State Papers Preserved in the Bombay Secretariat* (Home Series), edited by George W. Forrest, vol. i. p. 11.

lancie of our people directed by the Divine Providence of that greate protector that hath allwayes hetherto bestowed innumerable blessings uppon us hath prevented the end of that great mischeife intended. Our boats well manned on head of the headmost ship having with their grapnells ready for the purpose fastened on the boats so fired, and towing two of them (still burning) on the shoare, and the other two on the sands gave happie cause of great joye in our people for soe happie diliverance, and shame enough to our malitious enemy that hath thus basely in that kinde endeavoured ruines." [1]

The factory was fortified in 1642, and in 1646 its " quick stock " was valued at £83,000, and twenty years later it is said to have excelled all houses, except that of the Dutch, who had also been allowed to establish a factory. But though their factory had grown in wealth, the English factors had much to endure in the early days. In 1662 they state that " our last year's imprisonment and restraynt from food, the attempt of our deaths with many other sordid abuses, cryes vengeance on these infidels. And because our complaynts at home for justice cannot be heard, therefore are wee ye scorne of those people and our privelledges and honour trampled under by force in ye absence of our shipping." A more prosperous time however ensued when the brave and energetic Sir George Oxinden, who deserves to rank with Clive and Hastings as one of the illustrious founders of our Indian Empire, became chief of the factory. His defence of the factory when Shivaji, the founder of the Mahratta Empire, betrayed the town, was as gallant an affair as Clive's defence of Arcot. He informed the company in London that

" on ye 6th January, 1664, was brought a hott allarum yt Sevagy ye grand rebell of ye Deccan was within 10 or 15 miles of ye towne. The President sent for forty men from the ships to aid him in the defence, with whom wee your Ffactors servants joined and having drawn them out in ranke and file with drum and

---

[1] *Selections*, vol. i. p. 12.

trumpett your President in the head marcht through ye body of ye towne to ye Greene before ye Castle where ye Governour was ready to pop in upon the first notice of their approach. Wee past close by him, and so marcht on taking a great circle round that ye enemy was at the gates before wee could reach our house."

A Mr. Anthony Smith coming from Swalley was taken prisoner and came to Shivaji, who took 300 rupees

"ransome of him, and sent him ye next day to menace us, but before that we had received many threats. But wee still bidd him keepe his people out of ye reach of our gunns, elce wee would shoote them. Hee returned answere wee were friends, wee replied if soe, why did hee detaine an English man, take a horse out of our stable and make fences of your goods yt lay before ye coustume house; and also suffered them to bee plundered; all these things spoake him an ennemy, and therefore this President returned answere wee would not trust him or admitt of any further treaty, and therefore hee should send us noe more messages, and if hee did wee would kill ye messenger."

Shivaji also sent messengers to demand homage

"and yt if we refused it hee would raise our house to ye ground, and not spare a life.

"Wee replyed wee were here on purpose to maintaine your house to ye death of ye last man and therefore not to delay his coming upon us; by ye time he had broken Hodjy Saed Beagues house open, and had one nightes entire plunder out of it, which being so very neare us, as one wall to part both houses, wee feared they would strengthen yt place and afterwards annoy us, and by their multitudes force their way or undermine and blow us up, and yt seeing they did begin with their horse and foote to surround us, some then standing under our eaves for noe good, wee caused a party of foote to sally forth ye house and fight them; in which scufell we had 3 men slightly wounded, ours sleu a horse and man, some say two or three, but wee routed them. This good success animated us yet further to clear our quarters of them, and hearing they had taken their randevous in a Muskett or Moore Church joining close to our house, and also in Hodgy Saeds house warehouses, having out of feare of us not done him ye quarter of ye mischiefe they intended him. Whilst our men were clearing ye Muskett they in ye houses and warehouses opened ye doores and fled, soe wee shutt up ye doores and barracadoed them, and made a passage from our into his house, and kept a garrison in a belcony that cleared all ye streat and garded ye other house of ye Hodgies. When ye rebell had heard what was past of ye killing and routing his guards hee falls a threatning Mr. Smith, some time with ye loss of his head and some times to cutt of his hand, & at last causes him to write a noate to ye President, that if wee persisted in fighting against him hee would race our house to ye ground and bee our destruction. By this time wee had more assistance from ye ships, wherfore ye President wrote Mr. Smith, we would prosecute wt wee had begun, and not at all moved at his threate requiring him to save the labour of his servants running to and fro on messages, and come himself with all his army."

The approach of the Moghul army caused Shivaji to return from the town which he had plundered and laid waste.

" He hath carried away in gold, silver, and pearle, precious stones and other rich good to the vallue of many hundred thousand pounds, and burnt of other goods and houses to ye amount of as much more, so yt ye towne is utterly ruin'd and very little left either of riches or habitation. Ye rogue was very cruell ; Mr. Smith in ye time of his imprisonment was present when hee cutt of more than 26 hands in one day and many heads ; who ever hee was yt was taken and brought before him yt could not redeeme himself lost either his hand or his head, and his manner was first to plunder and then to cause ye owner of his house to give him some thing over and above to redeeme his house from being burnt, and yet ye perfidious villaine would fire it afterwards, although hee had obliged himself to ye contrary. Wee are now endeavouring to emprove this skirmage of ours to your profitt, by acclamations of ye townes people, as well they yt are sufferers as those whose houses were preserv'd, who laying aside their owne losses cry out in thousands for a reward from ye King to ye English yt had by their courage preserved them, when those to whom they were intrusted as the Governor etc a dared not shew his head."

SURAT

On the arrival of the Moghul army Sir George Oxinden received from the Commander

"great thanks for ye good service we did ye king and the country; whereupon your President having a pistoll in his hand layed it before ye Chiefe saying yt hee did now lay down his armes, leaving ye future care and protection of ye citty to them, which was exceedingly well taken; telling ye President hee did accept it and in reward of ye good service hee must give him a vest, a horse, and girt a sword about him; but your President told him these were things becoming a souldier, but we were merchants, and expected favour from ye King in our trade."[1]

The prosperity of the factory at Surat received a fatal blow by Bombay being ceded to the Company (1668) and being made the capital of the Company's possessions and the chief seat of their trade (1687). Surat was taken possession of by the English two years after the battle of Plassey (1757), and the conquerors assumed the undivided government of the city in 1800.

By means of old records and books of travel we gain an insight into the internal economy of the factory, and catch some interesting glimpses of the habits and life of the English in Surat in those days. John Fryer, M.D., Cantabrig., and Fellow of the Royal Society, writes from Surat, January 15, 1674-5: "The House the English live in at Surat is partly the King's Gift, partly hired; Built of stone and excellent Timber, with good Carving without Representations; very strong, for that each Floor is Half a Yard thick at least, of the best plastered Cement, which is very weighty. It is contrived after the Moor's Buildings, with upper and lower Galleries, or Terras-walks; a neat Oratory, a convenient open Place for Meals. The President has spacious Lodgings, noble Rooms for Counsel and Entertainment, pleasant Tanks, Yards, and an Hummum to wash in; but no Gardens in the

[1] *Selections*, vol. i. pp. 24–26.

City, or very few, though without they have many, like Wildernesses, overspread with Trees. The English had a neat one, but Seva Gi's coming destroyed it: It is known, as the other Factories are, by their several Flags flying."

The neat Oratory was the first place of worship founded by the English in India. Ten years before Fryer's visit George Oxinden informed the Company that they had

" seperated a place apart for Gods worship and decently adorned it, wherein stands your Library, and amongst them those severall volumes of ye holy bible in ye Languages which is much esteemed by those yt are learned amongst these people : yt if any eminent person come to your houses his greatest desire is to see the Chappell; wherfore wee entreate you for further ornament, to send us out a large table in a frame, gilded and handsomely adorned with Moses and Aaron holding the two tables containing the ten Commandments, the Lords Prayer and the Creed, written in letters of gould, and in ye midst at ye topp in triangles, Gods name writt in as many of these easterne Languages as Arabick, Persian, &c⁂ as can be procured; which if you please to honnor our Chappell with, it will bee a glory to our religion, as yt which is more taken than anything that they shall read beside, and yet our meaning is yt ye Commandments &c⁂ be wrot in ye English language." [1]

In the convenient place for meals the factors fared sumptuously every day. Their dishes and plates were of silver, " many and substantial," and were filled with the choicest viands prepared to please every palate by English, Portuguese, and French cooks. At dinner each course was ushered in by the sound of trumpets, and a band of music played during the meal. The English factors, even in those early days, had a sound knowledge of native character, and knew how to impress the Oriental mind. We are told that from the very outset the President adopted considerable show. When he went into the streets, " besides a noise of trumpets, there was a guard of English soldiers, consisting of a double

[1] *Selections,* vol. i. p. 31.

file led by a sergeant, a body of forty moormen and a flag-man carrying St. George's colours swallow-tailed in silk fastened to a single partizan." The President was carried in a Palki emblazoned with the royal escutcheon and lined with rich silks, and his Council were "in large coaches drawn by stately oxen." Fryer gives us a sketch of the native coach in which the factors rode. He was one of the old travellers who describes things as exactly as they see them, and this is the virtue which causes them to defy the power of oblivion. The works of Bernier, Ta-vernier, Terry, Hamilton, and Fryer, though two centuries have lapsed since they were first printed, still contain the most accurate and graphic accounts of India that have ever been published. These men were shrewd observers, and they note with care the physical appearance of the land through which they pass, the customs of the people, the hovels of the poor, and the palaces of the great. By simple speech they make us their companions in their wanderings. The modern traveller discusses the ryotwari system and the salt tax. Fryer tells us that the "Combies till the land and dress the corn with no remarkable difference from other Nations, they plough with Oxen, their coulters unarmed mostly, Iron being scarce, but they have hard wood which will turn their light grounds." "Their oxen are Little but all have a Bunch on their neck," "the women are Neat, well shaped and Affectionate to their children, Bearing them Naked on their Hips astraddle." By these touches he brings to our eyes and minds the ordinary life of the changeless East. His little sketch of the coach carries us into the very heart of a daily scene.

"Two large Milk-white Oxen are putting in to draw it, with circling Horns as black as a Coal, each Point tipped with Brass, from whence come Brass Chains across to the Headstall, which is all of Scarlet, and a Scarlet Collar to each, of Brass Bells, about their Necks, their flapping Ears snipped with Art, and from their

Nostrils Bridles covered with Scarlet. The Chariot it self is not swinging like ours, but fastened to the main Axle by neat Arches which support a Foursquare Seat, which is inlaid with Ivory, or enriched as they please ; at every Corner are turned Pillars, which make (by twisted Silk or Cotton Cords) the Sides and support the Roof, covered with English Scarlet Cloth, and lined with Silk with Party-coloured Borders; in these they spread Carpets, and lay Bolsters to ride cross-legged, sometimes three or four in one : It is born on two Wheels only, such little ones as our Fore-wheels are, and pinned on with a Wooden Arch, which serves to mount them : The Charioteer rides before, a-straddle on the Beam that makes the Yoke for the Oxen, which is covered with Scarlet, and finely carved underneath ; he carries a Goad instead of a Whip : In Winter (when they rarely stir) they have a mumjuma, or Wax-cloth to throw over it. Those for Journeying are something stronger than those for the Merchants to ride about the City or to take the Air on ; which with their nimble Oxen they will, when they meet in the Fields, run Races on, and contend for the Garland as much as for an Olympick Prize ; which is a Diversion, To see a Cow gallop, as we say in scorn ; but these not only pluck up their Heels apace, but are taught to amble, they often riding on them."

The merchants at home did not approve of the ostentation of their servants. They told the President that they would be better pleased if he would suppress his rising ambition and modify his inordinate love of display ; and to enable him the more readily to renounce all pomps and vanities they ordered that he should only be styled Agent, and reduced his salary to £300 a year. When Surat was taken possession of by the English in 1759 the commercial period came to an end. Fifty years went on, and when the East India Company assumed the entire government of the city and its dependencies, the Chiefship and Council were abolished, and a Lieutenant-Governor of the Castle was appointed. Three years later the title was changed into "Agent of Government at Surat." Surat, from being the seat of power and government, became a mere district of Bombay. The old factory, the scene of so much revelry and splendour, was converted into a lunatic asylum and a refuge for the native sick. Briggs, the author of *Cities of Gujarashtra*, who visited Surat in 1847, speaks of it as " a noble pile." " Lusty timbers of huge dimensions, and walls intended to last as long as any of those of ' the old houses at home,' barred windows below and heavy gates without, tell of other and glorious times." Thirty years ago, when we first visited Surat, what was left of the old factory was only a portion of the original lodge, which had been converted into a private dwelling. The fragment, however, deserves to be maintained with pious care by the State as one of the most interesting relics of our race. The factory at Surat in less than a century expanded into an empire which in extent of territory and in multitude of subjects rivalled Rome.

Leaving the English factory and proceeding to the north, we came to an open plot of ground with a cross which marked the site of the altar of the chapel of the Capuchins, who for a century, according to Hamilton in *A New Account of the East Indies* (1700–1720), " practised surgery gratis to the poor Natives of what Persuasion soever." Close to the church was the French lodge, of which only the lines of the foundations remain. Behind the French lodge are a few rooms of the Portuguese factory, " a fortification built for a never waning dominion ; strong, durable, impregnable to the native host : a receptacle for the pomp and pageantry of life."

The sepulchral ruins in the cemetery of Surat, massive and ponderous in their elaborate masonry, are all that is now left to remind the traveller of the pomp and show of former days. The old factors were of the same mind as poor Cleopatra :

> " Let's do it after the high Roman fashion,
> And make Death proud to take us."

The most stately monument is that erected over those " most brotherly of brothers, Christopher and Sir George

Oxinden." There is no weak affectation or sentimentalism in George Oxinden's tomb ; but it is worthy of the man who, with a handful of Europeans, held his factory against the

TOMB OF THE OXINDEN BROTHERS.

whole Mahratta army. It is forty feet in height and twenty-five in diameter, and includes two domes, with staircases and galleries, supported on massive pillars. It appears from

the Latin inscription that the lower dome was first built
to commemorate Sir George's brother Christopher, and was
surmounted by one to commemorate himself. Christopher's
epitaph has too much of the ledger about it to please. It
laments his short life, for it was only possible to reckon his
days, and not his years, before death required the account.
" Do you ask, my masters, what is your profit and loss ?
You have gained sorrow, but he has lost his life ; *per contra*
let him write, ' Death to me is gain.' " We may quote one
more from the many quaint epitaphs to be found in the
Surat cemetery :

" In memory of Mary Price, wife of William Andrew Price, Esq.,
Chief for affairs of the British nation and Governor of the Moghul's Castle and Fleet of Surat, who, through the spotted veil
of the small pox, rendered a pure and unspotted soul to God,
expecting but not fearing death which ended her days. April
the thirteenth, Anno Domini 1761. *Aetatis suae* 23.

> " ' The virtues which in her short life were shown
> Have equalled been by few, surpassed by none.' "

From the English cemetery we pass over, as Fryer did, to
the Dutch tombs, " many and handsome, most of them
Pargetted." They stand in a neglected patch of ground
studded with fruit-trees, and some wild parasite is bursting
asunder their walls. " Grand, noble, for the expanse of
ground it covers, its height, its peculiar style of sculpture
is the mausoleum erected over the last resting-place of Mr.
Van Rheede, to whom Oriental history pays the tribute of
eulogy in denominating the *Maecenas of Malabar*. At a period
when European residents in India wholly directed their
attention to mercantile adventure, or attempted political
aggrandizement, he could spare the leisure to devote to
scientific research ; and his labours have provided Holland
with many valuable manuscripts and other equally important curiosities, while some of his statements still challenge enquiry. His *Hortus Indicus Malabaricus*, a work in

DUTCH TOMBS.

twelve volumes folio, is an evidence of his literary exertions." The tomb approaches in shape a decagon with a double cupola of great dimensions and a gallery above and below supported on handsome columns. "In the centre of the chamber a single tombstone marks a vault with more occupants than the Dutch officials." A wooden tablet recounts the particulars of "Hendrik Adriaan Baron Van Reede," who died, aged 56, on the 15th of December, 1691. "The noble pile," as Ovington calls it, was built to eclipse that of Sir George Oxinden's. Nothing now remains to remind the traveller of the "one-hundred-and-seventy fortified stations in this India," which the Dutch once held, except a few ruined bastions of their old forts, the massive tombs in the old cemeteries dotted about the coast, and a few volumes of Dutch records in the archives at Madras and Bombay.

III

AHMEDABAD

TO the traveller, Ahmedabad, the capital of Gujarat will always be a city of interest as containing some of the most perfect and the most characteristic forms which Saracenic architecture assumed in India. It has also a history which has an interest, studied on the spot, among the monuments of the city. The province of Gujarat was for centuries the seat of very flourishing Hindu dynasties, and the story of their rise and fall is being traced by European and native scholars (with their newly created respect for historical accuracy) from inscriptions engraved on sheets of copper, on coins, and carved on stones. These have been compelled to yield up the secrets which litera-ture disdained to preserve. The Hindu writers, who in ancient days wrote historical legends, inform us that Vama Raja, in the eighth century, about the time the Mercians were conquering Wessex, founded the Chavada dynasty and built the famous capital Anahelavada,[1] about sixty miles north-east of Ahmedabad on the limpid stream of the Saravasti. It was his minister who erected the renowned town of Champanir, thirty miles from Baroda. The house of Vama Raja reigned over Gujarat for upwards of a century. It was succeeded by the Solanki family, whose greatness was founded by Mula Raja, said by an illustrious sage to be " the benefactor of the world. He was generous-minded, full of all good qualities. All kings worshipped him

[1] Tod's *Travels in Western India.*

as they worshipped the sun, all subjects who abandoned
their own country found a happy residence under his protection." Mula Raja was succeeded by his son, Chámunda
(A.D. 997), and during his reign Mahmud of Ghazni
burst into India, penetrated into Gujarat, and took the
capital Anahelavada. He then attacked the far-famed
temple of Somnath, desecrated the beloved Pagan shrine,
and stripped it of its treasures. The story of Mahmud
striking the idol of Somnath with his mace and the jewels running out is however one of the mock pearls of history. The
real object of worship at Somnath was not an image but a
simple cylinder of stone—a lingam. It is described as five
cubits high, two of which were set in the ground, and it was
destroyed by a fire lighted round it to split the hardness of
the stone. For a year Mahmud of Ghazni lingered in
Gujarat, delighted with the garden of Western India; and
its broad fertile plains, adorned with magnificent trees,
were so great a contrast to his rocky and barren home that
he entertained the thought of settling there, but on mature
deliberation determined to return to his own dominions.
His invasion was but a passing inroad. After he left,
Gujarat enjoyed many years of peace and prosperity, and
the splendour of its capital increased. It was during the
reign of Sidh Raja the Magnificent that the province reached
the zenith of its glory. Then Anahelavada was said to be
the richest town in India, and marvellous stories are told
of its markets, its palaces, its schools, and its gardens,
where, amidst sweet-scented trees, the learned studied and
taught philosophy and religion. Sidh Raja ranks high
among Hindu monarchs and he is described by his chroni-
clers as " the ornament of Goojat-land." Of his character
we are told that he was " the receptacle of all good qualities,
as great in kind actions as he was in war ; the tree of deserts
to his servants." Sidh Raja reigned for forty-nine years
(A.D. 1094–1143), and on his death, as he left no son, the

throne passed to a distant relative. The last of the line was Bhima Deva, who repelled an invasion made by Muhammad Ghori, but Kulub-ud-din, a favourite Turkish slave, revenged his master's defeat by driving Bhima Deva from his capital. The Muhammadans however did not remain in Gujarat, and Anahelavada continued to be the capital of a Hindu kingdom.

It was not till a century later that Gujarat was conquered by the Muslims and passed under the rule of the Viceroys of the Emperor of Delhi. These Viceroys in course of time grew more and more powerful and Gujarat became the seat of an independent Muhammadan dynasty. The second Sultan of this house, Ahmed Shah, founded in 1411 the capital Ahmedabad on the banks of the Saburmati and on the site of several Hindu towns. He built a citadel of much strength and beauty and he laid out his city in broad, fair streets. Bringing marble and other rich building materials from a long distance he raised magnificent mosques, palaces and tombs, and by encouraging merchants, weavers and skilled craftsmen he made Ahmedabad a centre of trade and manufacture. Under able rulers the kingdom increased in riches and power. The splendid buildings at Ahmedabad and the ruins of Champanir testify to the wealth of the sovereign, and travellers from beyond the sea bore witness to the prosperity of the kingdom. The Portuguese traveller Duarte Barbosa, who visited Gujarat in A.D. 1511 and A.D. 1514, informs us that " inland he found the capital Champanir a great city, a very fertile country of abundant provisions, and many cows, sheep, goats and plenty of fruit, so that it was full of all good things "; and Ahmedabad " still larger, very rich and well supplied, embellished with good streets and squares with houses of stone and cement." The Sultans of Gujarat gradually enlarged their territory and the sway of Bahadur Shah extended from Somnath to Bijapur. He died fighting the Portuguese, who had become the masters of the sea that washed his dominions. After his death the power of his successors began gradually to wane and the kingdom was impoverished and harassed by the constant quarrels of the turbulent nobles. In 1572, a party of them called on the great Akbar, who, meeting with little opposition, entered Gujarat and made Ahmedabad a province of his empire and appointed a Viceroy. With the annexation of the province by Akbar there began a time of far less architectural splendour but of incomparably better government and well-being.

The Sultans of Ahmedabad did what the Muhammadan conquerors have always done wherever their victorious arms have reached ; they oppressed their infidel subjects, forbade their worship, destroyed their temples and converted the material to their own uses. In Gujarat they stole not only the materials for building their mosques and tombs, but also the architectural style of the Jains—the adherents of one of the two great heresies from Brahmanism, which arose in the sixth century. Mahāvīra, the founder or reformer of Jainism, with his eleven chief disciples, may be regarded as the first open seceders from Brahmanism, unless one assigns the same date to the revolt of Buddha. " The two schisms have so much in common," says Hopkins in *The Religions of India*, " especially in outward features, that for long it was thought that Jainism was a sub-sect of Buddhism. In their legends, in the localities in which they flourished, and in many minutiæ of observances they are alike. Nevertheless, their differences are as great as the resemblance between them, and what Jainism at first appeared to have got of Buddhism seems now rather the common loan made by each sect from Brahmanism."

Mahāvīra, the reputed founder of his sect, was, like Buddha, of aristocratic birth. At the age of twenty-eight he set forth on his mission and betook himself to asceticism. He wandered as an ascetic into many lands, preaching, converting and enduring the scorn of the wicked. "He was beaten and set upon by sinful men, yet he was never moved to anger." Thus it was that he became the Arhat (venerable), the Jina (victor), the Kivalin (perfect sage). The teaching of the founder became known as Jainism, as Buddhism is the teaching of Buddha the Enlightened. Jainism and Buddhism were merely two out of the dozen heretical sects of importance agitating the region about Benares at the same time. The Jains, as Hopkins says, " drifted westward, while the Buddhist stronghold remained in the east (both of course being represented in the south as well); and so, whereas Buddhism eventually retreated to Nepal and Tibet, the Jains are found in the very centres of old and new (sectarian) Brahmanism, Delhi, Mathura, Jeypur Ajmer." Jainism however never became a dominant creed. Like Quakerism, it found its chief supporters among the rich middle class and to the Peases and Barclays of Western India we owe the costly Jain temples. The faith is still followed by the great banking families of Gujarat. When the Muhammadans conquered the province and built their Mosques they insisted on the essential features of their own style, the minaret and pointed arch, but as they had to employ Hindu architects they adopted the pillared halls and the traceries and rich surface ornament of the vanquished people. But the confounding two distinct and opposite styles of architecture is not a complete success. The Hindu worked out in rock-hewn cavern and dark-pillared hall those ideas of fear and gloom with which his religion associates the divinity. The Muhammadans expressed the simple ideas of glory and praise to an all powerful Jehovah. All the Muslim wants is a courtyard with a tank for ablution, roofed cloisters to shelter the worshippers, a niche in the east wall to indicate the direction of Mecca, a pulpit for the Friday sermon and a tribune or raised platform from which the Koran is re-

THE JUMMA MUSJID.

cited and prayers intoned. There must be, if possible, a minaret from which to call the faithful to prayer, but the dome is not an essential feature. The first mosque which Ahmed Shah built (1414) illustrates the Moslem's desire to destroy the temples of the heathen and to use their materials to erect his own fane. The mosque itself is founded on the site of ancient temples, and the rows of pillars supporting the dome were taken from infidel shrines. The very carving on the balustrade is Hindu. Nine years after he had built his own private chapel, Ahmed Shah enriched his new capital with the Jumma Musjid, which Fergusson considers to be one of the most beautiful mosques in the east. Quitting the crowd that blocks the streets, we pass through a mean portal into the courtyard of the Jumma Musjid, paved with fine white marble. The first vision overpowers and captivates, but the enchantment does not endure. It has not the special lasting charm which attaches to a building which has some feature peculiar to itself. The three hundred lofty columns supporting the domes are too crowded and their fantastic sculpture seems out of place. It is a Hindu temple converted into a mosque and the soul has gone. On the marble wall opposite the entrance are the words which represent the pride and the humility of the Muslim : "This spacious mosque was erected by Ahmed Shah, a faithful slave of Allah, seeking the mercy of God. He alone is good, He alone is to be worshipped ! " We may however admire the exquisite finish of the delicate fretwork and the ornament of the tower, all that is left of the famous shaking minarets. "A little force at the arch of the upper gallery," an ancient traveller states, made both of them shake "though the roof of the mosque remained unchanged." Forbes, in his *Oriental Memoirs*, describes them " as elegantly proportioned and richly decorated " and " each minaret contains a circular flight of steps leading to a gallery near the summit for the purpose of convening

RANI SIPRI : THE TOMB.

the people to prayer, no bells being in use among the Muhammadans. From these you command an extensive view of Ahmedabad and the Sáburmáli winding through a wide campaign." The minarets were thrown down by a great earthquake in 1819, " both of them breaking off at the sill of the window whence the call to prayers used to be chanted."

A door in the east wall of the Jumma Musjid leads to the tomb of its royal founder and his two sons. It is a massive structure surmounted by a dome and lighted at intervals by windows of fine fretwork. Beyond Ahmed's stately mausoleum is the burying ground of his favourite sultanas. A narrow and dirty lane leads to it. Mounting some steps we reach a platform, and passing through a lofty gateway enter a rectangular court surrounded by a trellised cloister. In the centre are the tombs of the two queens, one of white marble richly carved, girt with an Arabic inscription in minute relief, the other of black marble inlaid with mother of pearl. And beautiful is the contrast between the black and white marble tombs, the simplicity of the form and the richness and delicacy of the details.

The effect of the Jumma Musjid may be more over-whelming, but there is no building in Ahmedabad which is more pleasing to the eye, none which more thoroughly com-mends itself to the critical judgment, than Rani Sipri's mosque.[1] It is a Hindu building and it carries out logically the principles of Hindu architecture. No arch, as Fer-gusson points out, is employed anywhere either construc-tively or for ornament, and the minarets, though so ex-quisite in design, are not minarets in reality ; they have no internal stairs and no galleries from which the call to prayer could be recited. They are pure ornament of the most

[1] Rani Sipri was the wife of a son of Ahmed Shah, and her mosque and tomb, says Hope, in *Architecture of Ahmedabad*, were completed in A.D. 1431, probably by herself during her lifetime. according to a very general custom.

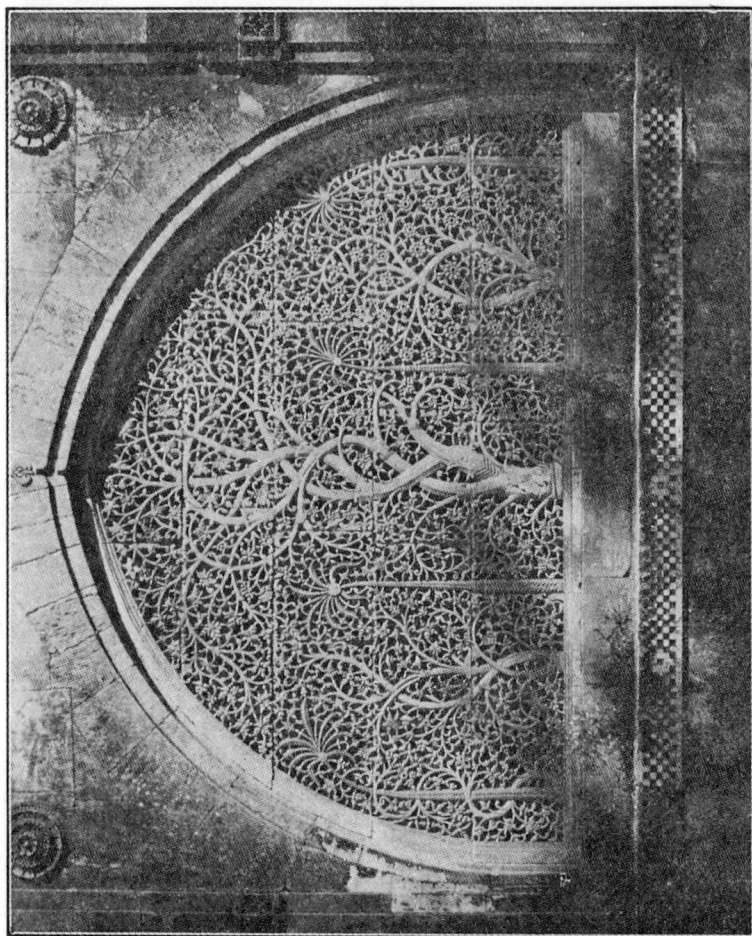

SIDI SAID'S MOSQUE. WINDOW OF PERFORATED MARBLE.

71

graceful kind. The mausoleum, built; like the mosque, of red sandstone, has a substantial grandeur which Fergusson calls heavy, but there can be no difference of opinion as to the marvellous beauty of the carving of the parapet round it. The Queen's Mosque (in Mirzapur), also built about the same time, has that same wealth of beauty in its details but it is very different in style and general effect. It shows how impossible it is to combine the Muhammadan arcuate style with the Hindu trabeate architecture and preserve harmony. "Although," as Fergusson says, "the architects had got over much of the awkwardness that characterized their earlier efforts in this direction they had not yet conquered them." They did not conquer them until the buildings, though not in every detail, became essentially Muhammadan. Shah Alum's tomb; the Hindu temple of Swámee Názáyen, the windows and the tracery of the niches of the minarets of the Queen's Mosque show how the Hindu sculptor could use his chisel with as free and delicate hand as Raphael could his pencil. It is however from the windows in a desecrated mosque in the Bhadar, or old castle, that we gain the highest conception of his faculties. Upon their construction and ornamentation he concentrated all his powers of invention. "It is probably," says Fergusson, "more like a work of nature than any other architectural detail that has yet been designed even by the best architects of Greece or of the Middle Ages." They remind one of the fairy water-works in the poet's enchanted caverns.

> "Sometimes like delicatest lattices,
> Cover'd with crystal vines : their weeping trees
> Moving about, as in a gentle wind ;
> Which, in a wink, to wat'ry gauze refined,
> Pour into shapes of curtain'd canopies
> Spangled and rich with liquid broderies
> Of flowers."

Nowhere does one feel oneself more thoroughly in an

SHAH ALUM : THE SAINT'S TOMB.

73

eastern city of past times than in the narrow streets of
Ahmedabad, thick with ancient houses, none so poor as
not to have a doorway or a window or a wooden pillar
carved finely. The wide main street is spanned by the
Teen Durwaza or Triple Gateway which the royal founder
built. It led into the Maidan Shah or Royal Square, the
outer enclosure of the Bahdar or Citadel. J. Albert de
Mandelslo, who visited Ahmedabad in 1638, and was the
guest of the English President, writes : " He brought me
to the great market-place called *Meydan Schach* or the
King's Market, which is at least 1,600 feet long, and half as
many broad, and beset all about with rows of palm-trees and
date-trees, intermixed with citron-trees and orange-trees,
whereof there are many in the several streets, which is not
only very pleasant to the sight, by the delightful prospect it
affords, but also makes the walking among them more convenient, by reason of the coolness." Not far from the
Royal Square was the King's Palace. " Over the gate there
was a kind of curtain or stage, for the music, consisting of
violins, haw-boys and bagpipes which play there in the
morning, at noon, in the evening and at midnight, as they
do in Persia and all other places where the prince professes
the *Mahumetan* religion. All the apartments of the house
were sumptuous, gilt and adorned with painting, according
to the mode of the country ; but more to their satisfaction,
who are pleased with diversity of colours, than theirs, who
look for invention, and stand upon the exactness of invention." The palace has been converted into a jail and the
apartments have been covered with whitewash according to
the mode of our civilized government. The gate yet stands,
and over it in Persian are the words : " The House of
Goodness and Favour," a strange inscription for a jail.

When Mandelslo visited Ahmedabad, Azam Khan was
viceroy and " the gentleman belonging to the embassy sent
by the Duke of Holstein to the great Duke of Muscovy and

THE SWAMEE NÁRÁYEN'S TEMPLE.

75

the King of Persia " gives us a vivid account of the splendour and riches of his court. " I was credibly informed," he writes, " that he was worth in money and household stuffs ten crou or carroas Ropias, which amounts to fifty millions of crowns, the cro being accounted at a hundred Lake Ropias, each whereof is worth fifty thousand crowns. It was not long before that his daughter, one of the greatest beauties in the country, had been married to the Mogul's second son, and the *Chan*, when she went to the court, had sent her attended by twenty elephants, a thousand horses, and six thousand waggons loaded with the richest stuffs and whatever else was rare in the country. His Court consisted of above 500 persons, 400 whereof were his slaves who served him in his affairs and were all dieted in the house. I have it from good hands that his expense in housekeeping amounted to about 5,000 crowns a month, not comprehending in that account that of his stables, where he kept five hundred horses and fifty elephants." Mandelslo went " along with the English merchant to visit the Governor and found him sitting in a pavilion or tent which looked into his garden. He was clad in a white vestment, according to the Indian mode, over which he had another that was longer, of *Brocadoe*, the ground carnation lined with white satin and above a collar of sables, whereof the skins were sewed together, so as that the tails hung down over the back." As soon as he saw them come in the Viceroy made them sit down " by the lords that were with him." After despatching several orders he went and inspected certain troops drawn up in the court. " He would see their arms himself, and caused them to shoot at a mark, thereby to judge of their abilities and to augment the pay of such as did well at the cost of the others, out of whose pay there was so much abated." Seeing him thus employed, Mandelslo and his companion, the President, would have taken their leave, " but he sent us word that we should dine with him."

On his return the Governor asked the Dutchman where he had learnt the *Turkish* language and whether he had ever been at Constantinople. " I told him I had never been there but had employed the little time abroad in the province of *Schirwan* and at *Ispahan* in learning that language, which is as common there as that of the country." The Governor stated that Schirwan was his country, and having known that Mandelslo had particularly known the King of Persia he asked him what he thought of that monarch. " I made answer, that he was a prince of a graceful aspect and person, and one that had understanding and courage enough to be obeyed in his kingdom. He asked me whether he still reigned as a tyrant, and continued his former cruelties. I answered that age having moderated his youthful extravagances, his government began also to be more moderate." The Governor replied : " That he was content to believe that Schach Sessi was an understanding person, but that even as to that there was no more comparison between him and the *Mogul* than there was between the poverty of the one and the vast wealth of the other, the Prince his master being able to maintain a war against three kings of *Persia*. I was loth to enter into any contestation upon so ticklish a subject, and therefore only told him that it was indeed true, there was not any comparison between the gold and wealth of Persia, and what I had already seen of the Mogul's kingdom ; but that it must be withal confessed that Persia had one thing which could not be had elsewhere, and was in effect inestimable, which was the great number of *Kissilbachs*, with whose assistance the King of *Persia* might attempt the conquest of all *Asia*. Which I said purposely, knowing the Governor was a Kissilbach, and that he could take no offence at such a discourse. Accordingly he discovered his satisfaction thereat, not only in saying that he must grant it to be true, but also, when turning to one of the lords who was a Persian as well as himself, he said to

him, *Walla beksade, jasehi a-damdar, chassa adamlar souer*,
that is to say, I believe this young gentleman hath courage
when he speaks so well of those that have."

Mandelslo states that the Viceroy was " a judicious understanding man, but hasty and so vigorous that his Government inclined somewhat to cruelty," and relates an occurrence which most certainly shows that the Governor was
somewhat inclined to cruelty. The Governor, he tells us,
one day being desirous of entertaining " the two principal
directors of the English and Dutch trade," sent for twenty
women-dancers, " who, as soon as they were come into the
room fell a singing and dancing, but with an activity and
exact observation of the cadence, much beyond that of our
dancers upon the ropes. They had little hoops or circles
through which they leaped as nimbly as if they had been so
many apes, and made thousands of postures, according to
the several soundings of their musick which consisted of a
Tumbeck or Timbrel, a Haw-boy and several Tabours."
After they had danced about two hours the Governor sent
for another troupe, who first pleaded illness for not coming ;
and when he sent a second time " they also were refused as
they had another and more pleasing engagement elsewhere,
saying they knew well enough the Governor would not
pay them." " He laught at it, but immediately commanded out a party of his guard to bring them to him, and
they were no sooner entered into the hall ere he ordered
their heads to be struck off. They begg'd their lives with
horrid cries and lamentations ; but he would be obeyed,
and caused the execution to be done in the room before all
the company, not one of the lords then present daring to
make the least intercession for those wretches, who were
eight in number. The strangers were startled at the horror
of the spectacle and inhumanity of the action, which the
Governor, taking notice of, fell a laughing, and asked them
what they were so much startled at. 'Assure yourselves,

gentlemen,' said he, 'that if I should not take this course, I should not be long Governor of Amadabaī.' "

Hard by the Teen Durwáza stands a large upper-roomed building which was once the Dutch factory. Near it was the English factory, but neither the building nor its site can be identified. Mandelslo says: " The English house or lodge is in the middle of the city, well built, and hath many fine and convenient apartments, with spacious courts for the disposal of merchandises. Master *Roberts* (the Chief) brought me first into his own chamber, which look'd into a little flower garden, in which there was a Fountain. The floor was cover'd with tapestry, and the pillars which sustained the structure were set out with silk-stuffes of several colours, and above a great white tassel according to the custom of the great ones of the country. We had a collation, after which he show'd me the whole house, and brought me into a very fair chamber, with a large closet in it, which he had design'd for my lodging. We supp'd in a great hall, whither the Dutch deputy came after supper to see us, with some of his merchants, with whom I had occasion to be acquainted at Suratta. After he was gone the whole company conducted me to my chamber, where my host kept me company till after midnight. After, that there might not be aught wanting in my entertainment (which in answer to the recommendatory letters I had brought from the President, he would needs have in all things extraordinary) he sent for six women-dancers, the handsomest could be found in the city."

When Captain Best made a trading agreement with the local authorities at Surat (1613) he provided for an establishment at Ahmedabad. The following year Thomas Aldworth having a house and having secured brokers, the factors began to make extensive purchases which, owing to the absence of any European rival, they did with sufficient cheapness. On January 21, 1615, Aldworth set out for Surat "with forty carts laden with indigo and cloths; and an escort which the local government increased because murders and robberies had been committed a few nights previously close to the walls of the city." On February 5, the caravan arrived at Surat, when "the goods were shipped on board of the vessels lying off Swali." In August, Aldworth started again for Ahmedabad. Soon after his arrival there he was smitten with a severe illness, and longing for the sea breeze he had himself carried out of the city on his way back to Surat. But his weakness increased rapidly and he died on October 4, at the village of Neriad. "All is now ended," wrote his friend, Kerridge, " and I destitute by want of so dear a friend, the greatest cross I could have felt in this country." Kerridge now took charge of the Ahmedabad factory. He was a man of imperious temper and a dispute with a native merchant over some indigo led to his being fined and imprisoned. Sir Thomas Roe went, on January 24, 1616, " to the Durbar to visite the king." Jehangir, " having looked curiously and asked many questions of my presents," demanded what he required of him.

" I answered: Justice. That on the assurance of his Majesties *Firmaen* sent into England, the king, my master, had not only giuen leaue to many of his subjects to come a dangerous voyadge with their goodes, but had sent mee to congratulate the amytye so happely begunne betweene two soe mighty Nations, and to confirme the same: But that I found the English seated at Amadaus enjured by the Gouernor in their Persons and goodes, fined, exacted upon, and kept as prisoners: that at eurie Towne new customes were taken of our goodes passing to the port, contrarie to all justice and the former Articles of trade. To which hee answered hee was sorry: it should be amended; and presently gave orders for two *firmanes* very effectually according to my desire to be signed, one to the Gouernor of

Amadavaz to restore mony exacted from Master Kerridge, and to vse the English with all fauour. The other to release all Customes required on any pretence on the way, or if any had beene taken to repay it ; of his owne accord wishing mee, that if these gave me not speedy remedy, I should renew my complaynt against the disobeyour, and hee should be sent for to answere there. And soe hee dismissed mee."

When Roe accompanied the Emperor to Ahmedabad he found there a large party of English factors carrying on an extensive trade. The city attracted the commerce of the east. " There is not," says Mandelslo, " in a manner any nation or any merchandise in all Asia which may not be had at Amadabath." The labour of an industrious and ingenious people was employed in the manufacture of silk and cotton fabrics of every description, in metal work, wood and ivory carving, and in inlay. " 'Tis true, they seldom use any silk in that country, much less any out of Persia, because it is somewhat too coarse and too dear, but they ordinarily make use of that of China, which is very fine, mingling it with that of *Bengala*, which is not quite so fine, but much beyond that of Persia, and much cheaper.. They also make there great quantities of gold and silver *Brocadoes*, but they put too much thin lace into them, so that in goodness and substance they come not near those of Persia, though some of them amount in the country to eighteen crowns the piece." At the time when Mandelslo was in Ahmedabad " they had begun to make a new kind of stuff of silk and cotton with flowers of gold which was very much esteemed, and sold at five crowns the ell ; but the inhabitants were forbidden the wearing of it, upon this account, that the king reserv'd it for his own, yet not so strictly but that he permitted Forraigners to buy of it, to be transported out of the king-dom. They make there also all sorts of sattins and velvets of all sorts of Colours—taffata, sattins for linings, of both Thread and silk, Alcatifs or Carpets, the ground Gold, Silk or

Yarn, but not so good as those of *Persia*, and all sorts of cotton." The commerce of Ahmedabad has declined, but a considerable number of persons are still employed in the manufacture of objects of taste and ornament. The gold-smiths yet make a number of well-arted things, round neck-laces, bracelets, nose-rings and earrings of chopped pieces of gold strung on red silk. " It is the finest archaic jewellery in India," says Sir George Birdwood, whose genius first revealed to the West the beauty and variety of Indian art. " The nail-headed earrings are," he adds, " identical with those represented on Assyrian sculptures." This jewellery is worn throughout India by the people as a safe investment. At Ahmedabad you will see in the streets little naked girls of perfect shape, whose neck and arms and ankles are shackled with jujubes of gold. Now and then one of them is enticed away and the tiny body found in a well without its orna-ments. The coppersmith yet hammers his brass pots and bestows all his skill in making finely cut brass screens and boxes covered with the most elaborate design for my lady's jewellery, sweets and spices. At Ahmedabad they still make quantities of gold and silver brocadoes, and the stuff of silk and flowers of gold (kincobs) is still esteemed by every chief in India and sold at more than five crowns the ell. The manufacture of the gold and silver thread used in them employ many skilful workers. The wire-drawer (tania) turns out six or eight hundred yards of thread from half an ounce of silver. " So great is his delicacy of touch that if desired the *tánia* can draw out half an ounce of silver into 2,000 yards of thread, a feat all the more wonderful that for boring the holes in his draw-plate the workman has no finer tool than the file pointed end of an old umballa steel." Hard by the goldsmiths an aged Muhammadan beats a book with a heavy-headed iron hammer. He is making gold foil for the confectioner, to cover his sweetmeats, and for the hemp-smoker to stretch across the bowl of his pipe in which the live coal is placed.   Yellow tin foil is wrought to deco-rate the images of the gods and the lintel and side-posts of the house-doors on high festivals.   An infinitely more im-portant art in which India was distinguished two thousand years ago still flourishes at Ahmedabad.   Within the potter's houses are shapes of clay " of all sorts and sizes great and small," and all of perfect form.   He uses red ochre, white earth, and mica to give them a light colour, and he polishes the great jars, in which the forty thieves hid, with a piece of bamboo or a string of agate pebbles.   Outside his mud den he sits and spins his primitive wheel as his forefathers did in the days of Menu, and the potter and his wheel carries you back a few thousand years.   On Christmas Eve we saw, as we drove to Sarkhej, a scene which Kalidasa, the Shakespeare of the Indian drama, de-picted fifteen centuries ago.   The Sabarmati River was low, and its sandy bed was lined with men and women and chil-dren, robed in vestments of the purest white, of azure, green, and purple.   Some of the damsels were chatting and exchanging gossip as they filled their copper jars, some were splashing in the stream whilst others—

> " Bolder grown,
> O'er a friend's head a watery stream have thrown,
> And the drenched girl, her long, black hair untied,
> Wrings out the water with the sandel dyed.
> Still is their dress most lovely, though their play
> Has loosed their locks, and washed their dye away,
> And though the pearls, that went their neck to grace
> Have slipped, disordered from their resting place."

A bullock cart, most primitive of human forms of conveyance, is crossing the stream.   " Listen, sisters (streams), kindly to him who praises you, who has come from afar with a waggon and a chariot ; bow down lowlily, become easily fordable. Remain, rivers, lower than the axle (of the wheel) with your currents."   Beyond the river the wide white road runs through a great plain with its dim memories dating back before the earliest dawn of history. Here the peasants have lived their rude simple lives for many a century; and have chanted their hymn for the ploughing season. "May the oxen (draw) happily, the men labour happily, the plough furrow happily." They have sown and reaped their grain, they have picked the snowy flake of cotton, they have planted the sugar-cane, they have cultivated mustard for oil-cakes to feed the oxen, while Rajpoot and Muslim have contended, and conquering races have come and gone.

Hard by the road are the remains of the mighty sepulchres of their conquerors, and from a crumbling wall shoots the sacred fig tree. "The revolving current of life," says one of their ancient hymns meant for all time and all mankind, " resembles the *Aswatha*, the eternal sacred fig-tree which grows with its roots above and its branches downwards."

After driving about three miles across the great plain clothed with groves of mangoes, lofty tamarinds with feathery leaves of bluish green and wide-spreading banyans, we saw in the distance a white dome glistening in the sun. It was the *roza* of Ganj Baksh, and a few miles further on the terrace on which the tomb stands was reached. Alighting from our carriage we passed through a covered gateway into a large flagged court on the right of which is a fairy kiosk, formed of sixteen slender columns supporting nine domes, and behind it rises the massive and stately tomb of the Saint Shaik *Ahmad Khattu Ganj Bakhsh*, the friend and spiritual guide of the royal founder of Ahmedabad. He belonged to an austere mendicant fraternity and tradition asserts, says Briggs, that no circumstance would induce him to alter his mode of life, though wealth and every sublunary honour within the gift of a powerful Muslim potentate were offered. There are many stories told of the holy Fakir. The most popular of these is the one told by the custodian to the pilgrims who from all parts of Gujarat resort to his shrine once a year.

" He was a saintly mortal, Ganj Baksh : he was free from the sensualities to which our race is prone ; his heart was ever with Alla (whose name be praised), and his thoughts with Muhammad (blessings upon our holy prophet) ; his life was one of Virgin purity; his death that of the beatified, Alla il Alla, etc. ; kings of the earth were admonished by him ; the holiest found him a friend. Wealth was profusely scattered at his feet, but he saw it not, received it not. Alla was his all. Before he passed from this world to the Paradise of our hopes, he built this *roza*. The labourers and artificers employed by him were daily paid their hire, and the good genii who supplied the funds deposited the exact quota to be appropriated beneath the carpet of the holy Ganj Baksh. Thus was built this delightful mausoleum to the memory of a saint whose virtues we can still revere, if our imperfections prevent a close pursuit upon his footsteps, Alla il Alla, etc."

Ganj Baksh did not erect the *roza*. It was begun the year the saint died (1445) by Sultan Ahmed's son Muhammad II., and completed six years later by Ahmed's grandson, Jalal Khan, better known as Kitub-ud-din. It is certainly a delightful mausoleum. The trellis work which encloses the tomb is wrought with lavish luxuriance of imagination and incredible perfection of detail. The brass lattice windows around the shrine also bear testimony to the power of the Hindu designer. The buildings possess two characteristics peculiarly their own, their pure Hindu style and their redundant richness. To the west of the Mausoleum is a large quadrangle with a mosque on its western face. It illustrates how during the twenty-five years that had rolled on since the building of the Jumma Mosque the architect had advanced in Muhammadan simplicity. It has the five domes of the Jumma Mosque but the pillars, as Fergusson points out, are fewer in number, more widely spaced and better arranged. " Except the Motee Musjid at Agra," he writes, " no mosque in India is more remarkable for simple elegance than this." The southern face of the quadrangle overlooks the great lake which Mahmud Begada excavated and surrounded with gigantic flights of steps and built on its border a splendid palace and harem. In a handsome tomb enclosed like the sepulchre of the Saint with well wrought trellis work lies Mahmud Begada and his sons, and a porch rich in carved niches supported by three pillars, miracles of size and perfection, separate it from the tomb of his Queen.

We had our dinner in the ruins of the Harem. The night was cool, and fragrant with orange blossoms. The stars shone from the depths of an eastern sky with steady lustre. The moonlight slept on crumbled wall and marble pillars. We reluctantly left the fairy haunt and drove back to the turmoil of the city.

IV

MOUNT ABU AND AJMER

THE journey onward from Ahmedabad will lead us as its next natural stopping-place to the isolated peak of Mount Abu, "the Saints' Pinnacle," the Rajpoot Olympus. The traveller who, after traversing the richly cultivated plain of Gujarat, mounts that lofty ridge will understand the influence which the physical features and situation of the country spreading out before him have exercised on the races who have lived on it. They are strongly marked. A little to the east of Mount Abu commences the chain of the Arvalis, or "mountains of strength," which stretch away in bold ridges towards Delhi, which has been, and always will be, the capital of India. Running north and south, they form the backbone of Upper India, and on the west lie the arid plains and ever shifting sand-hills of Marwar, Jesselmer, and Bikaner; on the east are the forests and plains of black loam furrowed by running streams, of Mewar Bundi, Kotah, Ajmer, and Jeypore. The vast and varied region which extends from the frontier of Sind on the west to the fort of Agra on the east, and from the sandy tracts of the Sutlej on the north to the Vindhya range separating it from the Deccan or "South," is known by the collective and classical denomination Rajast'han, "the abode of princes." "In the familiar dialect of these countries," says Tod, who has done for Rajpootana what the great Wizard of the North has done for Scotland, "it is termed *Rajwarra*, by the more refined *Raet'hana*, corrupted to *Rajpootana*, the common designation among the British to denote the Rajpoot principalities." Nature meant it to be the abode of chiefs. Tod, in his *Annals and Antiquities of Rajast'han*, the true Rajpoot epic alike in the vastness of its scope and in the completeness of its execution, has by pen and pencil revealed the beauty and variety of the land where the age of chivalry has not fled. Tod guides us through the Marcosi'hulli, or region of death (the emphatic and figurative name for the desert), to Bikaner, Jodpoor, and Jesselmer and the fair valley of Oodipoor. He conducts us on the east of the range through the Patar (table, *pat*, mountain, *ar*), or great Plateau of Central India watered by the Chumbul, the paramount lord of the floods and many a noble stream. " The surface of this extensive plateau," he tells us, " is greatly diversified." There are great rolling waves of country where the protruding rocks present not a trace of vegetation ; there are, besides, tracts yellow in harvest-time with ripened wheat and dotted with the roofs of a hardy and valiant yeomanry. There are ranges of rugged hills, while below them spread valleys with low meads, abundantly watered with numerous rills, and cultivation " raised with infinite labour on terraces, as the vine is cultivated in Switzerland and on the Rhine." There are beetling cliffs overhanging the rippling streams, crowned with the fortress-homes of the proud Rajpoot chiefs who claim their descent from the sun or from the moon, and whose ancestors have for ages exercised sovereign power. Every petty Rajpoot chief, and every member of his family or clan, believes with the intensity of an undoubting faith that he is of an ancient, illustrious, and royal descent. Tod tells us that each race has " its genealogical tree, describing the essential peculiarities, religious tenets, and pristine locale of the clan " that every Rajpoot should be able to repeat this creed, and that in point of fact " there is scarcely a chief of character for

88

knowledge who cannot repeat the genealogy of his line,"
though in these degenerate days many are satisfied with
referring to the family bard or chronicler. These genealogical tables are " the touchstone of affinities, and guardians
of the laws of intermarriage." Caste has ever prevented
the inferior class of society from being incorporated with
this haughty noblesse. Only those of pure blood in both
lines can hold fiefs of the crown. The highest may marry
the daughter of a Rajpoot, whose sole possession is " *a skin
of land* " ; the sovereign himself is not degraded by such
alliance. It is his blood, and not the number of his acres,
which ennobles the Rajpoot. He does not derive his title from
the land, but he gives his name to the land. The State takes
the name of the capital which is the residence and stronghold of the chief, and the capital takes the name of the
chief who founded it. The Rajpoot considers there are
two professions fit for a man—to conquer and to govern.
" The poorest Rajpoot of this day retains all the pride of
ancestry, often his sole inheritance ; he scorns to hold the
plough or to use his lance but on horseback." When a Rajpoot chief was unable to provide for a younger son he gave
him a horse and a lance, and the lad with some companions
went forth to serve some sovereign or to found a state.
He had learnt in his father's desert home or mountain eyrie
the business of war and the craft of government. Thus the
Rajpoot spread over the continent of India and influenced
its history. It is the desert and the mountain which have
influenced the historical process and feudal constitution of
Rajpootana, and has enabled the Rajpoot to maintain to
this day those social and religious institutions which make
Rajpootana one of the most interesting and romantic spots
in the continent of India.

On the summit of Mount Abu the marble Jain shrines
preserve the highest ideals of pure Hindu architecture.
And from them may be deduced interesting evidence bearing

upon the national character and creed. At a point where a lovely valley begins to close on an enormous plateau of granite, stands, warm and glowing, a mass of white marble. It is the four sacred shrines. Nine hundred years ago the most ancient of them was built by a merchant prince. The marble was not quarried from the mountain side, but it was transported some hundred miles and dragged up the steep mountain by a patient race to whom a century is but a day. Some years ago we were walking through a remote Deccan village and noticed a large stone pillar richly carved, lying by the roadside. We asked its origin and destination. The *Patel*, or head village officer, told us it was intended for the porch of the temple on the steep cliff overlooking the hamlet two miles away. " The villagers drag it," he added, " on great festivals, and, oh ! Sahib, in my lifetime they have moved it a hundred yards." He was bordering on fifty. " And see how much carving they have done," and he pointed to some eight inches of rich decoration. The old Brahman priest who accompanied us noticed our look of surprise and wonderment, and said, " You English are in such a hurry. There is the age of brass and the age of iron. They come and they go. Others have come and gone their way, and so you will go. But the pillar will reach the temple." In this spirit were these marble shrines at Abu hewn into transparent strength and the shafts erected above the marble courtyards ; " the white cupolas rise like wreaths of sea foam in the dawn." The desire of the Jain is to attain victory over all worldly desires to fill his soul, and so become divine. He therefore builds his temple to shut out the garish day and to give cool dark spaces shadowing forth the rest to which he looks forward. He filled the windows with marble tracery, through which the broken light falls, and a few beams fade away into the cell on to the image of the twenty-second deified saint, seated cross-legged and with folded hands. In the colonnade around are fifty-seven cells, and in each cell the identical image of the same god, with the same folded hands, with the same expression quiet, and so weary. It reveals the feelings of the worshippers, to whom salvation comes after eight births, when a man has started on the right road. And the first Jain of the long series of prehistoric prophets lived more than eight million years. " Patience is the highest good " is the Jain's creed.

About the centre of the Aravali range on the west side lies the British province of Ajmer-Merwara, surrounded by the Protected States of Rajpootana. The city, like the majority of Rajpoot cities, stands well. Situated in a fertile valley, it lies between a great lake and a magnificent isolated hill crowned with a fortress called Taragarh, the Home of the Stars. It is a spot which the first settlers would choose for a dwelling-place. It is a spot which, on account of its geographical position, the Muhammadan invaders would select as the centre of their operations against Rajpootana, and the dry climate of the plateau, three thousand feet above the sea, would be an attraction. Ajmer, " according to the traditional couplet and the poetic legends of its ancient princes, was visited by the first hostile forces which Islam sent across the Indus," and it became the favourite haunt of Moghuls and Pathans. Many are the traces of the heavy hand of the warriors and the conquerors who thought it glory and not shame to destroy the works of the Infidel and to turn them to the purpose of the believer.

The Arhai-din-ka-jhompra, or " the hut of two and a half days," is an example of how the Muhammadan conquerors took the chief Pagan shrines of a city as a trophy of their own faith. It is built on the western declivity of the mountain, and derives its name from its having occupied, as tradition tells, its magical builders only this short period in its erection. Tod, who gives a fine illustration of the " ancient Jain Temple at Ajmer," writes :—" The Temple is surrounded by a superb screen of Saracenic architecture,

JAIN TEMPLE, DELWARA.

92

having the main front and gateway to the north. From its simplicity, as well as its appearance of antiquity, I am inclined to assign the screen to the first dynasty, the Ghorian Sultans, who evidently made use of native architects. The entrance arch is that wavy kind, characteristic of what is termed the Saracenic, whether the term be applied to the Alhambra of Spain or the Mosque of Delhi, and I am disposed on close examination to pronounce it Hindu. The entire façade of this noble entrance, which I regret I cannot have engraved, is covered with Arabic inscriptions. But, unless my eye much deceived me, the small frieze over the apex of the arch contained an inscription in Sanscrit, with which Arabic has been commingled, both being unintelligible. The remains of a minaret still maintain their position on the right flank of the gate, with a door and steps leading to it for the *muezzim* to call the faithful to prayers. A line of smaller arches of similar form composes the front of the screen. The design is chaste and beautiful, and the material, which is a compact limestone of a yellow colour, admitting almost of as high a polish as the *jaune antique* gave abundant scope to the sculptor." Fergusson endorses Tod's estimate of the beauty of the screen and its decoration. He writes :—" Nothing can exceed the taste with which the Cufic and Togra inscriptions are interwoven with the more purely architectural decoration, or the manner in which they give life and variety to the whole without ever interfering with the constructive lines of the design. Nothing in Cairo or in Persia is so exquisite in detail, and nothing in Spain or Syria can approach them for beauty of surface decoration. Besides this, they are unique. Nowhere else could it be possible to find Muhammadan largeness of conception, combined with Hindu delicacy of ornamentation, carried out to the extent and in the same manner." The description of the pillared hall which now forms the mosque, given by Tod, is both picturesque and accurate. " Its plan is simple and consonant with all the more ancient temples of the Jains. It is an extensive saloon, the ceiling supported by a quadruple range of columns, those of the centre being surmounted by a range of vaulted coverings, while the lateral portion, which is flat, is divided into compartments of the most elaborate sculpture. But the columns are most worthy of attention ; they are unique in design, and, with the exception of the cave-temples, probably among the oldest now existing in India. On examining them, ideas entirely novel, even in Hindu art, are developed. Like all these portions of Hindu architecture their ornaments are very complex, and the observer will not fail to be struck with their dissimilarity ; it was evidently a rule to make the ornaments of every part unlike the other, and this I have seen carried to great extent. There may be forty columns, but no two are alike. The ornaments of the base are peculiar, both as to form and execution ; the lozenges, with the rich tracery surmounting them, might be transferred not inappropriately to the Gothic cathedrals of Europe. The projections from the various parts of the shafts (which on a small scale may be compared to the corresponding projections of the columns in the *Duomo* at Milan) with the small niches still containing the statues, though occasionally mutilated, of the Pontiffs of the Jains, give them a character which strengthens the comparison. The elegant *Cámácumpa*, the emblem of the Hindu Ceres, with its pendant palmyra-branches, is here lost, as are many emblematical ornaments, curious in design and elegant in their execution. Here and there occurs a richly carved corbeille, which still further sustains the analogy between the two systems of architecture, and the capitals are at once strong and delicate." The central vault consists of a series of diminishing amulets (or rings), richly ornamented, converging to the apex, from which projects a heavy stone pendentive carved in open work. Tod supposes that the Hindu shrine was built two centuries before Christ, but

94

General Cunningham infers, " but with some hesitation,"
that most of the temples which furnished materials for the
building of the great mosque must have been erected during

THE ARHAI-DIN-KA-JHOMPRA.

the eleventh and twelfth centuries. The great mosque,
according to an inscription on one of the minarets, was
completed during the reign (A.D. 1211–1236) of Altamish,

95

a slave of Kutb-ud-den, to whom he had given his daughter
in marriage, and was therefore built seven years later than
the Kutb Mosque at Delhi.[1]   In the latter the Mazinah, or
Muezzin's tower, for calling the faithful to prayer, is a distinct
and separate building, known as the celebrated Kutb Minar.
But in the Ajmer Mosque we have the earliest example of
a pair of Muezzin towers in two small minars, which are
placed on the top of the screen wall over the great centre
arch.   " The tops of both of these minars are now ruined,
but enough still remains to show that they were sloping
hollow towers, with twenty-four faces or flutes alternately
angular and circular, just like those of the Kutb Minar."
All who have seen the two mosques will agree with Cunningham that " in gorgeous prodigality of ornament, for
beautiful richness of tracery, and endless variety of detail,
in delicate sharpness of finish, and laborious accuracy of
workmanship, all of which are due to the Hindu masons,
these two grand Indian mosques may justly vie with the
noblest buildings which the world has yet produced."   We,
however, consider that the mosque at Ajmer is far more
interesting than its rival at old Delhi.

Above the mosque towers " the fortress of the goatherd."
" Aja Pal[2] was, as his name implies, a goatherd," says Tod,
" whose piety in supplying one of the saints with daily libations of goat's milk procured him a territory.   Satisfied with
the scene of his early days, he commenced his castle on the
serpent-mount in his own province ; but his evil genius
knocking down in the night what he erected in the day, he
sought out another site on the opposite side of the range,
hence arose the far-famed Aja-mer.   The towers and battlements built by Aja-Pal still remain, but the palaces of the

[1] " The Mosque at Ajmir was commenced apparently in the
year 1200, and was certainly completed during the reign of Altamish,
A.D. 1211-1236."   *History of Indian and Eastern Architecture*, by
James Fergusson, p. 510.
[2] Aja—Goat—Pal—Nourisher ; hence an epithet for a king.

Cohans have long since fallen into ruin. It is, however, good to ascend the mountain and see the green valley, the wide sheet of silver men call Ana Saugur,[1] the splintered pinnacles and granite hills in the golden morning sunshine. Beyond the red hills stretches the yellow desert, " The Kingdom of Death."

Nine centuries have rolled on since Ana Raja constructed Ana Saugur, one of the most perfect of lakes. Jehangir, " The Conqueror of the World," adorned its bank with the Doulat Bagh (The Garden of Splendour), filled with fruit and flowers, where he with his consort, Nur Jehan (The Light of the World), might find repose away from the cares of State. Shah Jehan (Lord of the World), his son, erected the marble pavilions reflected in its seductive water. The Garden of Splendour was a pleasant retreat for the luxurious Emperor from the fortified palace erected by the Great Akbar, when Ajmer became, after the fall of Chittore, an integral portion of the Moghul Empire, and gave its name to a Subah or province which included the whole of Rajpootana. Though Chittore, " The Rock of their Strength," had been despoiled and bereft of all symbols of regality, the Rajpoot warriors maintained a gallant and long protracted struggle. But they had to yield to the hosts of Delhi, and " the crimson banner," which for more than eight hundred years had waved in proud independence over the head of the Gehloles, was now to be abased to the son of Jehangir. Jehangir, in his auto-biography, which deserves to rank with the immortal diary of Pepys, writes : " Pleasing intelligence arrived of the intention of Rana Umra Sing to repair and make his obedience to me. My fortunate son Khoorum had established my authority and garrisons in divers strongholds of the country of the Ranas." The noble Umra, who had so long and sig-nally foiled the Imperial armies, is one of the Paladins of Rajpoot chivalry. " He was beloved of his chiefs for the

---

[1] Saugur—Sea or Lake.

qualities they most esteem, generosity and valour, and by his subjects for his justice and kindness, of which we can judge from his edicts, many of which yet live in the columns or the rock." Umra informed Prince Khoorum that he would "send his eldest son to attend and serve the Emperor, as did other Hindu princes," but the proud Rajpoot chief added, "on account of his years he would hold himself excused from attending in person." Jehangir, delighted at the submission of so formidable an enemy, writes : " I forgave the Rana, and sent a friendly firmaun that he might rest assured of my protection and care, and imprinted thereon, as a solemn testimony of my sincerity, my 'five fingers' (punja) ;[1] I also wrote my son, by any means by which it could be brought about, to treat this illustrious one according to my wishes." Khoorum offered to withdraw every Muhammadan from Mewar if the Rana would but receive the Emperor's firman outside his capital. "This his proud soul rejected ; and though he visited Prince Khoorum as a friend he spurned the proposition of acknowledging a superior or receiving the rank and titles awaiting such an admission." Umra determined to abdicate the throne. Assembling his chiefs and disclosing his determination, he made the teeka [2] on his son's forehead, and observing that the honour of Mewar was now in his hands, forthwith left the capital and

[1] " The giving of the hand amongst all nations has been considered as a pledge for the performance or ratification of some act of importance, and the custom among the Scythic or Tatar nations, of transmitting its impress as a substitute, is here practically described. I have seen the identical firman in the Ranas' archives.   The hand being immersed in a compost of sandal-wood, is applied to the paper, and the palm and five fingers (punja) are very distinct.   In a masterly delineation of Oriental manners (Carne's *Letters from the East*) is given an anecdote of Mahommed, who, unable to sign his name to a convention, dipped his hand in ink, and made an impression therewith.   It is evident the prophet of Islam only followed an ancient solemnity, of the same import as that practised by Jehangir." —*Annals of Rajpootana*, vol. i. p. 362.

[2] Teeka, a small round sacred mark.

secluded himself in a palace on a cluster of hills, "nor did he from that hour cross its threshold, but to have his ashes deposited with those of his fathers." Umra's son proceeded to Ajmer, "paid his respect, *and his rank* was commanded to be at the request of my son immediately on my right hand, and I rewarded him with suitable khelats." Sir Thomas Roe, who was present at the Durbar, states that "the son of Ranna, his new Tributary, was brought within the little rayle, the King embracing him by the head. . . . His guift was an Indian vyder (broad dish) full of silver, upon yt a carved silver dish full of gould. Soe he was led towards the Prince." The gallant races which by the wise policy of Akbar and Jehangir became the strongest supporters of the Moghul Empire, were hopelessly alienated by the fanatical persecutions of Aurangzeb. He made Ajmer his headquarters during the war with Mewar and Marwar, brought about by his own bigotry. The Rajpoots in their mountain fastnesses defied for many a month and many a year the armies of the Moghuls. On the death of Aurangzeb the three great Rajpoot chiefs, the Rana of Oudepoor, the Raja of Marwar, Ajit Sing, and the Raja of Jeypore, Jey Sing II., obtained from his successor an acknowledgment of virtual independence. The daughter of Ajit Sing married the Moghul Emperor Farukshir, whom Hamilton, the English doctor, cured of a troublesome disease, and obtained from the grateful monarch the first grant of land to the East India Company. Farukshir was thrown into a dungeon, his eyes being put out, and he was strangled by command of the Barha Seiads (that is, descendants of the prophets), the Warwicks of Delhi. The King-makers put two other puppets on the throne, but the third puppet, Muhammad Shah, proved too strong for them, and the power of the Seiads went for ever. When Ajit Sing heard of the overthrow of the vigorous and able Seiads and the disorder of the Moghul government, he struck a blow for sovereignty. He advanced against Ajmer, and drove the Muslims from the city. "He slew the King's governor, and seized on Tarragurh. Once more the bell of prayers was heard in the temple while the bang of the Mesjid was silent.[1] Where the *Koran* was read the *Puran* [2] was now heard, and the *mindra* [3] took the place of the mosque. The Kazi made way for the Brahman, and the pit of burnt sacrifice (homa) was dug, when the sacred kine was slain." The enthusiastic chronicler adds, " The records were always moist with inserting fresh conquests." Ajit Sing assumed every emblem of sovereign rule. " He coined in his own name, established his own *guz* (measure) and *seer* (weight), his own courts of justice, and a new scale of rank for his chiefs." But Ajit's independence was of short duration. According to the chronicle, in the following year (1721) the Moghul Emperor (Muhammad Shah) prepared a formidable army and the contingents of the twenty-two Satraps of the Empire. "In the month of Sawun (July) Tarragurh was invested. . . . It had held out four months, when through the prince of Amber (Jey Sing) Ajit listened to terms, which were sworn to on the *Koran* by the nobles and the king ; and he agreed to surrender Ajmer." In 1721 the Rajpoot bard states "Ajit went to heaven." In plain prose, he was murdered by his two elder sons, Abhe Sing and Bukht Sing, who were by the same mother, a princess of Boondi. " To Bukht Sing, who was with his father, the eldest brother wrote promising him the independent sovereignty of Nagore (where they then were), with its five hundred and fifty-five townships, as the price of murdering their common sire. Bukht crept one night to his father's bed, and from a pallet on which were placed the arms of Ajit he took his sword and slew him. The mother was awakened by the blood of her lord moistening her bosom. Her cries awoke the faithful Rajpoots who lay in the ad-

[1] The call to prayer of the Muslim.   [2] Puran—Puranas.
[3] Mindra—Mandir—a temple pagoda.

jacent apartments, and who, bursting into the chamber, discovered their prince dead. " The assassin fled to the roof of the palace, barring the gates behind him, which resisted all attempts to force them until morning, when he threw into the court below the letter of his brother, exclaiming, ' This put the Mahraja to death, not I.' " " On Asar the 13, the dark half of the moon of 1780 (1730)," says the chronicle, seventeen hundred warriors for the last time marched before their lord. " They placed his body in a boat,[1] and carried him to the pyre made of sandal wood and perfumes, with heaps of cotton, oil, and camphor. The Nazir (Head of the Harem) went to the Queen's Palace, and as he pronounced the words ' Rao Sidaôe,' [2] the Chohani queen with sixteen damsels in her suite came forth. ' This day,' said she, ' is one of joy ; my race shall be illustrated ; our lives have passed together, how then can I leave him ? Of noble race was the Bhattiani queen. She put up a prayer to the Lord who wields the discus (Krishna). ' With joy I accompany my lord ; that my fealty (sati) may be accepted rests with Thee.' In like manner did the Gazelle (Mirgavati) of Derawul, and the Tuar queen of pure blood, the Chaora Rani and her of Shekhavati invoke the name of Heri as they determined to join their lord. For these six queens death had no terror, but they were the affianced wives of their lord ; the curtain wives of affection, to the number of fifty-eight, determined to offer themselves a sacrifice to Agni (the fire). ' Such an opportunity,' said they, ' can never occur.' While thus each spoke Nathoo the Nazir thus addressed them ' This is no amusement : the sandal wood you now anoint with is cool ; but will your resolution abide, when you remove it with the flames of Agni ? When this

---

[1] A vehicle formed like a boat, perhaps figurative of the soul crossing the " Voiturna," or Styx of the Hindu. *The Annals of Rajast'han*, vol. ii. p. 92.

[2] Rao Sidao, the King is perfected, or the King is dead.

scorches your tender frames, your hearts may fail, and the desire to recede will disgrace your lord's memory. Reflect and remain where you are. You have lived like *Indrani* (the Queen of Heaven), nursed in softness amidst flowers and perfumes ; the winds of heaven never offended you, far less the flames of fire.' But to all his arguments they replied; ' The world we will abandon, but never our lord.' They performed their ablutions, decked themselves in their gayest attire, and for the last time made obeisance to their lord in his car. The drum sounded ; the funeral train moved on ; all invoked the name of *Heri*.[1] The countenances of the Queens were as radiant as the sun. They mounted the pyre and as the smoke emitted from the house of flame, ascended to the sky, the assembled multitudes shouted *Khaman, Khaman* (well done, well done). The pile flamed like a volcano ; the faithful queens laved their bodies in the flames, as do the celestials in the lake *Mansurwar*.[2] They sacrificed their bodies to their lord, and illustrated the race whence they sprang."

As one of the queens ascended the pyre she pronounced the anathema so terrific to the ears of the patriotic Rajpoot— " May the bones of his murderer be consumed out of Maroo." [3] Abhe Sing became sovereign, and he bestowed on his brother, Bukht Sing, not only Nagore, but also Jhalore. Abhe was appointed by the Emperor Viceroy of Ahmedabad, and Ajmer became a part of Marwar. It was during his reign that Nadir Shah invaded India, but the summons to the Rajpoot princes to put forth their strength in support of the tottering throne of Timour was received with indifference. Not a chief of note led his myrmidons to the plains of Kurnal, and Delhi was invested, plundered, and its

---

[1] Heri Krishna is the mediator and preserver of the Hindu triad ; his name alone is invoked in funeral rites.—*The Annals of Rajasthan*, vol. ii. p. 94.

[2] The sacred lake in Thibet.

[3] Marwar is a corruption of Maroo-war. The region of death.

monarch dethroned without exciting a sigh. Abhe Sing died in 1750 (seven years before Plassey), and was succeeded by his son, Ram Sing, who had more than his share of the pride and impetuosity of his race. He demanded the instant surrender of Jhalore. The request insolently made was courteously refused. "War was decided on; the challenge was given and accepted, and the plains of Mairta were fixed upon to determine this mortal strife in which brother was to meet brother and all the ties of kin were to be severed by the sword." All lovers of Tod know how the heir of Mehtri, with his father and brothers, sealed his fealty with his blood on the fatal field of Mairta. "He had long engaged the hand of a daughter of a chief of the Nirookas, and was occupied with the marriage rites, when tidings reached him of the approach of the rebels to Mairta. In the bridal vestments, with the nuptial coronet (mor) encircling his forehead he took his station with his clan on the second day's fight, and obtained a bride in Indra's abode." After a desperate struggle Ram Sing was defeated, and flying south he joined the Mahratta leader Jey Appa Sindia, with whom he concerted measures for the invasion of his country. Rajpoots of every rank rose to oppose this first attempt of the Mahrattas to interfere in their national quarrels, and led by Bukht in person advanced to meet them. Bukht encamped in the passes near Ajmer. Hither one of the queens of the Prince of Amber, a niece of Bukht, repaired, and to her was entrusted by her husband the task of murdering her uncle, who had demanded his assistance against Ram Sing. The mode in which the deed was effected is told by Tod :

" A poisoned robe was the medium of revenge. Raja Bukht, soon after the arrival of his niece, was declared in a fever ; the physician was summoned : but the man of secrets, the vedya, declared he was beyond the reach of medicine, and bade him prepare for other scenes. The intrepid Rahtore, yet undismayed, received the tidings even with a jest. ' What ! Sooja,' said he, ' no cure ? Why do you take my lands and eat my produce, if you cannot combat my maladies ? What is your art good for ?' The vedya excavated a small trench in the tent, which he filled with water ; throwing into it some ingredient, the water became gelid. ' This,' said he, ' can be effected by human skill ; but your case is beyond it ; haste, perform the offices which religion demands.' With perfect composure he ordered the chiefs to assemble in his tent ; and having recommended to their protection, and received their promise of defending the rights of his son, he summoned the ministers of religion into his presence. The last gifts to the church and these, her organs, were prepared ; but with all his firmness, the anathema of the Satis, as they ascended the funeral pyre on which his hand had stretched his father, came into his mind ; and as he repeated the ejaculation, ' may your corpse be consumed in a foreign land ! ' he remembered he was then on the border. The images which crossed his mental vision it is vain to surmise : he expired as he uttered these words : and over his remains, which were burnt on the spot, a cenotaph was erected, and is still called Booro Dewul, the ' Shrine of Evil.' "

The feudal chiefs of Marwar recognized, and swore to maintain the rights of Beejy Sing, the son of Bukht. He led them to the plains of Mairta, but the cohorts of the Rajpoot clans were unable to withstand the well-served artillery of the Mahrattas. After a desperate contest " The Lord of Marwar, who on that morning commanded the lives of one hundred thousand Rajpoots, was indebted for his safety to the mean conveyance of a cart and pair of oxen." After this victory the cause of Ram Sing was triumphing, and the Mahrattas were spreading over the land of Maroo when the assassination of their chief checked their progress.

" A Rajpoot and an Afghan, both foot soldiers on a small monthly pay, offered, if their families were provided for, to sacrifice themselves for his safety by the assassination of the Mahratta commander. Assuming the garb of camp-suttlers, they approached the headquarters, feigning a violent quarrel. The simple Mahratta chief was performing his ablutions at the door of his tent, which as they approached they became more vociferous, and throwing a bundle of statements of account on the ground, begged he would decide between them. In this manner they came nearer and nearer, and as he listened to their story, one plunged his dagger in his side, exclaiming ' this for Nagore ! ' and ' this for Jodpoor ! ' said his companion, as he repeated the mortal blow. The alarm was given ; the Afghan was slain ; but the Rajpoot called out ' thief,' and mingling with the throng escaped by a drain into the town of Nagore.''

The siege lasted for six months after the murder, when a treaty was made under which the Mahrattas abandoned Ram Sing to " his evil star " on the condition of receiving a fixed triennial tribute. The fortress and district of Ajmer was surrendered in full sovereignty to the Mahrattas, in *moondkati*, or compensation, for the blood of Jey Appa. " The monsoon was then approaching ; they broke up and took possession of this important conquest, which, placed in the very heart of these regions, may be called the key of Rajpootana." For sixty-two years the Mahrattas remained masters of the key of Rajpootana. The Rajpoot chiefs were too weak and divided by intestine feuds to be able to oppose the extortions and indignities of the Mahratta predatory rulers, and when the power of the Mahrattas decayed, their provinces were harassed by the Pindaree freebooters and the Afghan mercenaries of Amir Khan. Central India, including Rajpootana, was laid waste, villages burnt, the ryots tortured in order to extort the discovery of their scanty store, because the Power to whom the sovereignty of India had passed would not realize that an Imperial position entails Imperial obligations. The Imperial policy of Wellesley which established a close bond of connexion between the British Government and the principal States of India was abandoned by his successors, Cornwallis and Barlow, acting under the orders of their masters at home. The doctrine of non-interference was introduced, a policy which under the specious guise of moderation was a policy of weakness and a cruel dereliction of duty. The Rajpoot chiefs claimed the protection and interference of the British power on the grounds of justice. Sir Charles Metcalfe, Resident for Rajpootana, wrote : " They say that there always has existed some power in India to which peaceable States submitted and in return obtained its protection. . . . The British Government now occupies the place of the great protecting Power, and is the natural guardian of the peaceable and weak ; but, owing to its refusal to use its influence for their protection, the peaceable and weak States are continually exposed to the oppressions and cruelties of robbers and plunderers, the most licentious and abandoned of mankind." The robbers and plunderers now ventured to extend their depredations into British territory. The Marquis of Hastings, who when in Parliament attacked the policy of Wellesley, saw, soon after he assumed the office of Governor-General, that it was the only practicable policy. The British authority must be supreme throughout India. The British Government must be lord paramount over all the sovereigns and princes of the continent. After having brought to a successful issue his war with the Nepalese the Governor-General determined to make effective preparations for the crushing of the Pindarees. The freebooters looked for support to Daulat Rao Sindia as the most powerful of the Mahratta princes. But the measures of Lord Hastings were so speedy and effective that Sindia was compelled to associate with the Company against the Pindarees, and he had to consent to the abrogation of a clause in a former treaty which restrained the British Government from forming engagements with the Rajpoot States. In 1818 a treaty was made with Sindia by which the British Government received Ajmer and other districts and ceded lands of equal value. The history of Ajmer is no longer a romantic tale of sieges and battles or chivalrous deeds of valour, neither is it a tale of wrong and robbery. It is the prosaic

story of a people advancing in prosperity and civilization
under a settled government, and it would be impossible to
exaggerate the good that has been effected in the Protected
States of Rajpootana by our influence and example. When
a mighty famine arose in extensive and populous provinces of
our Indian Empire the chiefs of Rajpootana vied with the
British Government in alleviating the sufferings of the
people. Following the example set them by noble English
ladies, consorts in the burdens of Empire, chiefs in whose
kingdoms infanticide and suttee had prevailed for ages are
building hospitals for native women, and are securing the
services of lady doctors to alleviate the sufferings of the
inmates of the harem.

About three miles from the Fortress-palace of Akbar
stands in park-like grounds a handsome marble pile which
illustrates the gulf between the suzerainty of the English
and the suzerainty of the Mahratta and the Moghul. It is
the Mayo College, founded by the great ruler whose name
it bears, for the education of young Rajpoot princes. At
a great durbar which he held for the reception of the chiefs
of Rajpootana in October, 1870, Lord Mayo made a speech
so illustrative of what our policy and feelings towards the
nobles and the people of India should be that it cannot be
too often quoted :

" I, as the representative of the Queen, have come here to tell
you, as you have often been told before, that the desire of Her
Majesty's Government is to secure to you and to your successors
the full enjoyment of your ancient rights and the exercise of all
lawful customs, and to assist you in upholding the dignity and
maintaining the authority which you and your fathers have for
centuries exercised in this land.

" But in order to enable us fully to carry into effect this our
fixed resolve, we must receive from you hearty and cordial
assistance. If we respect your rights and privileges, you should
also respect the rights and regard the privileges of those who are
placed beneath your care. If we support you in your power,

we expect in return good government. We demand that everywhere throughout the length and breadth of Rajpootana justice and order should prevail ; that every man's property should be secure ; that the traveller should come and go in safety ; that the cultivator should enjoy the fruits of his labour, and the trader the produce of his commerce; that you should make roads and undertake the construction of those works of irrigation which will improve the condition of the people, and swell the revenue of your States ; that you should encourage education and provide for the relief of the sick.

"And now let me mention a project which I have much at heart. I desire much to invite your assistance to enable me to establish at Ajmer a school or college which should be devoted exclusively to the education of the sons of the Chiefs, Princes, and leading Thakoors of Rajpootana. It should be an institution suited to the position and rank of the boys for whose instruction it is intended, and such a system of teaching should be founded as would be best calculated to fit them for the important duties which in after-life they would be called upon to discharge. It would not be possible on this occasion to describe minutely the different features of such an institution, but I hope to communicate with you shortly on the subject ; and I trust you will favour and support an attempt to give to the youth of Rajpootana instruction suitable to their high birth and position.

"Be assured that we ask you to do all this for no other but your own benefit. If we wished you to remain weak, we should say, 'Be poor, and ignorant, and disorderly.' It is because we wish you to be strong that we desire to see you rich, instructed, and well-governed. It is for such objects that the servants of the Queen rule in India ; and Providence will ever sustain the rulers who govern for the people's good.

"I am but here for a time ; the able and ardent officers who surround me will, at no distant period, return to their English homes ; but the power which we represent will endure for ages. Hourly is this great Empire brought nearer and nearer to the throne of our Queen. The steam vessel and the railroad enable England year by year to enfold India in a closer embrace. But the coils she seeks to entwine around her are not iron fetters, but the golden chains of affection and of peace. The hours of conquest are past ; the age of improvement has begun.

"Chiefs and princes, advance in the right way, and secure

to your children's children, and to future generations of your subjects, the favouring protection of a power who only seeks your good."

Thus spoke the strong and worthy representative of a Queen who during her long and illustrious reign laboured to exercise her power for the good of India, and shared in the joys and sorrows of her Indian subjects. History will record how she won their affection. The presence in that magnificent pageant on Coronation Day, of Sindia and his hereditary foes the Maharaja of Jeypore and the Regent of Jodpore, bore witness to the personal loyalty which she created among the chiefs and princes of India. After their reception at Buckingham Palace by her son, one of the most illustrious and proudest of the feudatory chiefs, struck by the splendour of the scene and the dignity and kindness of his Emperor, declared he was now proud to be a feudatory of the Empire. The frequent visits of Indian princes to England should be indeed discouraged, because they are fraught with evil to themselves and their subjects. But it might be sound policy to expect that every chief before he ascends the *musnud* should pay a visit to England and present his *nuzzur*, and receive from the hands of the Emperor the emblems of sovereignty.

The feudal castle at Ajmer, where Jehangir held his Durbar and received the feudatory princes and the Ambassador from His Majesty King James I., has long since been converted into a public office. On each side of the fine gate facing the city can be seen the windows which answer to the " Jarruco wyndow " (Audience window) where Roe found the Emperor when he went to pay his respects on the Nau-roz, or New Year's Day feast. The Emperor was busy in receiving and giving presents. What he bestowed he let down " by a silke stringe rouled on a turning instrument " ; what was given him " a venerable fatt deformed ould matron " pulled up at a hole with such another clue. "At one syde in a wyndow were his two Principall wifes whose Curiositye made them breake litle holes in a grate of reede that hung before yt to gaze on mee. I saw first their fingers, and after laying their faces close, nowe one eye, nowe another; sometyme I could discerne the full proportions. They were indifferently white, black hayre smoothed vp; but if I had no other light, their diamondes and Pearles had sufficed to show them. When I looked vp they retyred, and were so merry that I supposed they laughed at mee." "The emperor suddenly rose and all retired to the Durbar and sat in the Carpette, attending his Commen." Not long after Jehangir appeared and descended the stairs "with such an acclamation of health to the King as would have out-cryed Cannons. At the foot of the stairs one came and buckled on his swoord and buckler, sett all ouer with great Diamondes and rubys, the belts of gould suteable."

"Another hung on his quiuer with 30 arrowes and his bow in a Case, the same that was presented by the Persian Ambassador. On his head he wore a rich Turbant with a Plume of herne tops, not many but long : on one syde hung a ruby vnsett, as bigg as a Walnutt ; on the other syde a diamond as great ; in the middle an emralld like a hart, much bigger. His shash was wreathed about with a Chayne of great Pearle, rubys, and diamondes drild. About his Neck hee carried a Chaine of most excellent Pearle, three double ; so great I neuer saw ; at his Elbowes, Armlettes sett with diamondes ; and on his wristes three rowes of seuerall sorts. His handes bare, but almost on euery finger a ring ; his gloves, which were english, stuck under his Girdle ; his Coate of Cloth of gould without sleeues upon a fine *Semian* as thin as Lawne ; on his feet a payre of embrodered buskinges with Pearle, the toes sharp and turning vp. Thus armd and accomodated, hee went to the Coach, which attended him with his New English seruant, who was Clothed as rich as any Player and more gaudy, and had trayned four horses, which were trapped and harnassed in gould veluetts. This was the first hee euer sate in, and was made by that sent

AJMER.

III

from England, so like that I knew it not but by the Couer, which was a gould Persian velvett. Hee gott into the end ; on each side went two Eunuches that carried small maces of gould sett all ouer with rubies, with a long bunch of white horse tayle to drive away flyes ; before him went drumes, ill trumpettes, and loud musique, and many Canopys, quittasolls and other strange ensignes of Maiestie of Cloth of gould sett in many Places with great rubyes, Nine spare horses, the furniture some garnished with rubyes, some with Pearle and emraldes, some only with studdes enameld. The Persian Ambassador presented him a horse. Next behind came three *Palenkees* ; the Carriages and feete of on Plated with gould sett at the endes with stones and couered with Crimson velvett embrodered with Pearle, and a frengg of great Pearls hanging in ropes a foote deepe, a border about sett with rubyes and emeralldes. A footman carried a foote stoole of gould sett with stones. The other two were couered and lyned only with Cloth of gould. Next followed the English Coach newly couered and trimed rich, which hee had given the queene Normahall, who rode in yt. After them a third of this Cuntry fashion, which me thought was out of Countenance ; in that sate his younger sonns. After followed about 20 Eliphantes royall spare for his owne ascending, so rich that in stones and furniture that they braved the sunne. Euery Eliphant had diuers flages of Cloth of siluer, guilt satten, and taffeta. His Noblemen hee suffered to walke a foot, which I did to the gate and left him. His wiues on their Eliphantes were carried like Parrakitoes half a Mile behynd him.''

No gorgeous Imperial pageant now rolls down the street of Ajmer. But there are few towns in India where you can enter so into the heart of the East and feel its life about you as Ajmer, with its old houses and their carved marble balconies overhanging its narrow and tortuous bazaars, alive with many races. They come to trade, for Ajmer is an important entrepôt, and they come—Rajpoot, Jat, Mahratta, Muhammadan—to visit the shrine of the Saint Khwaja Mueyyin-ud-din Chisti, known as Khwaja Sahib, whose miracles are renowned all over India. The great Akbar once made a pilgrimage on foot to this place to implore at the saint's tomb the blessing of male offspring. Many are the legends stated about the holy man. According to a popular tradition it was at Medina " the City " a voice came from the tomb of the Prophet calling for Mueyyin-ud-din, and directing him to go to Ajmer and convert the infidels. He obeyed the call. On reaching Ajmer he took up his abode on the hill overlooking Lake Anasagar, whose margin he found lined with idol temples. The idolaters made frequent attempts to slay him. But when they came in sight of the Saint they were rooted to the ground, and when they attempted to cry *Ram, Ram*, only ejaculated *Rahim, Rahim*.[1] They begged his forgiveness, and invited him to take up his residence in the town. He chose the site on the southern side of the city close to the wall, where the Dargah now stands. Here he lived working miracles till his death in 1235. The charm of the Dargah lies in its fine gateway, the marble courtyard glistening and sparkling in the sun, the tall trees planted around the tombs, which cast a cool and refreshing shade, and the grey mountain towering above. The marble mosque built by Shah Jehan has the radiant purity of the pearl mosque built by him at Agra. The monarch who erected the mosque at Ajmer, the pearl mosque at Agra, and the Taj Mahal, left the world richer than he found it.

[1] They tried to cry Ram, Ram, the Hindu Rama, and they were forced to cry the Muhammadan name ' Rahim ' for the Merciful God.

V

JEYPORE

FROM Ajmer the open tableland spreads eastward towards Jeypore, which stands on a sandy and barren plain sixteen hundred feet above the sea, surrounded on three sides by stony hills. From this point the Aravell range no longer forms an unbroken barrier against the desert. Ajmer whispers the mediaeval enchantment of the East : Jeypore proclaims itself a prosperous modern town. It owes its political importance to being the capital of one of the two chief States of Rajpootana, and its prosperity to being a great commercial centre for the trade between Delhi and Agra and Rajpootana. Though Jeypore is a modern prosperous Hindu city, the State to which it gives its name has a respectable antiquity. The chiefs of Jeypore claim their descent from Kash, the second son of Rama, who was the fifty-seventh of the line of Surajbans, or Sun-begotten kings, and therefore may be allowed " the boast of heraldry." Rama ruled long and gloriously in Ajodhya (the blessed) in Oude, and when the city waxed and waned the royal kinsmen went forth and carved out chiefships for themselves. When Edgar was King of all the English (A.D. 967) Dhola Rao and his Kachwahas, after many and stubborn struggles with the local chiefs, obtained a solid establishment in a territory known by the name of Dhundar from (Tod says) a sacred mount of that name situated some-where on the western frontier of the present State. Half a century later and the Kachwa chief got possession of Amber, consecrated to Amba the Universal Mother, a flourishing town erected by the Mynas, the great, pure, unmixed race of Upper India, whose original home was in the range of hills called Kali-Kho, extending from Ajmer nearly to the Jumna. As Amber lies in a gorge of the hills, the Mynas proudly styled it Ghatta Rani, Queen of the Pass. The prosperity of the town increased with the power of her new masters, and having become their capital she gave her name to their chiefship. From the annals of Amber little fruit can be gleaned till her chiefs became intimately connected with the Moghul dynasty. The far sight of Akbar saw that the strength of the Moghul Empire could be only sustained by alliances with the princely families of the Hindus, and so bringing the Hindu States into the Imperial system. He himself had two Rajpoot queens of the houses of Jeypore and Marwar, and his eldest son, Prince Selim, afterwards Jehangir, was married to a daughter of Raja Bagwandas of Jeypore. " By what arts or influence Akbar," says Tod, " overcame the scruples of the Cuchwaha Rajpoot we know not, unless by appealing to his avarice or ambition ; but the name of Bhagwandas is execrated as the first who sullied Rajpoot purity by matrimonial alliance with the Islamite." Maun Sing, nephew, adopted son, and successor of Bhagwandas, was one of the ablest of Akbar's soldier statesmen. " As the Emperor's lieutenant, he was entrusted with the most arduous duties, and added conquests to the Empire from Khoten to the ocean. Orissa was subjugated by him, Assam humbled and made tributary, and Cabul maintained in her allegiance. He held in succession the governments of Bengal and Behar, the Dekhan and Cabul." Maun Sing did much for his own capital, and commenced the palace, uniting it to the feudal castle of the former kings, some portions of which may still be seen.

He was succeeded by two unworthy successors, debauchees

who reigned but did not govern. The influence of Jeypore declined, and the princes of Jodpoor took the lead in the Imperial Court. Then, at the instigation of the celebrated Joda Bae, daughter of the Raja of Bikaner, Jey Sing, a grand-nephew of Maun, was raised by Jehangir to the throne of Amber. The chronicle relates that "the succession was settled by the Emperor and the Rajpootni in a conference at the balcony of the seraglio, where the Emperor saluted the youth below as Raja of Amber, and commanded him to make his salaam to Joda Bae, as the source of this honour. But the customs of Rajwarra could not be broken ; it was contrary to etiquette for a Rajpoot chief to salaam, and he replied, ' I will do this to any lady of your Majesty's family, but not to Joda Bae ' ; upon which she good-naturedly laughed, and called out, ' It matters not ; I give you the Raj of Amber.' " The chivalrous Jey Sing or Mirza Raja, the title by which he is best known, was qualified to restore and invigorate a kingdom. During his reign Amber reached the zenith of its prosperity and magnificence. By the construction of a dam he had formed the beautiful lake of Tal Koutora, and he adorned the royal city with luxurious gardens. He added to the palace which Maun Sing began the Jey Mandir, the Diwan-i-Khas, and several other noble buildings, and he diligently strengthened it by enclosing it within a wall. To the Empire he also rendered great service. Aurangzeb bestowed on him the *munsub*, or command of seven thousand horse, and he led many a campaign at the head of his valiant tribesmen. Aurangzeb sent him to crush the upstart Deccan robber Shivaji, who defied the armies of the Moghul. After a vigorous campaign of some months Mirza Raja brought the great Mahratta leader to bay at the Fort of Purandhar. Shivaji made several ineffectual sorties, and Jey Sing opening negotiations, a treaty was ratified.

" It was stipulated that Shivaji with his son Sambhaji should go and pay his respects to the kings at Delhi, and that Mirza

Raja's son, Ram Sing, should accompany him, and introduce him to the King, and obtain for Shivaji the royal pardon. When they parted Mirza Raja presented Shivaji with many valuable presents." [1]

Shivaji was coldly received by Aurangzeb, and he would have been murdered if Jey Sing's son had not discovered the plot. Three years later (1608) Jey Sing died. Tod states he was poisoned at the instigation of Aurangzeb, whose jealousy and resentment he had aroused. The chronicle says :

" He had twenty-two thousand Rajpoot cavalry at his disposal, and twenty-two great vassal chiefs who commanded under him ; that he would sit with them in *durbar*, holding two glasses, one of which he called Delhi, the other Satarra, and dashing one to the ground, would exclaim, there goes Satarra, the fate of Delhi is in my right hand, and this with like facility I can cast away."

" These vaunts reaching the Emperor's ear, he had recourse to the same diabolical expedient which ruined Marwar, of making a son assassin of his father. He promised the succession to the *Gadi* of Amber to Keerut Sing, younger son of the Raja, to the prejudice of his elder brother, Ram Sing, if he effected the horrible deed. The wretch, having perpetrated the crime by mixing poison in his father's opium, returned to claim the investiture, but the King only gave him the district of Kamah. From this period, says the chronicle, Amber declined."

Thirty years after the death of Mirza Raja, Jey Sing the Second, better known as Siwai Jey Sing, mounted the *musnud*. The title Siwai, which his descendants adopt to this day, was given him by the Moghul Emperor. " The word means one and a quarter, and is supposed to measure the superiority of the bearer to all contemporaries,

[1] *The Selections from the Letters, Despatches and other State Papers Preserved in the Bombay Secretariat Mahratta Series.* Edited by George W. Forrest.

whom the unit signifies." In vulgar English, Jey Sing was considered head and shoulders above the rest. He showed marked capacity as a statesman and legislator, and to his capacity as an engineer and architect the city he founded bears testimony. Of his proficiency in mathematics and astronomy men of science of Western reputation have borne witness. " He had erected observatories, with instruments of his own invention, at Delhi, Jeipoor, Oojein, Benares, and Mathura upon a scale of Asiatic grandeur ; and their results were so correct as to astonish the most learned. He had previously used such instruments as those of Ulug Beg (the Royal astronomer of Samarcand), which failed to answer his expectations. From the observations of seven years at the various observatories he constructed a set of tables. While thus engaged he learned through a Portuguese missionary, Padre Manuel, the progress which his favourite pursuit was making in Portugal, and he sent 'several skilful persons along with him' to the Court of Emanuel. The King of Portugal despatched Xavier de Silva, who communicated to the Rajpoot the tables of De la Hire." Jey Sing writes :

" On examining and comparing the calculations of these tables with actual observation it appeared there was an error in the former, in assigning the moon's place, of half a degree ; although the error in the other planets was not so great, yet the times of solar and lunar eclipses *he* " (Jey Sing speaks of himself in the third person) " found to come out later or earlier than the truth by the fourth part of a *ghurry*, or fifteen *puls* (six minutes of time)."

Jey Sing had Euclid's Elements, the treatises on plane and spherical trigonometry, and Napier on the construction and use of logarithms, to be translated into Sanskrit ; he also collated for himself a table of stars, which he called Tij Muhammad Shahi, the preface of which he thus opens :
" Let us devote ourselves at the altar of the King of

kings, hallowed be His name! in the book of register of whose power the lofty orbs of heaven are only a few leaves; and the stars, and that heavenly courser the sun, small pieces of money, in the treasury of the Empire of the most High."

From inability to comprehend the all-encompassing beneficence of His power, *Hipparchus* is an ignorant clown who wrings the hand of vexation; and in the contemplation of his exalted majesty, Ptolemy is a bat, who can never arrive at the sun of truth; the demonstrations of Euclid are an imperfect sketch of the forms of His contrivance.

" But since the well-wisher of the works of creation, and the admiring spectator of the works of infinite wisdom, Siwai Jey Sing, from the first dawning of reason in his mind, and during its progress towards maturity, was entirely devoted to the study of mathematical science, and the bent of his mind was constantly directed to the solution of its most difficult problems; by the aid of the Supreme Author he obtained a thorough knowledge of its principles and rules, *etc*."

After entering the gates of the palace, on the right lies a cluster of stone buildings containing the instruments designed by the Royal mathematician. The present Maharaja has had the Kantra or Observatory restored, so it now stands as it did in the days of his illustrious predecessor. It was Jey Sing's coadjutor in science and history, Vedyadhar, a Jain of Bengal, who designed his new capital for him. " Jeypore," says Tod, " is the only city in India built upon a regular plan, with streets bisecting each other at right angles." It is the regularity of the plan of the city, the straight streets, the houses all built after the same pattern, which deprive it of one of the mystic charms of the East. The houses, all of a pale pink or violet colour, ornamented with paintings, look well in the bright sunshine, but we miss the gloom and shadow, the mystery and romance of an

Oriental city. The wide spaces, filled with a white and red crowd, present a gay scene, but it is merely spectacular. The Rajpoot cavaliers on their fine horses, the bullock carts, the palanquins, the camels, the donkeys, the richly caparisoned elephants making their way through the throng, merely seem to pass over a stage. The houses, pierced with small windows filled in with slabs of perforated stone, are mere scenery, mud walls made to look like houses, and painted pink. Jeypore is, as André Chevrillon says, "India of novels and the opera, fairy-like and incredible." The fairy-land of the Parisian opera, but not of the Arabian Nights.

The Maharaja's palace, surrounded by a lofty wall built by Jey Sing, stands on a large open space in the centre of the town. The only portion visible from the streets is a building " of a singularly vivid rose-colour, rising in the form of a pyramid, bristling with a nine-storied façade, composed of a hundred bell-turrets and sixty-five projecting windows, adorned with colonnettes and balconies, pierced in open-work with countless flowers cut out in the stone ; a vapoury, impossible construction. This is the palace of the Wind —the palace of the Wind. How enchanting the name." The palace is, however, a mere mask of stucco, and it is more fantastic than beautiful. The Chandra Mahal, which forms the centre of the principal palace, is also a pyramidal building seven stories high, but the architecture is of a far higher order than that of the Hall of the Winds. It overlooks the Royal gardens, which are extensive, and in their way extremely beautiful, full of fountains, mango and orange trees, and flowering shrubs. "The garden," says Bishop Heber, whose comparisons are always happy, " is surrounded by a high embattled wall, having a terrace at the top like that of Chester, and beneath it a common passage (as one of the Ministers of State who accompanied me told me) for the Zenanah to walk in." The Diwan-i-Khas, or Hall of Audience, which occupies the ground floor of the

Chandra Mahal, is "a noble open pavilion, with marble pillars, richly carved, rather inferior in size, but in other respects fully equal to the Hall of Audience at Delhi." Here the Bishop and the Resident "sat cross-legged on the carpet, there being no chairs, and we kept our hats on." The Maharaja was a minor, and the Government was at the time being conducted under the Regency of his mother— whose vices matched those of Theodora. The Bishop writes : " I was mortified to find that the rannee never appeared even behind the purdah, though we were told she was looking through a latticed window at some distance in front." " After the usual exchange of compliments," says the Bishop, " some very common-looking shawls, a turban, necklace, etc., were brought in as presents from the rannee to me, which were followed by two horses and an elephant, of which she also requested my acceptance." When the audience was over the Bishop and the Resident mounted their elephants and returned to the Residency, " the ran-nee's presents going before us." The Bishop, when he reached camp, had the old warning brought home to him, " Put not your trust in princes." " Of these presents it appeared that the elephant was lame, and so vicious that few people ventured to go near him. One of the horses was a very pretty black, but he also turned out as lame as a cat, while the other horse was in a poor condition, and at least, as my people declared, thirty years old." Eight years after Heber's visit (1825) the Rani died, and two years later the young Maharaja Jey Sing. It was supposed that he was poisoned by one Jota Rama, the paramour of the late Queen. On the death of the Maharaja the Agent of the Governor-General proceeded to Jeypore, which was a scene of corruption and misgovernment, and assumed the guardian-ship of the infant heir. The strong measures which he adopted led to the formation of a conspiracy by Jota Ram. " The Agent's life was attempted, and his Assistant was

JEYPORE—TEMPLE OF THE WINDS.

122

murdered." [1] The murderers were seized and executed by order of the Native Minister. A Council of Regency, consisting of five of the principal nobles, was formed, under the superintendence of a political agent, and, as has been the case with other Native States under similar circumstances, Jeypore was delivered from ruin and anarchy. " The army was reduced, every branch of the administration was reformed, and suttee, slavery, and infanticide were prohibited." Maharajah Ram Sing, when he was installed ruler, found a well-governed prosperous State, and he proved himself a capable administrator. He did good service during the mutinies, for which he received a grant of land and also the privilege of adoption. He took advantage of this privilege shortly before his death, and adopted a young relative belonging to a distant branch (the present Maharaja), who was a poor village lad of the true blood. Siwai Madhao Sing, the hundred and fortieth descendant in a direct line from Rama, proud of his descent, proud of his country, of her ancient customs and her ancient faith, has shown that the Rajpoot has not lost his capacity for government. His Royal city has public institutions which would do credit to any Western capital. The public garden of Jeypore has a good title to be considered one of the finest in India. Here are well-kept grass plots, with beds planted with ferns and roses, and shrubberies bright with sky-blue and blood-red flowers. In the centre of the garden stands the Albert Hall, whose foundation was laid by the King-Emperor when he visited the city as Prince of Wales. On the rocky slope of a hill that bears the name of *Nahargarh* (" The Tiger's Stronghold ") can be seen the word *Welcome* in gigantic white letters, another memento of his visit. The Albert Hall contains a large Durbar hall, and one of the best arranged

[1] *A Collection of Treaties, Engagements, and Sunnuds, relating to India and Neighbouring Countries,* compiled by C. A. Aitchison, B.C.S., vol. ii. p. 59.

museums in India. As we strolled through it we came upon
an interesting group. Three or four Rajpoots from the wilds,
with their women, whose faces were veiled, listening with
rapt attention to a guide who was dilating on the imitations
of the frescoes in the Ajanta caves. The silks and carpets,
the porcelain and clay vessels, are well worth a close study,
and it is instructive to go from the museum to the School of
Art and compare the work which is being done with the work
of the past. The pencil drawings are very nice, the inlaid
work is very pretty, but something has gone from the beauty,
an indescribable something, the soul of the artist. A School
of Art does the same kind and amount of good as the purely
external literary English education at the Maharaja's College, and it also works as much mischief.

It was refreshing to leave modern prosperous Jeypore and
spend a day at Amber, amidst all " the venerable pageantry
of time." It was a soft, cool morning in February when we
drove from the Residency to the old capital. The pavement was early alive with men performing their ablutions,
who filled the atmosphere with their gurgles as they cleaned
their teeth with a piece of stick, as their forefathers had done
some centuries before gas was introduced into Jeypore.
Emerging from the north-east gate, we found ourselves on
the white sandy road running through luxurious gardens
and garden houses, the trees glittering with their broad
leaves in the sun ; the parrots all awake, chirping, screaming,
flashing from branch to branch, peacocks, blue and white,
sunning their tails on the walls. Then we come to a large
lake covered with waterfowl, and alligators basking in the
sun on the bank. Horrid, evil-looking monsters, with the
hungry impudent stare of the Yogis (mendicants) who
sit around the tombs and ruined houses. The alligators are
also protected by the pious, and they increase and multiply
because no one is allowed under pain of severe punishment
to hurt or disturb them. In Jeypore, with its gas and its

English college, zoolatry still prevails, and the alligator is one of the monsters worshipped. It is sacred to *Kamadeva*, Love. On the bank of the lake the road passes through an ancient gateway in an embattled wall, which connects the two hills that enclose the valley of Amber. Here we find the elephants sent by the Maharaja to complete our journey, for the road now becomes too steep for carriages. The sight of the huge monster kneeling at the word of his driver (Mahaut) has long ceased to be novel, but will never cease to delight and surprise. When loaded he rose, and rolled slowly up the steep hill, like some ungainly, fat dame. On reaching the summit we passed through another gateway, and below us lay a deep glen, where by the margin of a small lake, a blur of hot colour, sleeps the ancient capital of Amber, a city of ancient temples and ruined palaces, a city of the dead. The crests of the hills on either side are glorified with castles built of pink sandstone, the relics of old Rajpoot story. Above the lake on its western side rises the old fortified palaces, whose white and yellow facade is broken by balconies and verandahs. The elephant rolled through a winding street of ruined houses and miserable huts till a sloped paved ascent leading to the palace was reached. Guarded on either side by embattled ramparts, and having at every turn a massive red sandstone gateway, it is a fitting entrance to the home of a Rajpoot chief.

Having got through the last handsome gateway, we found ourselves in a large quadrangle surrounded by great blocks of buildings formerly used as barracks and stables. Here we alighted. To be accurate, we had alighted two miles before, for we had discovered that the back of an elephant is, like the sea, not our natural home. Mounting a long flight of steps and passing through another gateway ornamented with brilliant frescoes, we reached a courtyard, the Court of Honour, paved with red and white sandstone. At one end rises the Diwan-i-Khas, a noble hall of audience. "A double

AMBER—RUINED CITY.

126

row of columns, supporting a massive entablature, forms three sides of the hall, which is roofed in by a vaulted and very lofty ceiling of great solidity ; the fourth side, which is walled up, facing the lake. The building is therefore in reality only a kiosk on a very large scale, and is perfectly open to the air. The hall is paved with marble, inlaid with colours, and a platform of white marble erected at one extremity, serves as a throne. The first row of columns are of red sandstone, with capitals of great beauty, on which elephants are sculptured, supporting with their trunks the sloping stone roof which descends from the cornice. The shafts of these columns are covered with a layer of smooth white stucco, which hides the magnificent sculpture. It appears that no sooner had Mirza completed the Diwan-i-Khas than it came to the ears of the Emperor Jehanghir, that his vassal had surpassed him in magnificence, and that this last great work quite eclipsed all the marvels of the Imperial city ; the columns of red sandstone having been particularly noticed as sculptured with exquisite taste and elaborate detail. In a fit of jealousy the Emperor commanded that this masterpiece should be thrown down, and sent commissioners to Amber charged with the execution of this order ; whereupon the Mirza, in order to save the structure, had the columns plastered over with stucco, so that the messengers from Agra should have to acknowledge to the Emperor that the magnificence, which had been so much talked of, was after all pure invention. Since then his apathetic successors have neglected to bring to light this splendid work ; and it is only by knocking off some of the plaster that one can get a glimpse of the sculptures, which are perfect as on the day they were carved." At the other end of the courtyard is the abode of the King, with its magnificent gateway, covered with mosaics and delicate paintings. The marble frameworks of the windows are carved out of single slabs, and vie with those of Ahmedabad in delicacy

and beauty. Passing through the Royal portal, we entered
a court surrounded by palaces in the centre of which is a
fragrant garden. On one side of the garden there is the
Jey Mandir, the marble pavilion built by the great Jey Sing.
The interior is divided into three great saloons, which are
inlaid from the ceiling to the floor with mosaics in various
colours and pieces of looking-glass, evidence of the taste of
the eighteenth century. It is a creature of Oriental gor-

COURT OF HONOUR, AMBER.

geousness marred by a touch of western influence. Above
the Hall of Victory is a Jas Mandir, or Alcove of Delight, a
marble kiosk with three fine apartments ornamented in the
same style as, but in better taste than those on the ground
floor. On one side, overlooking the precipice, are large
windows with delicate marble trellis-work, through which
the queens had broken glimpses of wild and magnificent
nature ; on the other side is a marble terrace overlooking
an Elysian garden of the citron, orange, and pomegranate.

From a balcony may be enjoyed one of the most striking prospects that can be conceived, the rugged green valley, the silver lake reflecting the castles and ruined palaces, the wild waste of sand, and the red hills stretching away to the north. The amber tints of the sky, the dark brown of the ruins, the pale grey shadows of the hills, make the whole effect as unreal as "the light that never shone on sea or land." On the other side of the Jey Mandir is the Sukh Nawas, or Hall of Pleasure, famous for its painting of a grove, and a channel for a rivulet to run through the apartments. It was a cool retreat for an Oriental monarch, but it lacks the true glory and loveliness of Eastern art. The simplicity and princely air of the Zenana is more in keeping with the proud Rajpoot and his queens, through whose veins love, passion, courage, and the stern justice of revenge throbbed and burnt. The harem was originally a sanctuary; it was prohibited to strangers, not because women were considered unworthy of confidence, but on account of the sacredness with which custom and manners invested them. European writers are apt to judge the harem by the standard of the Moghul Emperor's seraglio. Making the worst of this, however, yet Aurangzeb was better than his contemporary Louis XIV. If we judge from the Rajpoot bards, women could not have been held in slight esteem. The princess of Canouj, who was carried off by the Chohan Emperor of Delhi, is the Helen of Rajpootana. The Rajpoot bard, like Homer, separates her from her faults, and a noble woman remains. When the Muslim invades the land, she breaks the bonds of pleasure and passion, and tells her lover, "Victory and fame to my lord! Oh Sun of the Chohans! in glory, or in pleasure, who has tasted so deeply as you? To die is the destiny not only of man, but of the gods : all desire to throw off the old garment ; but to die well is to live for ever. Think not of self, but of immortality ; let your sword divide your foe, and I will be your ardhanga (half-body) hereafter." When the Rajpoot's hosts were ranged to advance against the Islamite, Sunjogta armed her husband. " In vain she sought the rings of his corslet; her eyes were fixed on the face of the Chohan, as those of the famished wretch who finds a piece of gold. The sound of the drum reached the ear of the Chohan; it was as that of a death-knoll on that of Sunjogta : and as he left her to head Delhi's heroes she vowed that henceforward water only should

AMBER—ROYAL PALACE.

sustain her! ' I shall see him again in the region of Surya, but never more in Yoginipoor (Delhi).' Her prediction was fulfilled; her lord was routed, made captive, and slain; and, faithful to her vow, she mounted the funeral pyre." By this act of faith the Sati not only made atonement for the sins of her husband and secured the remission of her own, but had the joyful assurance of reunion to the object whose beatitude she procured. A Princess of Haravati, one of the queens of the illustrious Jey Sing, is the Rajpoot conception of true female modesty. Her manners and garb, in accord with the simplicity of her provincial capital, subjected her to the badinage of the more refined court of Amber, whose ladies had added the Imperial costume to their own native dress. " One day, being alone with the prince, he began playfully to contrast the sweeping *jupe* of Kotah with the more scanty robe of the belles of his own capital ; and, taking up a pair of scissors, said he would reduce it to an equality with the latter. Offended at such levity, she seized his sword, and assuming a threatening attitude said, ' that in the house to which she had the honour to belong they were not habituated to jests of this nature ; that mutual respect was the guardian not only of happiness, but of virtue ' ; and she assured him that if he ever again so insulted her, he would find that the daughter of Kotah could use a sword more effectively than the prince of Amber the scissors." The Queen of Ganore is as grand as Lucretia. After having defended five fortresses against the foe, she retreated to her last stronghold on the Nerbudda River. She had scarcely left the boat when the assailants arrived in pursuit. The garrison were few in number, and the fortress was soon in possession of the enemy. The fame of the radiant beauty of the Queen of Ganore had reached the Muslim conqueror, and he begged her to reign over the fortress and himself. Denial was useless. The Khan awaited her reply in the hall below. " She sent a message of assent, with a complimentary reflection on his gallant conduct and determination of pursuit, adding that he merited her hand for his bravery, and might prepare for the nuptials, which should be celebrated on the terrace of the palace. She demanded two hours for unmolested preparation, that she might appear in appropriate attire, and with the distinction her own and his rank demanded." The two hours sped away. The Khan was summoned to the terrace.

" Robed in the marriage garb presented to him by the Queen, with a necklace and aigrette of superb jewels from the coffers of Ganore, he hastened to obey the mandate, and found that fame had not done justice to her charms. He was desired to be seated, and in conversation full of rapture on his side, hours were as minutes while he gazed on the beauty of the Queen. But presently his countenance fell— he complained of heat ; punkas and water were brought, but they availed him not, and he began to tear the bridal garments from his frame, when the Queen thus addressed him : ' Know, Khan, that your last hour is come ; our wedding and our death shall be sealed together. The vestments which cover you are poisoned ; you had left me no other expedient to escape pollution.' While all were horror-struck by this declaration, she sprung from the battlements into the flood beneath. The Khan died in extreme torture, and was buried on the road to Bhopal."

An ancient pagan scene, yet not without a charm even to the modern Christian world. And now, as the sun threw a violet haze over the mountains, we descended the hill, and cast a last look on the massive walls, the fairy kiosks, the slender balconies of the Royal Fortress, a fit home for knights of old.

VI

DELHI

DELHI is the Empress of Indian cities. She has often been sacked and left naked and desolate. But she could not be despoiled of the incomparable situation which marks her for the metropolis of a great Empire. Standing on her high battlements, the eye can sweep over a wide expanse of yellow country scarred by ravines and dotted with trees and gardens till it reaches a long range of barren hills bathed in orange and lilac. Scattered over this wild stretch of land are surviving ruins, remnants of mighty edifices, tombs of warriors and saints, which convey a more impressive sense of magnificence than Imperial Rome. They are memorials not of a single city but of supplanted nations. Eight centuries before the Latins settled on the plains of Latium and Campania a band of Aryans drove from here aboriginal savages and founded on the left bank of the Jumna the city of Indrapastha, which grew into a mighty kingdom. Then the Muslim appeared on the scenes, and Hindu civilization disappeared in smoke and ruin, and of all that it contained there is nothing left but an iron pillar which records that Raja Dhava, who erected it, " obtained with his own arm an undivided sovereignty on the earth for a long period." An old prophecy declared that the Hindu sovereigns should endure as long as the pillar stood. *Quamdiu stabit Colyseus stabit et Roma, quando cadit Colyseus cadit Roma—*

" While stands the Coliseum, Rome shall stand,
When falls the Coliseum, Rome shall fall."

When Delhi first became the capital of a Muhammadan Empire (1206) the founder Kutb-ud-Din (the Pole-star of religion), originally a Turki slave, was told the prophecy, but he showed his contempt for it by allowing the pillar to remain, for it was more gratifying to the pride of the Muslim conqueror to allow the idolater's pillar to stand in the courtyard of a great mosque built with the spoils of innumerable Hindu shrines. The great mosque is now in ruins, but the remaining arches, with their granite pillars, covered with inscriptions in the florid Cufic character, Bishop Heber considered to be " as fine in their way as any of the details of York Minster." Ibn Batuta, the Tangier traveller who saw the mosque little more than a century after its erection, describes it as having no equal either for beauty or extent. The Turki slave, not contented with erecting a mosque from the materials of the infidel temples, determined to build a tower which should mark the triumph of Islam over the foul worship that prevailed in them, and from whose summit the Faithful should hear the Muezzins (criers) proclaim the *Ezan* or public invitation to prayer in the name of God and His prophet. Far over the ruins of Delhi soars the tapering shaft which bears his name. By sublime massiveness and subtle alterations of proportion the architect has created a transcendent building. The purplish red of the sandstone at the base is finely modulated through a pale pink in the second story to a dark orange at the summit, which harmonizes with the blue of an Indian sky. Dark bands of Arabic writing round the three lower stories contrast with the purple red. The Hindus whom the Muslim conquerors employed to erect and embellish their buildings wrought cunningly and with knowledge. His great aim, as Ram Raz points out in his work on Hindu architecture, was to produce beauty by geometrical proportion. The height of the column (238 feet 1 inch) is exactly five times the diameter, and that of the lower story

twice the diameter. The plinth is a polygon of twenty
sides : the basement story has the same number of faces
formed into convex flutes which are alternately angular and
semicircular, the next has semicircular flutes, and in the
third they are all angular. Then rises a plain story, and
above it soars a partially fluted story, whose shaft is
adorned with bands of marble and red sandstone. A bold
projecting balcony, richly ornamented, runs round each
story and affords relief to the eye. After six centuries the
column stands as fresh as on the day it was finished.

In Delhi we have the martial violence and religious sentiment of Muhammadanism raised to the elevation of fine art.
Dark massive mausoleums scattered over the plain bear
testimony to the manly vigour of the Afghan rulers, and
convey the expression of authority and power appropriate
to the puritanical spirit which enabled the followers of the
Man of Mecca to spread their victorious arms over the world.
The stately palaces and jewelled shrines within the walls of
the city mark the decline of that spirit and the influence of
wealth, luxury, and climate on the Empire founded by the
brilliant audacity and warlike skill of Zaher ud din Muhammad (Light of the Faith), better known by his Tartar
sobriquet of Baber (the Lion). The blood of conquerors
ran in his veins. He was the sixth in descent from Tamerlane, and his mother was a Moghul of the race of Chengiz
Khan. It was not until after four unsuccessful expeditions
(1519–1526) into India that he won, on the fateful field of
Paniput, situated fifty miles from Delhi, the bloody and
decisive victory which gave him a firm footing in Hindustan.
Baber, in his authentic memoirs, a book full of human interest and of great historical importance, writes : " I
placed my foot in the stirrup of recollection, and my
hands on the reins of confidence in God, and I marched
against the possessions of the throne of Delhi and the
dominions of Hindusthan, whose army was said to amount

to 100,000 foot, with more than 1,000 elephants." "The Most High God," he adds, "did not suffer the hardships that I had undergone to be thrown away, but defeated my formidable enemy, and made me conqueror of this noble country."

Baber's wide dominions were divided between his two eldest sons : Camran received Afghanistan and the whole of the Punjab ; and Humayun, the eldest, became the second Moghul Emperor. Nine years after his succession, he was

MAUSOLEUM OF THE EMPEROR HUMAYUN.

driven from the Imperial throne by the Afghan of the tribe of *Sur*, called Shir Khan (" Lion-lord," from having killed a tiger by a single blow of his sabre). After sixteen years of privation and suffering, Humayun entered Delhi in triumph, and once again was sovereign of Hindustan. He did not long enjoy his prosperity. The year after regaining his throne, as he was descending some steps, his foot slipped, and he fell headlong to the bottom. He was carried into his palace, where, after lingering for four days, he expired.

Humayun was buried on the banks of the Jumna, and his widow and son, the Great Akbar, erected over his remains a noble tomb, which for chastity of design and delicacy of execution has never been surpassed. On a lofty square platform of red stone, adorned with arches, rises an octagonal mass of white marble and rose-coloured sandstone, crowned by a marble dome of the perfect Persian shape which forms so conspicuous a feature in all the Moghul buildings. At each of the four corners rises a superb arch about fifty feet high ; and as the shaft or cylinder on which a dome rises is never a pleasing feature, the cunning architect raised the wall about fourteen feet above the arch, and destroyed its monotony by minaret and pinnacle. No man better understood than the Eastern architect that " change or variety is as much a necessity to the human heart and brain in buildings as in books," and he therefore did not continue the high wall, but placed at each corner a small pavilion with a marble dome. In the northern arch of the building is a door which admits the visitor into the room containing a marble tomb. It is only a cenotaph, for in the corresponding room below lie the remains of Humayun, his widow, his infant daughter, and some of his descendants. Here the last Moghul Emperor had a humble grave prepared for himself. But he was not destined to occupy it. A quiet, reflective man, fond of letters, and endowed with some of the ability of Baber and Akbar, he had none of the energy and activity of his ancestors. He was stricken in age when the insurgent troopers rode into Delhi from Meerut on May 11, 1857, and, of all men, least fitted to deal with a crisis. He became a mere puppet in the hands of the mutineers, and when the British troops stormed the walls of his city the old Emperor fled to the Imperial mausoleum of his ancestors. He was pursued, and " the trembling old creature put the sword he had with him into the powerful hands of Hodson." Thus the last descendant of the house of Timur gave up his arms to an English subaltern, and was led away captive to await his trial. He was tried, found guilty, and sentenced to transportation for life. On November 7, 1862, died in prison at Rangoon the last of the Great Moghuls.

About a mile from the Mausoleum of Humayun is the Chausat Khambah, a hall of sixty-four pillars, which is the resting-place of the foster-brother of the Great Akbar,

THE KUTUB MINAR.

a contemporary of Queen Elizabeth, who consolidated and raised the Moghul Empire to its full height of splendour and power. The marble pillars so shiny, so smooth, which support the marble hall, have their capitals and base decorated with the most exquisite simple foliage. The outer pillars are connected by marble screens ten feet high, some pierced with lattice-work and others divided into panels, perfect models shewing how delicate and inventive

THE CHAUSAT KHAMBAH.

art can be. The whole building is a fine example of the chaste beauty of Moghul architecture before luxury destroyed both its purity and dignity. Not far from the Chausat Khambah is the Mausoleum of Safdar Jung, which is a striking illustration of the rapid decline of Moghul art. It is not unlike that of Humayun, but with all the vigour and freshness departed, and the decoration lacks the patient skill and crispness of the ornamentation of the earlier buildings. The mausoleum contains a handsome marble sarcophagus, but in a vault beneath, under a simple mound of earth, lies the body of him who bore the proud title of " Piercer of battle ranks." The inscription at the head informs us, " However great and pompous man may be in the presence of his fellow-men, he is small and humble before God." The sentiment of humility in the sight of God expressed on the Moghul tombs seems inconsistent with the proud sepulchres they built for themselves. But the Mussulman's tomb was his castle and his home. Outside the walls of a city he chose a piece of land, which he surrounded with a strong wall and one or more noble gateways, with rooms for residence. In the centre of a garden planted with cypresses and fruit-trees, on a lofty terrace, he erected a square or octagonal building covered by a dome, which was the festal hall. When death came and put an end to mirth, the founder knew that his pleasure-house would not descend to his heirs but be seized by the sovereign. No Muslim would, however, desecrate a cemetery. He therefore ordered his remains to be buried in the garden he loved, and by his side they laid his favourite wife. The proud dwelling was handed over to the care of a few priests, the garden fell into decay, and the place became the abode of " eloquent, just and mighty Death," who " hast drawn together all the far-stretched greatness, all the pride, cruelty, and ambition of men, and covered it all over with these two narrow words *Hic jacet.*"

During the reign of the first three Emperors, Agra was the capital of the Moghul Empire, but Shah Jehan transferred the seat of government to Delhi. He was a contemporary of our first Charles, and the time when the English people were struggling both in Parliament and on the battlefield for constitutional government was the golden age of Moghul rule. Shah Jehan governed his vast dominion, which extended from Bengal to the borders of Persia, with ability. humanity, and justice. The native historians of these times state that, although Akbar was pre-eminent as a conqueror and a law-giver, yet for the order and arrangement of his territory and finance no prince ever reigned in India that could be compared to Shah Jehan. Travellers from the far West have recorded the splendour of his court, his peacock throne—which the practised eye of European lapidaries valued at six millions of English money—his elephants and horses with their trappings of silver and gold. But Shah Jehan's greatest splendour was shown in the magnificent fabrics of marble and stone which he caused to be erected. In the centre of Delhi and on the highest eminence he had built the Jumma Musjid, or Great Mosque. Five thousand workmen were daily employed on it for six years, and it was not finally finished till the very year the royal founder was deposed from the Imperial throne. A noble flight of steps leads to a handsome gateway of red sandstone, passing through which one enters a vast platform surrounded by high walls broken by two graceful gateways, and containing cloisters for pilgrims. Facing the Eastern gateway on the Western side (for the follower of the Prophet must look towards Mecca when he worships) rises the Mosque, with its grand central arch flanked on either side by five of small dimensions. Above all rise three fine domes of white marble striped with black, and at each angle towering in the air stands a gigantic minaret composed of alternate stripes of marble and red sandstone, from whence the Muezzins call

141

the faithful to prayers. In the centre of the quadrangle is a marble reservoir of water in which three fountains play. Round it are groups of figures performing their ablutions before joining in the evening worship, for with the Muhammadans, as Gibbon notes, cleanliness is the secret of prayer, and the frequent lustrations of the hands, the face, and the body is solemnly enjoined by the Koran. Squatted below the arcades are old moulvies with flowing beards, teaching their scholars the Koran. A Muhammadan friend introduced me to a teacher renowned for his knowledge of history, and we conversed about rare old manuscripts and the Great Moghuls. History comes home to you in the city in which it was created ; and to hear the old scholar talk with pride and dignity of the Moghuls amidst the monuments of their glory and the witnesses of their fall, touched us with a profound pathos. The conversation was interrupted by the Muezzins' shrill call to prayer. From all parts of the square men hastened to the Mosque, and, as the old teacher bade me farewell, I quoted to him the words of the Prophet, " Masjids are the gardens of Paradise, and the praises of God the fruit thereof." And we watched below those enormous white rows of figures rise and fall as one man, as they praised the Lord.

Opposite the Great Mosque is the palace built by Shah Jehan, which was the home and abode of the Moghul Cæsars. Surrounded by a lofty granite wall with frowning battlements, it was a residence worthy of the descendants of the immortal Timur. The entrance was through a fine vestibule. " It consists," says Heber, " not merely of a splendid Gothic arch in the centre of the great gate-tower, but after that of a long vaulted aisle like that of a Gothic cathedral with a small octagonal court in the centre, all of granite, and all finely carved with inscriptions from the Koran and with flowers." A long fine red sandstone arcade is all that now remains of the old entrance to the palace. The hall opened

DISTANT VIEW OF THE PALACE.

143

into a large courtyard, from which a great bazaar extended
right and left, where sat and worked the royal manufac-
turers,—" goldsmiths, picture drawers, workmen in lace and
workmen in silk and purple-gold, and in all those sorts of
fine cloth of which they make turbans, girdles with golden
flowers, and those drawers of ladies that are so fine and
delicate." Passing through a great gate, over which was
the *Nobutkhana* or Music Hall, the visitor entered the great
court of the palace, in which " there is a great and stately
hall with many ranks of pillars, high raised, very airy, open
on three sides looking on to the court, and having its pillars
and ground painted and gilded. In the midst of the walls
which separate this hall from the Seraglio, there is an opening
or kind of great window, high and large, and so high that
a man cannot reach to it from below with his hand. There
it is where the King every day about noon giveth a general
audience to all ; which is the reason that this great hall is
called Am-kas, that is, place of audience or a place of meeting
common to great and small." François Bernier, who was
Court Physician to the Moghul Emperor towards the beginning of Aurangzeb's long reign (1658–1707), gives us a
striking picture of the Am-kas as he saw it at certain festivals
of the year.

" The King appeared upon his throne, splendidly ap-
pareled. His vest was of white satin, flowered and raised
with a very fine embroidery of gold and silk. His turban
was of cloth-of-gold, having a fowl wrought upon it like a
heron, whose foot was covered with diamonds of an extraordinary bigness and price, with a great Oriental topaz,
which may be said to be matchless, shining like a little sun.
A collar of long pearls hung about his neck down to his
stomach, after the manner that some heathens wear here
their great beads. His throne was supported by six high
pillars or feet said to be of massive gold set with rubies,
emeralds and diamonds. Beneath the throne there appear

the great nobles, in splendid apparel, standing upon a raised ground covered with a great canopy of purpled gold with great golden fringes and enclosed by a silver balistre. The pillars of the hall were hung with tapestries of purpled gold having the ground of gold ; and for the roof of the hall there was nothing but great canopies of flowered satin fastened with red-silken cords that had big tufts of silk mixed with threads of gold hanging on them. Below there was nothing

JUMMA MUSJID.

to be seen but great silken tapestries, very rich, of an extraordinary length and breadth."

The glory has departed from the Diwan-i-Am, but the pillars of marble inlaid with mosaic work which supported the marble canopy above the throne still remain to please the eye of the traveller. A little behind the Great Hall of Audience, separated from it by a garden gay with flowering shrubs, rises an airy pile of white marble overlooking the broad Jumna. It is the Diwan-i-Khas, or private Hall of Audience, world-renowned on account of the inscription which in letters of gold upon a ground of white marble ran round the cornice : "*Agar Firdaus rue zamin ast—hamin ast to, hamin ast to, hamin ast* (If there is a paradise on earth it is this, it is this, it is this)." The whole work is a masterpiece of refined fancy. On a marble platform rises a marble pavilion, whose flat-coned roof is supported by arches resting on a double row of marble pillars. The inner face of the arches, and the spandrels, and the pilasters which support them, are covered with flowers and foliage of delicate design and dainty execution, created in green serpentine, blue, *lapis lazuli* red and purple porphyry. The Moghul realized the prophecy, " I will make thy windows of agates, and thy gates of carbuncles, and all thy borders of pleasant stones." On that hall the artist Austin de Bordeaux concentrated all his powers of modulation and lavished the wealth of an Empire. The ceiling was of wood, painted red and richly decorated with gold ; it was also formerly encrusted with a rich silver foliage inlaid with gold. Tavernier, the French jeweller, valued it at twenty-seven million francs. In the centre of the pillared terrace was the Emperor's judgment-seat, hewn out of a solid block of natural crystal about " eighteen inches high and four feet in diameter " ; and in front of it three jets of clear water were continually kept playing. On state occasions His Majesty used the famous peacock throne, " so called from its having the figures of two peacocks standing behind it, their tails being expanded and the whole so inlaid with sapphires, rubies, emeralds, pearls and other precious stones of appropriate colours, as to represent life. The throne itself was six feet long by five feet broad ; it stood on six massive feet, which with the body were of solid gold inlaid with rubies, emeralds, and diamonds. It was surmounted by a canopy of gold, supported by twelve pillars, all richly emblazoned with costly gems, and a fringe of pearls ornamented the borders of the canopy. Between the two peacocks stood the figure of a parrot of

the ordinary size, said to have been carved out of a single
emerald." The peacock and parrot, Bernier states, were
made " by a workman of astonishing powers, a Frenchman by birth, who after defrauding several of the Princes of
Europe by means of false gems, which he fabricated with
peculiar skill, sought refuge in the Great Moghul's court,
where he made his fortune."

In a small court leading from the quadrangle in which the
Diwan-i-Khas stands is the Emperor's private mosque, the

THE DIWAN-I-KHAS.

Moti Musjid, or Pearl Mosque ; and well does it deserve its
name, for it is as chaste and as rich as it can be.   The domes
only are seen above the red sandstone walls which enclose the
mosque until the opening of two small fine brass gates, when
the gem bathed in sunlight lies before you.   But it is not
full and untempered sunshine, for the Eastern architect
designed with the sense of heat upon him and the value
of shade.   In the Moti Musjid, as in all other mosques, the
central dome is always the largest, both in bulk and interest
(as having the main archway), and the other two are sub-

ordinated to it. Behind the front arches there is another
row of three arches supported on marble pillars, and the
interchange of light and gloom in the three parallel aisles
rivets the gaze. To break the monotony of the rise of the
bulbous domes, are placed at the corners small minarets,
and to relieve the creamy whiteness of the marble the parapet has a rich tracing of tendrils. In grace, simplicity and
perfect proportion the Moti Musjid cannot be surpassed,
and it is a fine expression of what is best in the Moslem
creed. It was built by a devout Islamite, Aurangzeb, the
son of Shah Jehan, under whose sway the Moghul Empire
attained its widest limits. The Royal Baths, with their
luxuriant ornamentation, and the jewelled apartments for
the lights of the Seraglio, however, bear witness that the
dominion founded by the brave warriors from the Oxus
had already begun to subside into emasculate debility.
Rapid was the decline. Thirty years after Aurangzeb's
decease (February 21, 1707) Nadir Shah, the Persian
soldier of fortune, descended through the passes of Afghanistan and occupied and sacked Delhi. In the Diwan-i-Khas
he exchanged with the vanquished Emperor his own serviceable head-dress for the jewelled turban of Muhammad Shah.
Nadir Shah departed home, revealing to the free lances of
the North that the power of the Great Moghul was not
unassailable. The Afghans followed in his footsteps, and
three years after his departure they captured Delhi and
plundered the Imperial capital. Two years later the Mahrattas dealt the mortal blow. After a month's siege they
captured the city, desecrated the tombs and shrines, and
stripped the Diwan-i-Khas of silver and gold ornaments.
At the time (1788), when Burke in words of passionate eloquence was depicting the miseries caused by the wise administration of Hastings, a Rohilla chief made a sudden
attack upon Dehli, seized the Emperor Shah Alum (who
had bestowed the Diwani of Bengal on Clive), and in the

Diwan-i-Khas he struck out the monarch's eyes with his dagger. The unfortunate Emperor was rescued by the Mahrattas, but only to become in turn their prisoner, until he was released by Lord Lake. The English general was ushered into the royal presence at the Diwan-i-Khas and found the Great Moghul " seated under a small tattered canopy, the remnant of his royal state, with every external appearance of the misery of his condition."

Within the wall of the Citadel palace the English allowed him to hold a mock court, and though the power of the Great Moghul had perished, the title continued to attract the veneration of the natives. It was this spell which caused the mutineers, the morning they entered Delhi, to march to the palace crying, " Help, O King ! We pray for assistance in our fight for the faith " ; and in the Imperial Hall of Special Audience, the native officers waited on the Emperor and " promised to establish his rule throughout the whole country." Before the sun had set a descendant of the immortal Timur once more reigned in the Imperial City.

On the evening of May 11, 1857, fifty Christian people, men, women, and children, were brought to the palace and confined in an underground apartment without a window and only one door, so that little of light and air entered the dreary dwelling. After being confined for five days in this gloomy, pestilential dungeon, starved and insulted, but defying their tormentors to the last, they were led into a courtyard and hewn to pieces. The whole dark truth of what took place can never be told. But swift came the hour of retribution. A few months passed away, when the British soldiers stormed the palace and bivouacked in the Diwan-i-Am, the great Hall of Audience, where travellers from all quarters of the globe in the days of old had admired the magnificence of the Moghul Cæsars. On Sunday morning, September 20, the soldiers assembled in the Diwan-i-

Khas. It was no vain pomp or unmeaning ceremony, but the humble recognition of their merciful deliverance and final triumph. Through the Diwan-i-Khas rolled the words of our noble liturgy, and marble wall and gilded pillar echoed the cry that went forth from the depths of their brave hearts—" Not unto us, O Lord, not unto us, but unto Thy name be the praise."

During my last visit to Delhi I enjoyed a delightful experience. Lord Roberts, who was at the time making

THE PEARL MOSQUE.

a short stay in the Imperial capital, kindly undertook to describe to me on the theatre of their enactment the principal operations of the great siege which decided the destinies of India. One afternoon in March we made our expedition. Lord Roberts drove me first to the ramp which leads to the Cabul Gate, and here, alighting from the carriage, we walked up a narrow lane bounded on the right by the walls of the city, and on the left by houses with flat roofs, affording convenient shelter for sharpshooters. Sixty yards from the ramp the wall and lane suddenly bend, and on the

THE CASHMERE GATE.

city side there is a strong, lofty house, with a blank wall broken by only two windows. From one of these windows, in all probability, was fired the shot which proved fatal to John Nicholson. A tablet marks the spot where he fell. Of all the heroes who have made the Indian Mutiny our Iliad, none strikes the imagination like John Nicholson. Tall of person and of majestic presence, he well justified the title of " Lion of the Punjab." Strong and brave, he had the high moral grace which makes bravery and strength beautiful. He became to the wild races he governed a semi-divine figure, and they allowed him to drill them and lead them to Delhi. He reached the lane on the morning of the assault at the moment when the soldiers, seeing their leaders swept away by a torrent of grape and musketry, had begun to waver. Springing forward, Nicholson called with a stentorian voice upon the men to follow him, and instantly he was shot through the chest. Near the spot grows a tall and graceful tree ; and, as his favourite personal orderly, Khaja Khan Raus, an Afghan who stormed with him the breach at Delhi, informs us : " The General then desired to be laid in the shade, and said, ' I will remain here till Delhi is taken.' He then called for some cold water. At that time I ordered a dooly from Delhi, and sent Latief Khan (with the General) to the General Hospital in camp, where Dr. —— gave him some medicine and he became a little better." Lord Roberts, in his *Forty-one Years in India*, states that at the Cashmere Gate he found a dooly deserted by its bearers. On opening the curtains, he discovered Nicholson, who said that he was in great agony, and asked him to have him removed to the hospital. Lord Roberts, with some difficulty, collected four men and had him carried into camp. The Afghan orderly tells us that " On September 20 the victory at Delhi was complete, the faces of the rebels were blackened, and they fled. I went to the Sahib and told him of the victory. He was greatly delighted, and said, ' My desire was that Delhi might be taken before I die, and it has been so.' " The news of the capture of the Moghul Palace and the complete acquisition of the city consoled the death-bed of John Nicholson. From the first there was little hope, and the pain he suffered was most excruciating. " Throughout those nine days of suffering," wrote Neville Chamberlain, " he bore himself nobly ; not a lament or a sigh ever passed his lips, and he conversed as calmly and clearly as if he were talking of some other person's condition and not his own." His first care was for his country, and from his bed he aided the last military operations with his counsels. Day by day he grew weaker, but his intellect remained unclouded, and when life was fast ebbing away the stern warrior sent a message of tender humility to his oldest and dearest friend, Herbert Edwardes, and one to his mother, counselling her to be patient for his loss. " Tell my mother that I do not think we shall be unhappy in the next world." On the morning of September 23 the noble and fearless spirit of John Nicholson sped to the world " where God shall wipe away all tears." " He looked so peaceful," wrote the comrade who had watched by his bed. " The Sirdars of the Mooltanee Horse, and some other natives, were admitted to see him after death ; and their honest praise could hardly find utterance for the tears they shed as they looked on their late master."

Leaving Rampart Road, we drove through the Cashmere gate, and stopped to read the inscription on the simple tablet which that fine soldier Lord Napier of Magdala had erected to the gallant men who sacrificed their lives in blowing up the gate the day the guilty city was stormed. The band of heroes had to advance in daylight to the gateway in the very teeth of a hot fire from all sides. The powder-bags were coolly laid and adjusted by the advance party, when Lieutenant Salkeld advanced to do his duty. While endeavouring to fire the charge he " was shot through the leg and arm, and handed over the slow match to Corporal Burgess, who fell mortally wounded just as he had successfully performed his duty." Thus in a few prosaic words the official despatch records one of the most heroic deeds which illustrate the annals of England. On the slab are inscribed the names of the four sepoys who also took part in that brave deed. Two were wounded and one was killed. It is meet and right to honour the memory of those who, in spite of terrible tempta-tion, remain faithful to their colours. The history of the Mutiny abounds with examples of heroic deeds wrought by Englishmen ; it also abounds with examples of noble self-sacrifice displayed by sepoys for their officers.

Leaving the Cashmere Gate, we drove through a road lined with fine trees, till we came to a low wall which separates Ludlow Castle from the road. It was here on the morning of the assault that Lord Roberts saw Nicholson at the head of his column. Leaving the carriage, we walked through the grounds till we came to two blocks of masonry marking the site of the famous No. 2 Battery, which made the breach for our troops to enter. Three days before the assault it was completed. Lord Roberts writes : " I was posted to the left half of No. 2 Battery, and had charge of the two right guns. At eight o'clock on the morning of September 11 we opened fire on the Cashmere bastion and the adjoining curtain ; and as the shots told and the stones flew into the air and rolled down, a loud cheer burst from the Artillerymen and some of the men of the Carabineers and 9th Lancers, who had volunteered to work in the batteries. The enemy had got our range with wonderful accuracy, and immediately on the screen in front of the right gun being removed, a round shot came through the embrasure, knocking two or three of us over. On regaining my feet, I found that the young Horse Artilleryman who was serving the vent while I was laying the gun had had his right arm taken off. . . .

HINDU RAO'S HOUSE.

On the evening of September 13 Nicholson came to see whether we gunners had done our work thoroughly enough to warrant the assault being made the next morning. He was evidently satisfied, for when he entered our battery he said : ' I must shake hands with you fellows ; you have done your best to make my work easy to-morrow.' "

After leaving Ludlow Castle we proceeded along the road till we reached the top of the ridge where was enacted one of the great events of our nation's history. This rocky ridge, sixty feet above the city, was not only a coign of vantage for attack, but a rampart for defence. Below the centre, and extending to the left, the British camp was pitched in and around the old cantonment. Deserting the carriage, we walked to the military cemetery, where the majority of those who fell during the siege were buried. Of all desolate sights this is the most desolate. A few stunted trees stand within the enclosure, and every yard of ground is a raised mound covered with dried yellow grass. Interspersed among the mounds are a few substantial tombs. But this barren spot is full of soul-stirring associations, for here lies the dust of heroes. After some search we found the tomb of Lieutenant Quintin Battye, Commandant of the Guide Cavalry, who fell mortally wounded by a bullet from the ramparts. " Now I have a chance of seeing service," was his joyous exclamation, as he set forth with his corps from the frontier to Delhi. A keen soldier, good swordsman, and fine rider, there was every prospect of a splendid career for the intrepid lad. But he fell at his first fight, and as life ebbed away he murmured with his failing voice the old Roman saying engraved on his tomb, that it is well and proper for a man to die for his country. But for the heroes lying beneath the yellow mounds there is not the empty fame, " In the glistening foil set off to the world." Their names are not inscribed on tablets, but " the working of the good and the brave, seen or unseen, endures literally for ever, and cannot die."

Leaving the cemetery, we retraced our steps till we reached the Flagstaff Tower, which was one of our four great posts on the ridge during the siege, and was held by a strong infantry picquet. Farther on to the south of the Tower is an old Pathan mosque, whose stout walls also afforded shelter to a picquet. Not far from it was the Observatory erected by the great Rajpoot astronomer, a strong old building, near which our heavy gun battery was erected. Three hundred yards from the Observatory, we came to Hindu Rao's house, built by a Mahratta nobleman, who was in the old days famous for his hospitality. Our troops found it deserted, and occupied it. The enemy knew it was the key of our position, and all through the siege made the most desperate attempts to capture it. But the post of honour and danger was confided to Major Reed and his gallant Gurkhas, and all attempts to dislodge them were made in vain. At first Major Reed had only his own battalion and two companies of the 60th Rifles, but after a time the Guides Infantry was added, and on an alarm he was reinforced by two more companies of the 60th Rifles. The house in which he resided with his corps was within perfect range of nearly all the enemy's heavy guns, and was riddled through and through with shot and shell. He never quitted the ridge save to attack the enemy below it, and never once visited the camp until carried to it wounded the day of the assault.

On the extreme right of the ridge, where the lofty Memorial of the great siege now stands, the besiegers had a heavy gun battery, known as the Right Battery, which was twelve hundred yards from the city wall. From the steps of the Memorial we saw a sight of great beauty. Below us lay a stretch of broken ground dotted with green trees. Beyond it was a long line of purple walls, within which rose the fair city with its stately mosques and minarets. As we gazed, the white dome of the Jumma Musjid caught

a pale pink flush, and of a sudden the full glory of the
setting sun fell upon the tall red minarets, and a golden
glow swept over the blue waters of the Jumna. All was
peaceful now. It was hard to picture the mortal strife for
Empire which took place in that valley only a quarter of a
century ago.

Quitting with regret our point of vantage, we descended

NICHOLSON'S GRAVE.

the ridge, and drove back towards the city. As we approached the Cashmere Gate, Lord Roberts expressed his
intention of paying a last visit to the grave of John Nicholson, for his "forty-one years' service in India" had been
completed, and he was on his way home. Thirty-six years
before, the Commander-in-Chief, then a subaltern in the
Bengal Artillery, had marched out of Delhi the morning of

Nicholson's funeral. " It was a matter of regret to me," he writes in his modest autobiography, " that I was unable to pay a last tribute of respect to my loved and honoured friend and commander by following his body to the grave, but I could not leave the column." The old cemetery stands by the road, and is surrounded by lofty trees. The inside is bright with budding flowers and roses. Near the entrance is the grave of John Nicholson. A few roses were placed on the tomb by his old comrade, and he stood for many minutes gazing at the resting-place of his loved and honoured friend. He then joined us at the gate, and as we drove away, beyond the cemetery walls we had, through the trees, a glimpse of the breach through which Nicholson led his victorious soldiers. " I never saw any one like him," was the only remark that broke the silence.

We return through the Cashmere Gate to the city. Passing by the church, we reach an archway supported by two towers. This is the old gate which led to the Delhi Arsenal. The past in one flash of consciousness rushes back. Thirty years ago my father used often to drive me through that gate, and great was my boyish delight at the sight of all the guns and munitions of war. On a tablet above the archway are inscribed the names of the nine valiant, resolute men who, deserted by all their dependants, for some hours kept at bay a multitude of trained and disciplined men. Then the guns could no longer be worked. A shout of triumph rose from the walls. It was momentary. The signal was given and the train lighted. A crash of thunder followed, and the exulting assailants were dashed to pieces by the explosion of hundreds of shells and powder barrels. And the three hundred Spartans who in the summer morning sat " combing their long hair " in the passes of Thermopylæ have not earned a more lofty estimate for themselves than these nine modern Englishmen. A name on the tablet recalls a dear memory and a great sorrow. But the heart swells with

pride at the thought that his name will live long as men
reverence deeds of valour.

> " My Son,
> No sound is breathed, so potent to coerce
> And to conciliate, as their names who dare,
> For that sweet motherland which gave them birth,
> Nobly to do, nobly to die. Their names,
> Engraven on memorial columns, are song
> Heard in the future ; few, but more than wall
> And rampart, their examples reach a hand
> Far thro' all years, and everywhere they meet
> And kindle generous purpose and the strength
> To mould it into action pure as theirs."

VII

AGRA

A GRA, like Delhi, has been indebted, if not for its origin, at any rate for its importance, to the commercial and strategetical advantages of its position. The Jumna was the natural highway for the traffic of the rich delta of Bengal to the heart of India, and it formed from very ancient times the frontier defence of the Aryan stock settled in the rich plain between the Ganges and the Jumna against their western neighbours, hereditary freebooters who occupied the highlands of Central India. Along this great highway the early settlers built forts, planted trees, and cultivated their fields. The groves which lined the banks of the curling stream were the homes of the deities of their mythology. Foremost among these was Krishna, the Hindu Apollo, the royal god of light. About thirty miles south of Delhi, on the western bank of the Jumna, stands Bindraban, which means the Tulasi grove, or the grove of Holy Basil. As Daphne was turned into the laurel, hence sacred to Apollo, so Krishna's coy nymph was converted into a lovely shrub of Tulasi, alike sacred to him. At Bindraban Krishna passed much of his youth. In olden days an ancient tree was shown at whose root Krishna sat and played so divinely his celestial reed (bansuli) that all the wild beasts and reptiles of the forest assembled round him to listen. Here is the spot where, like Apollo, he slew a terrible python (Kali Naga), which by lying across the Jumna stopped its course and poisoned its waters. Here he stole the raiments of the maidens as they laved "their sweet limbs" in the stream. In the meads beside the waters he loved to sport with the cow-herds and milk-maids, and as he touched his reed one said, "Oh, favoured stream of Jumna, where Krishna deigned to drink." Another cried, "Melodious above all is the flute which resides for ever in his lips"; and another exclaimed, "Honoured above all existing animals are these cattle which the Creator Himself leads to pasture." Under the name of Gopala, Krishna is the pastoral Apollo who fed the herds of Armeties. Pan is not dead. The Hindu women as they call the cows and buffaloes home, hear his pipe, and the beautiful, brave, and amorous Krishna is the most beloved of all deities. Nine miles below Bindraban stands the sacred city of Mathura, the birthplace of Krishna. At the time when history begins to dawn on us it was the capital of an extensive kingdom of the same name. Four miles south-east from Mathura (Muttra), perched on some beetling cliffs, is Gokul (cow-stall), the suburb of ancient Mahaban, where Krishna was cradled. Mahaban means the Great Forest, and in the ravines and woods around the Moghul Emperors had their royal hunts and killed their tigers. Thirty-six miles below Muttra in a bend of the river lies Agra. No place was better fitted for an emporium and for a frontier fortress. It combined the advantages of the river, being at no time fordable, and yet being capable of navigation to boats of heavy tonnage throughout the year. Whether the genius of some far-seeing warrior or the natural development of traffic called Agra into being it is vain to surmise. It is equally vain to attempt to settle its high antiquity by the derivation of its name from the Sanskrit word *agre*, in front. Another suggested derivation is that Agra is the shortened form of Agrahara, a royal donation of land or village to Brahmins. We have the substantial evidence of ancient coins as to its Hindu origin, and

Jehangir in his autobiography tells us that before his father, Akbar, built the present fort, the town was defended by a citadel of great antiquity. For three hundred years the Afghans and other tribes came down from the north and founded kingdoms ; and their power radiated from Delhi and Agra. It was Sikandar, of the house of Lodi, the last of the Afghan dynasties, who realized the stragetic importance of Agra as a point for keeping in check his rebellious vassals to the south. He removed his court there, and Agra, from being " a mere village of old standing," says a Persian chronicler, became the capital of a kingdom. On Sunday, December 14, 1517, the year that Luther made his great " protest," Sikandar Lodi, one of the fiercest persecutors of the Hindus, died at Agra, after a reign of twenty-eight years. The suburb of Sikandar, now best known as the site of Akbar's tomb, was named after him. It was here, five years before his death, he built the fine red-stone summer-house where Akbar afterwards buried his wife, who is supposed to have been a Portuguese. Sikandar was succeeded by his son Ibrahim, who fell on the fateful field of Panipat, " having five or six thousand of the slain lying in heaps in a small space around him." On the very day of the battle Baber [1] pushed forward two detachments, the one to Delhi, the other to Agra, both to prevent the plunder and to secure the treasures of these cities. Next morning, says Baber, " we marched," and on the third day we encamped to the south of Delhi, between the Kutub Minar and the Jumna. On Friday, April 27, 1526, his name as Emperor was read in the public prayers at the Grand Mosque, and the following morning he proceeded " march upon march upon Agra." On reaching the suburb of that city he found the fort had not surrendered, though Humayun, his son, had blockaded it. In the citadel were the wives and children and some of the chief followers of Bakrama Jit,

---

[1] See Delhi.

the Hindu Raja of Gwalior, who, Baber states, "has governed that country for upwards of a hundred years." The Raja had been compelled to surrender his principality to Ibrahim, and was enrolled in his service. According to the charitable mode in which a good Muhammadan signifies the death of an infidel, Baber writes, "In the battle in which Ibrahim was defeated, Bikermajit was sent to hell." His wives and followers, in attempting to escape from the fort at Agra, were captured. Humayun behaved generously to the captives, and prevented their being plundered. "Of their own free will they presented to Humayun a Pish-kash (a present to a superior), consisting of a quantity of jewels and precious stones. Among these was one famous diamond which had been acquired by Sultan Alaeddin. It is so valuable that a judge of diamonds valued it at half the daily expenses of the whole world." This diamond was the Kohinoor, which Tavernier the jeweller, a competent judge, afterwards valued at £880,000 sterling. On Baber's arrival Humayun presented it to his father, who returned it to him.

On Thursday, May 10, the Emperor entered Agra, and took up his residence at Sultan Ibrahim's palace. It was the hottest season of the year, and Baber's followers began to long for their cool mountain homes. "Many men dropped down and died on the spot." The inhabitants in terror fled before them, "so that we could not find grain nor provender either for ourselves or for our horses. The villagers, out of hostility and hatred to us, had taken to rebellion, thieving and robbery. The roads became impassable." All these evils made his best men lose heart. They objected to remaining in Hindustan, and even began to make preparations for their return, but Baber was determined to found a Tatar empire in India. As soon as he heard of the murmurings among his troops he summoned a council of his nobles.

"I told them that empire and conquest could not be

acquired without the materials and means of war: That royalty and nobility could not exist without subjects and dependent provinces: That, by the labour of many years after undergoing great hardships, measuring many a toilsome journey, and raising various armies; after exposing myself and my troops to circumstances of great danger, to battle and bloodshed, by the Divine favour I had routed my formidable enemy, and achieved the conquest of the numerous provinces and kingdoms which we at present held: 'And now what force compels, and that hardship obliges us, without any visible cause, after having worn out our life in accomplishing the desired achievement, to abandon and fly from our conquests, and to retreat back to Kabul with every symptom of disappointment and discomfiture ? Let not any one who calls himself my friend ever henceforward make such a proposal. But if there is any among you who cannot bring himself to stay or to give up his purpose of returning back, let him depart.'"

Baber was speedily rewarded for his heroic firmness. " It was no sooner known," says Erskine, "that his invasion was not to be a temporary inroad, like those of Mahmúd of Ghaznae and the Great Taimur, but that he was to remain permanently in the country and govern it on the spot, than new fears and new hopes began to operate both on the natives and the Afghans. His generous policy, his manly deportment and known valour inspired his friends with confidence, and struck terror into his enemies." The consequence was soon visible. The Afghan chieftains were reduced to obedience. The decisive battle of Khanwa, near Biana[1] (March, 1527), and the storming of the great Hindu stronghold Chánderi on the south-east of Malwa, destroyed

---

[1] This decisive action has by Elphinstone and others been called the battle of Sikri city, which was called Fathpur, in honour of the victory (fath), because Sikri is not far from Khanwa, and Baber encamped there, and was joined by the garrison from Biana.

all hope of there ever being again a Rajpoot Empire. Three years after Panipat, Baber had brought Behar and Bengal under his sway. This is the last campaign of which we have the history from his own pen, and of the military events of the next fifteen months we hardly know anything. The silence of his diary was no doubt due to the decline in his health, which had become evident to all around him. The grave illness of his son Humayun, whose cultivated mind and sprightly wit rendered him especially dear to his father, was a mortal blow. The native historians inform us how Humayun was brought to Agra stricken unto death, and Baber, seated one day in his palace overlooking the Jumna, exclaimed that of all things his life was what was dearest to Humayun, as Humayun was to him ; that his life, therefore, he cheerfully devoted as a sacrifice for his son's, and prayed the Most High to vouchsafe to accept it. " The noblemen around him entreated him to retract the rash vow, and, in place of his first offering, to give the diamond taken at Agra, and reckoned the most valuable on earth ; that the ancient sages had said that it was the dearest of our possessions alone that was to be offered to Heaven. But he persisted in his resolution, declaring that no stone, of whatever value, could be put in competition with his life. He three times walked round the dying prince, a solemnity similar to that used in sacrifices and heave-offerings, and, retiring, prayed earnestly to God. After some time he was heard to exclaim, ' I have borne it away.' "

The Muhammadan historians declare that the son daily grew better while the father daily grew worse. Baber soon after died in his palace near Agra on December 26, 1530. He was only forty-eight, yet one of the most illustrious sovereigns that ever filled a throne. Erskine's portrait of him is worthy to rank with any in Clarendon's stately record :

" His character was happily compounded of most of the

qualities that go to form a great prince and a good man. He was bold, enterprising, full of ardour, and possessed of the commanding talents that sway and lead the mind of man. His temper was frank, confiding and gay, and maintained through life the freshness of youth. He had strong affections, the warmest of domestic feelings, was devotedly attached to his relations and friends, and ready to sympathize with the pleasures and the sufferings of human beings of every class. Keenly alive to whatever was grand and beautiful, he cultivated knowledge of every kind with unwearied assiduity and with proportional success. Glory in every shape inflamed his imagination, and he attained a rare eminence of power and renown. Yet no man's success could be more entirely his own."

Three days after the Emperor's death, Humayun ascended the throne, and during the brief intervals when there was not so much a state of tranquillity as a suspension of arms between the hostile monarchs, Agra was more often the royal city than Delhi. It was the post from which the Emperor took the field in his various campaigns against the Afghans, who still possessed vast estates and considerable power throughout India and were ready on the first signal to fly to arms. The Empire which the great Baber established required to be sustained by the firm and dexterous hand of the founder. Humayun had his father's quick intellect and his personal courage, but his mind was naturally indolent, and he never commanded the esteem of his subjects. After nine years of discord and confusion his army was dispersed and his camp taken at Kanaug by Shir Khan, an Afghan of great ability, caution, and enterprise.[1] Humayun fled from Agra to Lahore, and for five years Shir Shah, who had previously ruled Bengal and Bahar, reigned over Hindustan. He made Agra his headquarters, and is said to have built a palace within the walls of the old fort. On May 24, 1645, while conducting the siege of the fort of Kalinjer, the

[1] He was an Afghan of the tribe of Sur. He became the King of Delhi under the title Shir Shah.

key of Bandelkand, he was dreadfully burnt by the explosion of a tumbrel. " In spite of the excruciating pain which he suffered, he had fortitude enough to walk to the trenches, and directed that the accident should be concealed from his troops. Here he remained, and as from time to time new storming parties advanced to the assault, he cheered them on with his voice, issued occasional orders with astonishing composure, and sent away such of his officers as came about him, to join the action. The attack was continued with un-remitted vigour. As the cry to evening prayers was heard, news were brought to the King that the fort had fallen. ' Thanks be to Almighty God,' he said, and quietly expired." The Sur dynasty, which rose by the genius of Shir Khan, and was sustained by the talents of his son Selim, fell by the ignorance and vice of their successors. In 1555 Humayun returned to India, obtained a complete victory over Sikandra Shah and the Afghans at Sirhend, and once more ascended the musnud at Delhi. Agra surrendered without any resistance. After having arranged affairs in the Imperial city, he was about to proceed there, when, as he was descending some steps, his foot slipped and he fell headlong to the bottom. He was carried into his palace, where, after lingering for four days, he expired, on January 24, 1556. Humayun was succeeded by his son, Jalal-ud-din (the glory of the faith) Muhammad, called Akbar the Great, and few monarchs have so well deserved the title by which he is known in history. At his accession to the crown he was a little over thirteen, but he had been already trained in the rough school of war, and he possessed those qualities which Englishmen admire—good temper, vast muscular strength, and un-flinching courage. Among mountaineers remarkable for their feats of strength and bodily activity few outdid him in their national pastimes. He was fond of sport, and took a special delight in hunting the royal tiger and capturing herds of wild elephants. Three years after his accession

Akbar took up his residence in Agra and, pleased with its situation on the banks of the Jumna, " the waters of which has few rivals for lightness and taste," and, incited by its strategic position, he determined to make it the seat of his empire. The brick walls of the old citadel were fast crumbling away, and Akbar ordered his Lord High Admiral (Kasim K'han) to build on the same site a new fort at Futtehpore. A multitude of labours urged the conclusion of the work, but eight years passed before the stupendous fortress was completed. The strong and lofty walls of red sandstone, which glisten like jasper in the rays of an Indian sun, are a mile and a half in circuit, and all that could adorn the dignity of an Imperial residence, or contribute to the comfort or pleasure of its numerous inhabitants, were contained within them. The shape has been likened to a crescent and a triangle, with its base stretching for half a mile along the river bank on the east. The other two sides are almost of equal lengths, and at the angles are massive projecting bastions. On the north, towards the city, is the Delhi Gate, a massive pile flanked by two enormous octagonal towers of red sandstone, inlaid with white marble, and crowned by two domes.

After crossing a drawbridge which leads across the deep moat that surrounds the crenelated ramparts of the fort, and passing up a paved ascent, we drive across a barren square till we reach a broad flight of steps leading to a red sandstone platform. Mounting them, we come to a fine gateway. A door is thrown open, and we find ourselves in a quadrangle paved with white marble, and on either side is a marble colonnade with exquisite arches, supported on light pillars of perfect grace. Opposite is a marble mosque resting on finely proportioned Saracenic arches supported on a row of triple pillars, massive, and exquisitely carved at the base. The whole is crowned with three white marble domes, and elegant kiosks break the monotony, which a long straight line would present to the eye. No more pure and stainless sanctuary was ever created by man in honour of the Creator. On the entablature there is an inscription of black letters inlaid in the white marble, which informs us that the mosque " may be likened to a mansion of paradise or to a precious pearl " ; and that the building was completed in seven years, at the cost of three lakhs of rupees, in the twenty-sixth year of the fortunate reign of Shah Jehan, in the year of the Hegira one thousand and sixty-three (A.D. 1665), the year when the gay Charles

THE FORT, AGRA.

was on the throne of England and plague had devastated London.

A short distance from the Moti Musjid, or Pearl Mosque, lies the palace erected by Shah Jehan, under whom the Moghul Empire attained its highest limit of strength and magnificence. A somewhat mean portal leads to a square planted with trees and flowers and a few vines, which give to the courtyard the name of Anguri Bagh, or Grape Garden. White marble walks radiate from a marble plat- form in the centre, and the beds are after the manner of the

Moghul gardens, divided into numerous small compartments by ridges of red sandstone. Legend states that the soil was brought from Cashmere, and to this day its depth and richness are extolled by the gardeners. Around the courts are the apartments which the lights of the harem used to occupy, and opposite, on a raised platform of white marble, stands a fairy hall—the Khas Mahal, or reception room of the royal ladies. In front of the hall is a colonnade opening into the court. " The flat roof is supported on engrailed arches, springing from massive square pillars, whose base and capital are ornamented with sprays of flowers. Three smaller arches give access from the colonnade to the hall, and on the opposite side are three archways with windows overlooking the river." Here the fair captives enjoyed the fresh breezes of the morning, and gazed upon the blue waters of the Jumna and the palaces and gardens of the nobles which lined its banks. Here they could watch the Emperor review his troops, and, unseen, catch a glimpse of the gay cavalcade that surrounded him. It was the only glimpse which the captives had of the outer world. No male was admitted into the palace, except the Emperor, and the domestic work was entirely done by women. It was a paradise of luxury and splendour. All gold and silver stuffs and jewels and all things gorgeous and costly were provided for the inmates, but it was a prison. The description of the harem of the Emperor Akbar by his minister reveals how dreary the daily life must have been. He informs us the harem contained a separate room for every one of the women, whose number exceeded five thousand, who were divided into companies, with proper employment assigned to each individual. Over each of these companies a woman was appointed (darogha), and one was selected for the command of the whole, in order that the affairs of the harem, the writer adds, " might be conducted with the same regularity and good government as the other departments of the State." " Every one received a salary according to her merit. The pen cannot measure the extent of the Emperor's largesses, but the ladies of the first quality received from one thousand to sixteen hundred rupees, and the servants according to their rank—from two rupees to fifty-one per month. And whenever any of this multitude of women wanted anything, they applied to the treasurer of the harem, who, according to their monthly stipend, took care their wants should be supplied. The inside of the harem was guarded by women, and the most confidential were placed about the royal apart-

MOTI MUSJID—PEARL MOSQUE.

ments. The eunuch watched immediately on the outside gate, and at proper distances were placed the Rajpoots and porters ; and on the outside of the enclosure the Omrahs, the Ahdeeans, and other troops mounted guard according to their rank. But besides all the precautions above described, his Majesty depends on his own vigilance as well as on that of his guards." It would be impossible to imagine a less romantic and more monotonous existence. But in spite of all the Emperor's vigilance " the human need of loving," as Browning says, had to be gratified even in the harem, and was too strong for his precautions. Below the palace are some dreary vaults. In the most gloomy of them we see a pit, and over it a beam highly carved, and from the beam dangles a silken cord. Here the frail ones of the harem were hanged.

Returning to the light of day, we ascended the platform of the Khas Mahal, and walking to the right we came to a marble open lattice-work screen, beautiful from its extreme simplicity. The screen separates the reception-room from a pavilion hanging over the river, and the most sacred of sacred apartments—those which were occupied by the Emperor and the favourite inmates of the harem. Two square chambers united by an arch, with three graceful Saracenic arches opening into the marble court, form the pavilion. The walls are encrusted with jasper, carnelian, lapis-lazuli, agate and bloodstone, and the balconies and terraces are marble wrought into lace. Hard by "the jewelled and enamelled caskets" of Shah Jehan is the red sandstone palace, which bears the name of Jehangir Mahal. "Nowhere," states Fergusson, "is the contrast between the two styles more strongly marked than in the palace of Agra : from the red stone palace of Akbar, with its rich sculpture and square Hindu construction, a door opens into the white marble court of the harem of Shah Jehan, with all its feeble prettiness, but at the same time marked with that peculiar elegance which is found only in the East." The exact date of the building of the palace cannot be ascertained, but there is good reason to suppose that it was built before the time of Akbar or of Jehangir. To erect it only Hindu architects and artists must have been employed, and it is a noble example of the Hindu skill in building and the luxuriance of his imagination. But it is imagination disciplined by the study of art. In the whole building there is nothing mean and commonplace, and there is not a single inch of orna-ment lacking in originality. The Hindu mason has impressed his originality on Saracenic geometrical tracery. The palace addresses the eye by a few clear and forceful lines, and it appeals to the imagination by the richness of the work. It is entered from Shah Jehan's harem, through a noble archway forming the centre of three sides of a quadrangle. Never were pillars erected more slender and graceful than those which support this porch. The round capitals are richly and elaborately sculptured, and send out elegant brackets on each side from above their tops. It is impossible to imagine anything in better taste than the way niches and recesses in the walls are faced with white marble, beautifully carved into engraved work, the points of which terminate with graceful oval pendants. Making our way through corridors and halls, each more elegant than the other, we reached the grand open pillared hall on the north side. From the first row of pillars project brackets of exquisite workmanship, which support broad sloping eaves formed of thin slabs of stones. The roof, supported by stone cross-beams, with great dragons carved on them, is "a wonder of architectural constructive ingenuity."[1]

Passing from the grand court through corridors, we again came to the Anguri Bagh, and crossing the square we entered the Shisha Mahal, or the baths built for the inmates of the palace. " The Shisha Mahal, or house of glass, is both curious and elegant, although the material is principally pounded talc and looking-glass. It consists of two rooms, of which the walls in the interior are divided into a thousand different panels, each of which is filled up with raised flowers in silver, gold, and colours, on a ground-work of tiny convex mirrors ! The idea it impresses on the mind is that of being inside some curiously worked and arched box—so unlike is the apartment to a room ! The roof reminds you of the style of ceiling that prevailed during the time of Louis the

[1] *Archæological Survey of India*, vol. iv. pp. 126, 127.

XIV., and resembles the ceilings at Versailles. Pounded mica has the effect of silver. Fronting the entrance, in the second room, are three rows of niches for lights, and below, standing forward a little, there are more rows of marble niches for the same. From the top, the water pours out, and falls in a broad sheet over the upper lights, and is received below in a basin, from which it again pours forth in another fall *over* the lower row of lights, so that you see the lights burning *behind* the falling waters. The waters are then received in a fountain, which springs high and sparkles in the glare, and then, running over a marble causeway, fills another beautifully carved white marble basin, from the centre of which springs another fountain, which is in the first apartment." As we wandered through the baths we recalled to mind Lady Montagu's graphic description of the scene she witnessed in the Baths at Constantinople. She tells us that, as lightly clad as Eve before the fall : " They walked and moved with the same majestic grace which Milton describes of our general mother. There were many amongst them as exactly proportioned as ever any goddess was drawn by the pencil of Guido or Titian, and most of their skins shiningly white, only adorned by their beautiful hair, divided into many tresses, hanging on their shoulders, braided either with pearl or ribbon, perfectly representing the figures of the Graces."

From the Shisa Mahal we proceeded to the Saman Burj, or Jasmine Tower, the boudoir of the chief Sultana. It is a fairy pavilion, exquisitely carved in marble, and ornamented with flowers wrought in precious stones. The court below the pavilion is arranged in squares of coloured marbles, so that the inmates of the harem could enjoy the game of *pachisi*—somewhat similar to our draughts. A staircase leads from the Jasmine Tower to the Diwan-i-Khas, or hall of private audience. This finely proportioned hall opens by three arches on a lofty colonnade with a flat roof, supported by noble Saracenic arches springing from graceful slender pillars arranged in pairs. The bases of the pillars are ornamented with the purest of white marble

SAMAN BURJ—JASMINE TOWER.

flowers, traced so delicately on the stone that they seem rather drawn than sculptured ; and these are surrounded by a band of mosaic flowers of the brightest colours. Near the Diwan-i-Khas, on a terrace facing the river, is the great marble slab commonly called the Black Marble Throne of Jehangir. The stone has split through in a slanting direction in the middle, and the presence of iron in its composition has given it a reddish stain in one spot. Hence the legend that the throne emitted blood when desecrated by the foot of the infidel. Hawkins, who visited Agra during the reign of Jehangir, informs us that the black slab was used by the Emperor to pray upon. He writes :

" In the morning at break of day, the King is at his beads, praying, on his knees, upon a Persian lambskin, having some eight rosaries, or strings of beads, each containing 400. The beads are of rich pearl, ballace rubies, diamonds, rubies, emeralds, aloes, wood, *eshem* and coral. At the upper end of a large black stone on which he kneels there are figures graven in stone of the Virgin and Christ ; so turning his face to the west he repeats 3,200 words, according to the number of his beads."

On the other side of the court is a white marble slab on which the Vizier sat. It overlooks the *Machi Bhawan* (or Fish Tank), a vast courtyard of red sandstone, which has a tank in its centre and a series of chambers on two sides. On the east there is a platform where the grandees of the Court waited till they were admitted to a private audience with the Emperor. At a corner of the square is the Naginah Musjid, or Gem Mosque, which well bears out its name. This exquisite shrine of white marble stands in the centre of a small court, walled in with white slabs, and consists of three tiny aisles, supported on square plain pillars, from which spring Saracenic arches supporting the roof, which is crowned with three domes. This was the private mosque for the ladies of the harem. They had access to it by means of a screened passage, which led by the Diwan-i-Am to their apartments. Following this passage we came to the royal gallery, which overlooked the Diwan-i-Am, or hall of public audience. " It is a pavilion of white marble, inlaid with jasper and cornelian, in the form of flowers, ornamented scrolls, and sentences of the Koran. Below it is an immense slab of white marble, on which he (the Emperor) was accustomed to seat himself." Seated on the marble slab and looking down on the deserted hall and barren courtyard, the memory goes back to the scene which the Emperor witnessed when Agra had reached the meridian of its glory. Captain Hawkins, who was in high favour with Jehangir, writes :

" At three o'clock all the nobles then in Agra, who are in health, resort to court, when the King comes forth to open audience, sitting in his royal seat, and all the nobles standing before him, each according to his degree. The chiefs of the nobles standing within the red rail, and all the rest without, all being properly placed by the Lieutenant-General. The space within the red rail is three steps higher than where the rest stand, and within this red rail I was placed among the chiefest of the land. All the rest are placed in their order by officers, and they likewise are placed within another rail in a spacious place, and without the rail stand all kinds of horsemen and foot-soldiers belonging to his captains, and all other comers. At these rails there are many doors kept by a great number of porters, who have white rods to keep every one in order. In the middle of the place, right before the King, stands one of the King's sheriffs or judges, together with the chief executioner, who is attended by forty executioners, distinguished from all others by a peculiar kind of quilted caps on their heads, some with hatchets on their shoulders, and others with all sorts of whips, ready to execute the King's commands. The King hears all manner of causes in this place, staying about two hours every day for that purpose : or the Kings in India sit in judgment every day, and their sentences are put in execution every Tuesday."

It is interesting to know what manner of man was the Sovereign who was surrounded with so much splendour. Hawkins writes :

" After this he retires to his private chamber for prayers, when four or five kinds of finely dressed roast meats are set before him, of which he eats till his stomach is satisfied, drinking after his meal one cup of strong drink. He then goes into a private

SECUNDRA—AKBAR'S TOMB

room into which no one enters, but such as are named by himself, where for two years I was one of his attendants ; and here he drinks other five cups of strong liquor, being the quantity allowed by his physicians. This done, he chews opium, and being intoxicated, he goes to sleep, and every one departs to his home. He is awakened after two hours to get his supper, at which time he is unable to feed himself, but has it thrust into his mouth by others, which is about one o'clock in the morning, after which he sleeps the rest of the night."

The glory of the Moghul Empire was the transient glory of barbarous splendour and outward show. Neither property nor life was safe from tyrannical caprice. Hawkins, writing about Jehangir, states :

" While I was at his court, I have seen him do many cruel deeds. Five times a week he orders some of his bravest elephants to fight in his presence, during which men are often killed or grievously wounded by the elephants. If any one be sore hurt, though he might very well chance to recover, he causes him to be thrown into the river, saying, ' Despatch him, for as long as he lives he will continually curse me, wherefore it is better that he die presently.' He delights to see men executed and torn in pieces by elephants."

Not an English traveller, but a Muhammadan historian, relates the following anecdote concerning Akbar, the wisest and most tolerant of all the Moghul Emperors :

" At that time the Emperor used to retire for a long interval, after evening prayers, during which time the servants and courtiers used to disperse, assembling again when they expect his Majesty to reappear. That evening he happened to come out sooner than usual, to hear the news from the Dakhin, and at first found none of the servants in the palace. When he came near the throne and couch, he saw a luckless lamp lighter, coiled up like a snake, in a careless death-like sleep, close to the royal couch. Enraged at the sight, he ordered him to be thrown from the tower, and he was dashed into a thousand pieces."

The Moghul Emperors have left behind them some of the most beautiful buildings in the world as monuments of their

rule, and the English have erected some of the ugliest, but
the administration of the Moghuls will not bear comparison
with our more prosaic and less splendid rule. We have
given the natives peace, order, and security, for anarchy
and oppression. But it behoves England to ponder well
upon the task which her brave soldiers and illustrious
statesmen have set her in India. To preserve her Empire
she must do more than dig canals and build railways,
material monuments of dominion. The besetting sin of a
bureaucracy of foreigners is a blind belief in administrative
machinery. During our century of rule we have made but
little impression on the people. All we have done is to
civilize *administratively*, and in doing so not only old mis-
managements but "reforms and taxations new" have produced their inevitable harvest of misery and disaffection.
This cannot be met merely by legislation, but by the instruction and enlightenment of the people. Contact with
the West has created changes in social relations and religious
feelings, and the mental and moral agitation, the hopes and
aspirations of the educated classes, must not be ignored, but
guided by a wide, thorough, and liberal education. It is
very insecure to reign supreme on the frail foundation of
being the welcome composer of political troubles and the
constructor of great public works. The sewage system of
Rome was a wonder and model to the world, but the
Roman Empire perished.

Six miles from Agra on the Delhi road is situated the tomb
of the Great Akbar. We drive to it in the early morning,
when the air is cool and crisp, through a green aisle of
noble trees, from whose boughs chatter a host of green parrots.
The effigy of a horse in red sandstone attracts our notice,
and walled gardens, time-stricken mosques and tombs remind us of the days when the Moghuls ruled the land, and
Agra was one of the most splendid cities in the East. The
carriage stops at a massive square pavilion, whose terrace

is crowned by eight kiosks and four shattered white marble minarets. The façade is pierced by a lofty pointed arch, and ornamented by bold incrustations in coloured marble and by broad black inscriptions in the flowing graceful Persian character. The inscriptions set forth the praises of the monarch and the mausoleum. The name of the Emperor Jehangir, the son of Akbar, is given as that of the founder, and it is stated that the work was completed in the seventh year of his reign, corresponding to 1613 A.D. Jehangir in his autobiography informs us that in this year of his reign he went " on foot to see the resplendent sepulchre of his father."

" When I had obtained the good fortune of visiting the tomb, and had examined the building which was erected over it, I did not find it to my liking. My intention was, that it should be so exquisite that the travellers of the world could not say they had seen one like it in any part of the inhabited earth. While the work was in progress, in consequence of the rebellious conduct of the unfortunate Khusru, I was obliged to march towards Lahore. The builders had built it according to their own taste, and had altered the original design at their discretion. The whole money had been thus expended, and the work had occupied three or four years. I ordered that clever architects, acting in concert with some intelligent persons, should pull down the objectionable parts which I pointed out. By degrees a very large and magnificent building was raised, with a nice garden round it, entered by a lofty gate, consisting of minarets made of white stone."

Finch, who visited Agra about this time, writes :

" Nothing more finished yet after ten years' work. This tomb," he adds, " is much worshipped both by Moors and Gentiles, holding him for a great saint."

Hawkins states :

" It hath been fourteen years building, and it is thought will not be finished these fourteen years more. The least that works there daily are three thousand people ; but this much I will

SECUNDRA—AKBAR'S TOMB.

say, that one of our workmen will despatch more than three of them."

Passing through the gateway we come to a square planted with grand old trees, and carpeted with grass as green as an English lawn. It looks more like an English park than an Indian garden. At the end of a broad stone causeway rises the mausoleum on a raised red-sandstone platform. The lower story is pierced with ten large Moorish arches, and in the centre is a larger Moorish archway adorned with marble mosaic. Above this rise three storeys of diminishing size, all being of red sandstone, and marked by rows of kiosks of exquisite lightness and elegance of design. Above the last story is a white marble square, paved with white and coloured marble, around which runs a corridor of marble supported on the most delicate pillars ; and the whole is surrounded by an outer screen of marble divided into panels of marble trellis-work of the most beautiful pattern. The terrace has no roof. Finch says :

" It was to be inarched over with the most curious white and speckled marble, to be ceiled all within with pure sheet gold richly inwrought."

Fergusson considers if the tomb had been crowned with a domical chamber it certainly would have ranked next the Taj among Indian mausoleums. To have crowned it with a dome might have destroyed the characteristic features of the building, and any canopy but that of the vault of heaven would certainly have diminished its romance. To look at the bright blue sky roofing the white marble tomb and to watch the sunlight on the beautiful flowers carved on it reveals the poetry and genius of the designer. In Persian characters are inscribed the ninety-nine names or attributes of the deity from the Koran. "Verily there are ninety-nine names of God ; whoever remembers them shall enter Paradise." At the head of the monument are carved the words "Allah Akbar" (God is great). But the mortal remains of the Great Akbar lie not beneath this tomb, but in a vault beneath the ground floor.

The first apartment of the building is the Sonehri Mahal, or chamber of gold. The sides and ceiling of the vaulted room are in compartments, which bear traces of having been ornamented with flowers, raised in gold, in silver, and enamel. And an inscription in gold raised upon a blue ground runs around it. From the Golden Room a long narrow passage leads to a plain gloomy chamber, and beneath a simple marble tomb lies the Great Akbar. Finch states that the coffin was made of gold.

The Emperor who puts questions of sceptical philosophy to Muslim moulvies, Hindu sages, Christian missionaries, who conversed familiarly with men of letters, and who was a wise and strong ruler, is one of the most striking figures in history. At the time when in England the fires of Smithfield were alight, and men suffered torture and death for their religion, Akbar established entire toleration throughout his dominions. A Muhammadan historian writes :

" Learned men of various kinds and from every country, and professors of many different religions and creeds, assembled at his Court, and were admitted to converse with him. Night and day people did nothing but inquire and investigate. Profound points of science, the subtleties of revelation, the curiosities of history, the wonders of nature, of which large volumes could only give a summary abstract, were ever spoken of. His Majesty collected the opinions of every one, especially of such as were not Mohammedans, retaining whatever he approved of, and rejecting everything which was against his disposition and ran counter to his wishes. From his earliest childhood to his manhood, and from his manhood to old age, his Majesty has passed through the most diverse phases, and through all sorts of religious practices and sectarian beliefs, and has collected everything which people can find in books, with a talent of selection peculiar to him, and a spirit of inquiry opposed to every (Islamitic) principle. Thus a faith based on some elementary principles traced itself on the mirror of his heart, and as the result of all the influences which were brought to bear on his Majesty, there grew, gradually as the outline on a stone, the conviction in his heart that there were sensible men in all religions, and abstemious thinkers and men endowed with miraculous powers, among all nations."

The historian adds :

" In A. H. 986 the missionaries of Europe, who are called Padris, and whose chief Pontiff, called Pápà (Pope), promulgates his interpretations for the use of the people, and who issues mandates that even kings dare not disobey, brought their Gospel to the King's notice, advanced proofs of the Trinity, and affirmed the truth and spread abroad the knowledge of the religion of Jesus. The King ordered Prince Murad to learn a few lessons from the Gospel, and to treat it with all due respect, and Shaikh Abu-l-Fazl was directed to translate it. Instead of the inceptive ' Bismullah,' the following ejaculation was enjoined : ' *In nomine Jesu Christe*,' that is, ' Oh ! thou whose name is merciful and bountiful.' Shaikh Faizi added to this, ' Praise be to God ! there is no one like Thee—Thou art He ! ' "

Akbar not only took an interest in the different sects of the Hindus, but also in their classical language. The learned, but bigoted, Abdul-Kadur states :

" On a third night the King sent for me, and desired me to translate the ' Mahabharat ' in conjunction with Nakeb Khan. The consequence was that in three or four months I translated two out of eighteen sections, at the puerile absurdities of which the eighteen thousand creations may well be amazed. Such injunctions as one never heard of. What not to eat, and a prohibition against turnips ! But such is my fate, to be employed in such works. Nevertheless, I console myself with the reflection that what is predestined must come to pass."

However, the other great Indian epic pleased him better, for he writes :

" In this year the King commanded me to make a translation of the *Ramayana*, a composition superior to the *Mahabharat*."

The translations from the Sanskrit, which were made by command of Akbar, appear to have been executed under

TOMB OF ITIMAD-UD-DAULA.

the superintendence of the poet Feizi (most excellent), the brother of the Minister Ab-ul-Fazl (the father of excel lence). The two brothers were the Emperor's dearest friends, and to them he poured out all the doubts and aspirations of his soul. It was Ab-ul-Fazl who persuaded his sovereign " that the seal and asylum of prophecy was no more to be thought of than as an Arab of singular eloquence, and that the sacred inspiration recorded in the Koran were nothing else but fabrications invented by the ever-blessed Mahomed." To Ab-ul-Fazl we owe the *Ain-i-Akbari*, or code of regulations drawn up under the direct supervision of his master. It contains the best record of Akbar's policy and of the conditions of the country under his rule. The brutal murder of his Minister caused the Emperor profound grief, and he survived his faithful servant and friend only three years. In September 1605 after a reign of forty-nine years, almost equal in extent as it was in brilliancy to that of his great contemporary, Elizabeth, Akbar was stricken with a mortal illness. He seemed anxious to die reconciled to the Muslim faith, and a Muslim priest was summoned, who came and read the Muhammadan confession of faith. When finished, Akbar threw his arms round his son's neck and spoke to him parting words of advice. " My servants and dependants,—When I am gone, do not forget the afflicted in the hour of need. Ponder word for word on all I have said, and again forget me not." Then the life of the great Akbar—philosopher, warrior, and statesman—ebbed quietly away. His son has left us the following delineation of his intellectual character :

" My father used to hold discourse with learned men of all persuasions, particularly with the Pandits, and was illiterate, yet from constantly conversing with learned and clever persons, his language was so polished, that no one could discover from his conversation that he was entirely uneducated. He understood even the elegancies of poetry and prose so well that it is impossible to conceive any one more proficient."

The son has also drawn the following graphic portrait of the Emperor :

" He was of middling stature, but with a tendency to be tall, wheat-colour complexion, rather inclining to dark than fair, black eyes and eyebrows, stout body, open forehead and chest, long arms and hands. There was a fleshy wart, about the size of a small pea, on the left side of his nose, which appeared exceedingly beautiful, and which was considered very auspicious by physiognomists, who said it was the sign of immense riches and increasing prosperity. He had a very loud voice, and a very elegant and pleasant way of speech. His manners and habits were quite different from those of other persons, and his visage was full of godly dignity."

Leaving the tomb of Akbar, we drove to another mausoleum beyond the Jumna. It is situated in a walled garden, to which there are four gateways of red granite, ornamented with black and white marble. On a raised platform stands the mausoleum—a square building with an octagonal tower, somewhat squat in proportion, at each corner. The beauty of the building is due to its being entirely built of white marble, and being covered throughout with a mosaic in *pietra dura*. It was early in the seventeenth century that Italian artists, principally from Florence, taught the Indians the art of inlaying this marble with precious stones, and the tomb of Itimad-ud-Daula is probably one of the first, and certainly one of the most splendid examples of that class of ornamentation in India. It is impossible to agree with the criticism of Fergusson, that, " as one of the first, the tomb of Itimad-ud-Daula was certainly one of the least successful specimens of its class. The patterns do not quite fit the places where they are put, and the spaces are not always those best suited for this style of decoration." The mosaic at this mausoleum is more Oriental, more bold, and more true to nature than the decoration of the screen at the Taj, where Italian influence has debased the art to the ʃ eebleness and falseness of a Florentine paper weight. Above the central chamber there is a marble pavilion on a slightly raised platform. It has a canopy-shaped roof with wide projecting eaves, and is supported on twelve marble pillars with marble screens of exquisite pattern, wrought like lace, between them. In the pavilion are two altar tombs like those in the chamber below, where are interred the remains of Mirza Gheas Bey, a Persian adventurer from Tehran whose surname was Itimad-ud-Daula, and his wife. The sides of the chamber are lined with marble inlaid with mosaic, and the ceiling is most elaborately ornamented with gold and silver, and coloured flowers raised in compartments which are fast becoming tarnished and effaced. The side chambers are panelled with marble, inlaid with mosaic, plain and effective, and the ceilings are adorned with flowers and the graceful long-necked Persian vase. Facing the river there is an ornamental red sandstone building, where we sat and watched the sun bathe the white domes of the Moti Musjid rising above the pink ramparts of the fort. Down below us are the gay waters of the Jumna, and a wide boat laden with straw is floating down the stream. In the far distance, enveloped in a veil of woven light or luminous haze, are the marble dome and minarets of the Taj. The Taj is the expression in marble of wedded love, the Itimad-ud-Daula of filial affection. It was erected by Nur Jehan, who was hardly inferior to Elizabeth in intellectual power, while in beauty and voluptuous grace she was equal to Mary Stuart, to commemorate the memory of her father, Mirza Gheas Bey, who was created Vizier by his Imperial son-in-law, Jehangir. The life of Nur Jehan is a romance from the cradle to the grave. Her father was a native of Tartary, which he quitted to seek his fortune at the Court of Akbar. He was so poor that, placing his wife on a horse, he himself was obliged to perform the journey on foot. Before he reached his destination a daughter was born to him, to whom he gave the name

TAJ-MAHAL.

of Nur Mahal, or light of the palace. His talents gained him the favour of Akbar, who made him Chancellor of the Exchequer. The daughter born in the desert grew up to be a woman of surpassing beauty, and one day, when paying a visit to the Queen, she met the heir-apparent, and won his heart by dropping her veil, as if by accident, and in the graceful confusion occasioned by the incident, allowing her beautiful eyes to rest upon his. The young Prince desired to make her his wife, but the Emperor refused to allow the marriage, and tried to put Nur Jehan out of his son's way by causing her to be married to a young Persian nobleman —Shir Afghan Khan—who received high employment in Bengal. When Jehangir ascended the throne he commanded the divorce of Nur Jehan, but the husband refused, and after several ineffectual attempts the Emperor caused him to be slain. Nur Jehan was brought to Delhi. The Emperor, in a fit of remorse, however, refused to see her, and granted only a paltry allowance for the support of herself and her slaves. To supplement her scanty means, Nur Jehan, who was endowed with ability as well as beauty, proceeded to work pieces of rich embroidery, and to paint silks and sell them to the inmates of the harem. The money gained she spent in embellishing her apartments and adorning her slaves. She herself, to suit the character of a poor widow, affected a plain and simple dress. The fame of her skill and her taste spread far and wide, and reached the ears of the Emperor. His curiosity was aroused, and one day he surprised her in her apartments. She arose and saluted him, and with downcast eyes stood before him attired in simple dress. Her stature, shape, beauty, and voluptuous grace revived the old passion. Astonished at the contrast between her simple attire and the splendour which surrounded her, the Emperor asked : " Why this difference between the Sun of Women and her slaves ? " With a woman's wit she replied : " Those born to servitude must dress as it shall please those whom they serve ; these are my servants, and I lighten the burden of bondage by every indulgence in my power, but I, who am your slave, O Emperor, of the world, must dress according to your pleasure and not my own." The gentle sarcasm pleased the Emperor, and the reconciliation was complete. Nur Mahal became the wife of Jehangir, and from the day she was married she virtually took the reins of government into her own hands. A Muhammadan historian writes :

" Day by day her influence and dignity increased. First of all she received the title of *Noor Mahal,* ' Light of the Harem,' but was afterwards distinguished by that of *Noor Jahan Begam,* ' Light of the World.' All her relations and connexions were raised to honour and wealth. . . . No grant of lands was conferred upon any one except under her seal. In addition to giving her the titles that other kings bestow, the Emperor granted Noor Jahan the rights of sovereignty and government. Sometimes she would sit in the balcony of her palace, while the nobles would present themselves, and listen to her dictates. Coin was struck in her name, with this superscription : ' By order of the King Jehangir, gold has a hundred splendours added to it by receiving the impression of the name of Noor Jahan, the Queen Begam.' On all *farmans* also receiving the Imperial signature the name of ' Noor Jahan, the Queen Begam,' was jointly attached. At last her authority reached such a pass that the King was such only in name. Repeatedly he gave out that he had bestowed the sovereignty on Noor Jahan Begam, and would say, ' I require nothing beyond a *sir* of wine and half a *sir* of meat.' It is impossible to describe the beauty and wisdom of the Queen. In any matter that was presented to her, if a difficulty arose, she immediately solved it. Whoever threw himself upon her protection was preserved from tyranny and oppression ; and if ever she learnt that any orphan girl was destitute and friendless, she would bring about her marriage, and give her a wedding portion. It is probable that during her reign no less than 500 orphan girls were thus married and portioned."

After leaving the tomb of Itimad-ud-Daula we re-cross

the old pontoon bridge, and proceeding down the road which skirts the river we reach the great goal of our pilgrimage—the Taj. No building has been more often described, drawn, and photographed. But no drawing or photograph can give any idea of so rich and poetical a subject. No description can shadow forth the whole, combined out of marble dome, fair minarets, and fragrant garden. Words cannot express the multitudinous richness of its ornamentation, perfection of form, and minuteness of decoration, each lending assistance to the other. This is the true charm of the Taj. It is like unto one of those daughters of the gods who were most divinely fair. It is the fashion now to say that the Taj is lacking in strict architectural beauty. A well known writer states : " The truth is that the Taj is not an architectural group altogether satisfactory." No doubt in parts of the Taj genius is brought into jeopardy by unskilfulness : but the divine gift prevails. If a man possesses the sentiment of form the Taj will please him. As we sit on the steps of one of the minarets in the cool air of the evening and gaze upon the marble dome, and the smooth, broad front of marble, warm in the rays of the setting sun, across the memory comes Keats' line—" In form and shape, compact and beautiful." What has been said of Keats' St. Agnes Eve may be applied to the Taj—" A monody of dreamy richness."

VIII

FATTEHPUR-SIKRI

THE air is crisp and bright on the December morning we leave Agra to drive to Fattehpur-Sikri. We pass fields waving in green wheat, with patches of bright red poppies scattered about. From them there comes the monotonous wail of the ryot's song as he drives the bullocks that draw the water from the well, and from the cluster of bushes there arises the shrill cry of the partridge. Peasants strong and well knit, and young girls with graceful figures, are tramping to the town to sell their produce. Fine white oxen with spreading horns dragging heavy carts go by. Large substantial villages are passed and naked urchins with large eyes ask for *bucksheesh* as we stop at the roadside well to change horses. Then we see in the horizon a stone wall with battlements and round towers, and within it rises a rocky high ridge crowned with buildings. This is Fattehpur-Sikri, the summer residence of the great Akbar. The legend of its foundation is familiar to all. Akbar returning from one of his campaigns halted at the foot of the hill. At this time he and his wife—a Hindu princess of the Jeypore family—were in deep grief at the loss of their twin children. On the top of the hill resided a very famous and holy hermit, Shekh Salem Chishli, who promised them a son and heir if they would take up their abode at the place. They consented, and either the salubrity of the air or the spiritual exertions of the holy Father led to the birth of a son, who was called Salem, which name he bore till he mounted the throne as Emperor Jehangir. The tomb of the holy man stands on the highest part of the plateau, and is surrounded by high red walls, which gave it the appearance of a fortress. Approaching it from the Dafter Khana, or Record Office, of Akbar, now used as a travellers' bungalow, we come to a fine gateway, passing through which we enter a quadrangle of about five hundred feet square, with a very lofty and majestic cloister all round. Bishop Heber rightly said that there is no quadrangle either in Oxford or Cambridge fit to be compared with it, either in size or majestic proportions or beauty of architecture. Opposite rises a majestic mosque, and on the right is the marble mausoleum of the Saint, surrounded by the tombs of his descendants. " One cannot but feel deeply impressed on entering this silent and deserted court ; the long sombre galleries, surmounted by a thousand cupolas; the gigantic gateway resembling a *propylon* of Karnak ; and the noble mosque which forms a dark red framework to the mausoleum of the Saint, the dazzling whiteness of which is heightened by the foliage of the trees overhanging it. In the whole effect there is a mixture of severe grandeur and soft harmony which has always characterized Indian Islamism." The tomb of the Saint is entirely of white marble, and the walls are nothing but a curtain carved in open fretwork of the most exquisite geometrical patterns. A deep cornice of marble upheld by brackets of the most elaborate Hindu design intercept the rays of the sun. Behind an inner screen inlaid with mother-of-pearl, is the sarcophagus of the Saint, which is also inlaid with mother-of-pearl and covered with rich stuffs. Numerous dirty strings are tied in the holes of the screen. They have been placed there by women who are desirous that the spirit of the Saint thould do for them what the prayers of the Saint did for the wife of Akbar. Near the tomb is the mosque which Fergusson considers to be one of the finest in India. A chronogram over the main arch informs us that it is the duplicate of the Holy Place at Mecca,

TOMB OF SHEKH SALEM—FATTEHPUR-SIKRI.

197

and that it was built in 1571. It is crowned with three domes, and a handsome arch leads to the central chapel, whose vaulted roof is ornamented with a variety of geometrical patterns painted in the most delicate tints, and the floor is paved with marble. On each side of the central mosque are chapels with lofty square Hindu pillars. From the mosque we proceed to the great northern gateway. But to speak of it as a gateway conveys no meaning of the building. It is a triumphal arch, and compared with it the Arch of Constantine or the Arch of Titus is poor. It was erected to commemorate the conquest of Khandesh by Akbar. An inscription below the spring of the arches illustrates how the pride and arrogance of the Muslim is united with extreme religious humility. In the height of his triumph the victorious Emperor remembered, " Said Jesus, on whom be peace! The world is a bridge; pass over it, but build no house on it. He who hopeth for an hour, may hope for an eternity. The world is but an hour, spend it in devotion, the rest is unseen." Passing through a half domical entrance we reach some lofty steps, from which we look down upon ruined palaces and mosques encircled by the walls of the Imperial city; and beyond the stone battlements stretches a green country, and the monotony of the wide plain is broken by the dim outlines of blue hills. Descending the steps and walking through a narrow lane we arrive at an old mosque, which probably had once been a Hindu temple, for it is entirely Hindu in its character, and between Hindu pillars have been inserted arches. The curved brackets are exactly similar to those in the Saint's tomb. It is said that the mosque was built by the stone-cutters of the neighbourhood for Salem, and that here he taught his disciples. Near the mosque is an enclosure with a tomb, where lies buried Salem's son. Legend states that the infant one day noticed his sire was dejected. Though only six months of age and he had never spoken before, he

THE BOLAND DARWAZA—FATTEHPUR-SIKRI.

sat up in his cradle and asked his father the cause of his grief. The Saint replied : " Oh, my son, it is written that the Emperor will never have a son unless some other man will sacrifice for him the life of his own heir ; and surely no one is capable of such an act." " If you will allow me," cried the child, " I will die in order that his Majesty may be consoled." And before the father could reply the obliging infant expired. Nine months later Jehangir was born.

Leaving the tomb of the precocious infant we again mount the steps and devote some time to looking at the fine outer arch, which has a character of elegance combined with boldness of invention. The grey and pink sandstone columns, the marble ornaments, the bold flowing Arabic characters on the white ground, all lend grace to one of the finest portals in the world. This was the opinion of Finch, who visited it two centuries ago. He writes :

" At the head of this street stands the King's house, or Moholl, with much curious building : beyond which, on an ascent, is the goodliest mosque in all the east. It has a flight of some twenty-four or thirty steps to the gate, which is, in my opinion, one of the loftiest and handsomest in the world, having a great number of clustering pyramids on the top, very curiously disposed. The top of this gate may be distinctly seen from the distance of eight or ten miles. Within the gate is a spacious court curiously paved with stone, about six times the size of the Exchange of London, with a fine covered walk along the sides, more than twice as broad and double the height of those in our London Exchange, supported by numerous pillars all of one stone ; and all around about are entrances into numerous rooms very ingeniously contrived. Opposite the grand gate stands a fair and sumptuous tomb, most artificially inlaid with mother-o'-pearl and inclosed by a stone balustrade curiously carved, the ceiling being curiously plastered and painted. In this tomb is deposited the body of a *calender* or Mahometan devotee, at whose cost the whole of this splendid mosque was built. Under the courtyard is a goodly tank of excellent water ; none other being to be had in the whole extent of the city, except brackish and corroding, by the use of which so great a mortality was

occasioned among the inhabitants of this city, that Akbar left
it before it was quite finished, and removed his seat of empire to
Agra, so that this splendid city was built and ruined in the space
of fifty or sixty years."

Leaving the mosque and passing the houses of Akbar's
two great friends—Ab-ul-Fazl, the compiler of the Ain-i-
Akbari, and his brother the poet, we enter by a lofty and
richly carved gate a large quadrangle, on the north and
south sides of which are a series of apartments roofed with
sloping slabs covered with blue enamel. This is called the
Jehangir Mahal or Jodh Bhai Mahal, on the supposition that
it was the residence of the Hindoo princess Jodh Bhai, the
mother of Jehangir. Jodh Bhai was, however, the wife and
not the mother of Jehangir. Who was the mother of Jehangir is uncertain, but her son reverently informs us that she
was called Mariam Zamanah, or Mary of the Period, thus
showing the respect with which she was regarded, for the
Muhammadans hold in reverence the memory of the Virgin
Mary. To this circumstance is probably due the legend that
Akbar had a Christian wife called *Bibi Mariam*. From the
palace we proceed to what is supposed to have been the
Christian lady's residence, and over the door one is
shown what is supposed to have been an Annun-
ciation. But it is so faded that it is difficult to make
out the figures, and the frescoes, which tradition says
represented scenes from Firdusi's poem the *Shah-nama*,
have faded beyond hope of restoration. The house was
once profusely gilded and painted, from which it derived
its name, Sonehri Manzil, or Golden Palace. Akbar may
have wished that the residence of his Hindu consort should
surpass in magnificence the residence built almost opposite
by Rajah Birbal for his daughter. The Hindu Minister
had won the heart of the Emperor by his wit and love of
letters, and it was he who led his master from the straight
path of orthodoxy. The house he erected for his daughter

proves that he had a keen appreciation of the beautiful. But it does not seem to be a house, but a casket in red sandstone, carved and ornamented after the pattern of some ebony or sandalwood casket. Not a piece of wood is used in the whole edifice, but the whole building and its entire ornamentation remind us that the Hindu architects loved to imitate their old structures, which were entirely of wood. Wood lent itself to the Hindu genius for elaborate ornamentation, for it could with facility be carved. At Fattehpur-Sikri the Hindu found red sandstone so soft that it could be easily chiselled clean and sharp; and he covered every inch of it with ornaments perfect in taste and design. But his love of ornament led him sometimes to outwardly curve a stone bracket meant to represent a wooden truss, and so destroyed the impression of reality and durability. The limitation and strength of the Hindu intellect is vividly illustrated in his architecture. He is endowed with great powers of analysis, and a rich imagination which displays itself in the variety and richness of his work, but he is lacking in the power of invention. He laid a large slab across his columns of stone, and he made the whole beautiful by rich carving; but he never thought of creating the radiating arch, and its complement, the radiating dome. The rooms in the upper story of Birbal's house are, it is true, crowned by massive domes, but these are due to Muhammadan influence. The ceilings of the rooms below, fifteen feet square, are constructed of slabs fifteen feet in length and one foot in breadth, which rest upon bold cornices supported by deeply arched pendentives. The rooms are examples of the best and most perfect manual skill, and it is impossible not to admire them, because the work is good and strong and the ornaments so finished; but it is not certain that the ugly goblins and formless monsters carved on an old cathedral front do not give more pleasure. There is the joy of life and vigour about them;

but Birbal's house affords one only sensuous delight. Near it rises a fanciful construction called Panch Mahal—the " five palaces "—which consists of four platforms each smaller than the one beneath, and supported on rows of columns which diminish in number from fifty supporting the ground floor to four supporting the small kiosque. The thirty-five columns which support the second terrace are all different, and illustrate the way the Hindu architect treated the pillar. Unlike the Greeks and Romans, who make their columns always round, the Hindu constructed his of every shape. There is also no fixed intercolumniation in the Hindu architecture, as is found in the Grecian, but the spaces allowed between pillar and pillar in different Hindu buildings are found nearly to coincide with the Grecian mode of intercolumniation, though in many instances they differ widely from it ; and the same, perhaps, may be said of the Egyptian colonnades. " The Indian pedestals and bases are made more systematically, and afford by far a greater variety of proportions and ornaments than the Grecian and Roman. In the European architecture the form and dimensions of the pedestals and bases are fixed by invariable rules, with respect to the orders in which they are employed ; but in the Indian the choice is left to the option of the artists. The capitals of the Grecian columns invariably mark the distinction of the several orders : those of the Indian are varied at pleasure, though not without regard to the diameters and length of the shaft ; and the forms of the plainest of them, though they have nothing in common with the Grecian order, are found, at a distant view, to bear some resemblance to the Doric and Ionic capitals ; but those of a more elaborate kind are sometimes so overloaded with a sort of filigree ornament as to destroy the effect of the beautiful proportion of the whole." There has been some discussion as to the use of the Panch Mahal, since it could not have been used as a habitation, and commanding a view of the

Harem, strangers could not have been admitted to it. But it must be borne in mind that Eastern despots did not erect buildings merely from consideration of use. This elaborate and quaint erection moreover may have been constructed to enable the Emperor to enjoy the cool air on a summer's night.

From the Panch Mahal we entered the Khas Mahal, and walking to the south we arrive at the *Khwabgah*, or sleeping place. Ascending a narrow staircase we come to a small, well-proportioned room of red sandstone without any ornament. This was the bedroom of the Great Akbar. Opposite is the light and elegant Diwan-i-Khas with its handsome balcony and well carved balustrades. On the left is a small red building used as a girls' school. Above it towers the elegant Panch Mahal. On the right is the apartment occupied by Akbar's chief wife, Ruquina Sultana Begam.[1] Descending the steps we walk across the court to it. Upon the decoration of this little palace, the Hindu has concentrated all his powers of imagination and invention. Here we see the splendid caprice of the East. Here is carved in stone the rich and lavish life of the tropics. On the panels round the room the Hindu has carved the palm, beneath whose trunk, according to Moslem tradition, was born the holy Son of Mary, and the cypress which grew in the Moslem's terrestrial paradise, and we have cunningly wrought pheasants perching on trees, and the tiger wandering through the jungle. The vine and the pomegranate clasp the shafts. The roof is carved in geometrical patterns as rich and careful as the skill of man can make them. From each door we gaze on two pillars, also luxuriantly carved, and the bright light of the sun falls upon the cool green leaves of the graceful neem

[1] "But from the Hindu nature of the building, it is most probable that it was the dwelling of Akbar's Hindu Consort, the daughter of Raja Bihari Mal, known as Mariam-uz-Zamani."—*Agra*, by Syad Muhammad Latif, p. 156.

tree. The jewelled and enamelled marble caskets which
Shah Jehan constructed for his mistress excite admiration
by their voluptuous beauty, and about the Taj hovers the
poetry of death : about the apartment of the Stamboul
Begum hovers the poetry of love.

With deep regret we left it and walked to the Diwan-i-Am,
a small redstone hall, with a deep redstone balcony, on each
side of which is a redstone screen. To this balcony Akbar
arrayed in robes of State used to repair each day and inquire into and redress the grievances of the people who used
to crowd the courtyard below. It was here he used to
receive the strangers who used to flock to his court from all
parts of the earth. Here he received the Jesuits of Goa who
brought him the leaves and seeds of tobacco, and it was at
Fattehpur-Sikri the *hookah* is supposed to have been invented. From the Diwan-i-Am the Emperor passed to the
Diwan-i-Khas, or Privy Council Chamber. It is a lofty hall,
in the centre of which is an enormous column of red sandstone, which terminates at some distance from the ceiling
in a capital richly carved in the Hindu style. This capital
forms a platform encircled by a light balustrade, and from
it radiate four stone causeways leading to four niches in the
buildings. Legend states that the Emperor used to take
his seat on the platform, his Ministers occupying the niches,
while the ambassadors, commanders, and nobles, who had to
transact business, remained below. It is also supposed that
this hall is the place mentioned by Badaoni, where Akbar
held his religious controversies. We have mention of a
building as possessing four *aiwans*, one for each class of
religionists, and it is possible that the disputants occupied
the four corners, while the Emperor sat in the middle.
Wearied of work or religious controversy, the Emperor proceeded, when the heat of the afternoon began to decline,
to the court nigh at hand, marked out by alternate squares
of black and white marble as a *puchisi*-board. The game is

played by four players with four pawns apiece, and the
moves are regulated by throwing three long dice, the highest
throws being twenty-five, from which the game derives its
name.. The object of the game is to get one's four pawns
into the centre square of the board. Akbar played it in an
Imperial manner with sixteen handsome slave girls as pawns.
North of the *puchisi*-board is the Ankh Michauli, or hide-and-
seek place, where it is said Jehangir used to play at hide-and-
seek as a child. Judging from the building it was more
probably used as a treasury. Close to the Ankh Michauli is
a small platform shaded by a canopy, where, according to
tradition, sat a Hindu teacher tolerated by Akbar. It is a
building of the purest Jain architecture, each of the architraves being supported by two highly carved struts issuing
from the mouths of monsters and meeting in the middle.

From the Khas Mahal we proceed to a large quadrangular
building known as the Mint. It is a kind of barbican with a
large number of dark vaults and a hall described as the Hall
of Account. The writer of that rare work, *The Wanderings
of a Pilgrim*, states :

" The *taksal* (the mint) is at this place ; in it rupees were first
coined ; unlike the circular rupees of the present day, those
coined by Akbar are square ; he also coined square gold mohurs
and eight anna pieces of the same form. The square rupee,
if *without a blemish*, is reckoned of great value ; it is used in
conjuring the truth out of thieves, who are much afraid of it,
and often confess the truth from a belief in its virtues. If a rich
native can obtain one of Akbar's rupees, or, what is better, an
Akbarabadee gold mohur, he puts it away with his hoard of
riches, firmly believing that by its virtue robbers will be prevented
from discovering his gold."

Forbes, in his *Oriental Memoirs*, tells us that Akbar
restricted the coinage of gold to four places—Agra, Bengal,
Ahmedabad, and Cabul. Silver coin was allowed to be
struck in fourteen cities, including the preceding four ;
mints for copper coin were appointed in twenty-eight cities.

" Great attention was paid to assaying and refining the various metals and to every department of the mint and treasury. The gold and silver intended for the current coin of the realm, when brought to the greatest degree of purity, was committed to the most celebrated artists, to give each specimen the perfection of beauty. It is well known that coins, medals, and signets of the Mahometan princes have no portrait or armorial bearings cut in the die from which the coin is to be stamped, as is generally practised in Europe : it is usually impressed with the name of the reigning monarch, the date of the year in the Hegira, and perhaps some appropriate or flattering title. In the reign of Akbar were struck those immense gold masses, distinguished as the immortal coins. The largest, called Henseh, weighed upwards of one hundred tolahs, in value one hundred lual jilaly mohurs, not much short of two hundred pounds sterling, estimating the gold mohur at fifteen silver rupees of half a crown each ; others were of half that value ; from which they diminished to the small round mohur, valued at nine silver rupees ; some of these were marked with flowers, especially the tulip and the rose, but never with the represen-tation of any animated form. In the place of such emblems, Akbar had moral sentences and tetrastichs from the Persian poets, the praises of the Almighty, or his own titles, engraved on the die in a most beautiful manner." On the reverse of the Henseh was written : " The best coin is that which is employed in supplying men with the necessaries of life, and that benefits the companions in the road to God." On some of the smaller coins were the following inscriptions in Persian characters, some of them ornamented with a tulip and wild rose : " God is greatest ! " on the reverse, " O Defender," " God is greatest ! mighty is His glory ! " with the date.

As we leave the Mint to return to Birbal's house, where we are going to spend the night, the sun begins to sink swiftly down the horizon, and the people returning from the fields drive their cattle through the deserted streets, and flocks of goats come up through the lanes, and crop the bushes that are now springing from the palaces of Akbar. Then the sky, soft and tender as an Italian one, is tremulous with starlight, and the moon rises above the horizon like a ball of fire. Swiftly she mounts the sky and whitens the country below, and spreads sheets of light over the dark mosques and deserted palaces of the city. This is India not of heat, toil, and cruel separation, but of romance and beauty. But the very beauty only lends itself to sad thoughts, for as we gaze on the boundless starlit depths over-head, there comes to us—

> " The self-same song that found a path
> Through the sad heart of Ruth, when, sick for home,
> She stood in tears amid the alien corn;
> The same that oft-times hath
> Charm'd magic casements, opening on the foam
> Of perilous seas, in faery lands forlorn."

IX

LUCKNOW

WITHIN fifty years after the death of Aurangzeb, the foundations of the Empire which Baber created and Akbar, Jehangir and Shan Jehan consolidated, were undermined to the centre and the Viceroys of the provinces established independent kingdoms for themselves. In the south the Turki Chin Kilich Khan, better known as Nizam-ul-Mulk (Regulator of the Kingdom), a capable commander of great personal courage and proud spirit, made himself *de facto* sovereign of the wide dominion which his descendants, the Nizams of Hyderabad, govern this day. In Hindustan the Persian Sádat Khan, whose original name was Muhammad Amin, carved out of the great Gangetic plain the modern kingdom of Oude.   Dow, the historian, spoke of his grandson as " the infamous son of a yet more infamous Persian pedlar," a phrase which raised the ire of Burke. Sádat Khan's ancestors were, as Burke stated, " of noble descent," tracing their origin to the Prophet himself : and they had been long settled at Naishapur in Khorásán. His father had served the Moghul Emperor, and on the son coming to India he was appointed by the Emperor, Governor of Agra.   He took an important part in the overthrow of the Saiads,[1] and for his services he was appointed by the Emperor Muhammad Shah, Subahdar of Oude (1720).   Historians do not agree as to whether Sádat Khan in concert

[1] See Ajmer.

with Nizam-ul-Mulk, called in the Persian soldier of fortune, Nadir Shah, but there is no doubt that their rivalry led to the defeat of the Moghul Army at Kurnal (1738) and the subsequent sack of Delhi. Sádat Khan was taken prisoner and died before the close of the year. "Ajodhya (the ancient capital) and Lucknow were the places at which he chiefly resided, and having assumed for his crest the fish which is still, so to speak, the arms of Oude, he changed the name of the well known fort of Lucknow from Kila Likna (so called after the founder, one Likna Ahur) to Machi Bhawan or the fish-house." Sádat was succeeded by his nephew and son-in-law, who was appointed by the Moghul Emperor, Vizier of the Empire, or Prime Minister, and so was the first to be called Nawab Vizier ; but he lost the favour of the Emperor and was superseded as Premier of the Empire by Ghazi-ud-din, the grandson of Nizam-ul-Mulk. He retired to his own kindgom and died in 1756. He was succeeded by his son, Shuja-ud-daulah, who had married the Bhow Begum, a Persian lady, but by no means, as Burke alleged, " of the first birth and quality in India," for her grandfather had been Aurangzeb's head cook. Her grievances have been immortalized by the fervid oratory of the accusers of Warren Hastings. But those who knew her describe her as a woman of uncommonly violent temper. " Death and destruction is the least menace she denounces upon the most trifling opposition to her caprice." Her main object was the extirpation of the English and their power in Hindustan. Her husband, jealous of their growing ascendancy on the coast, and having the Nawab of Mursheda bad and the titular Emperor of Delhi in his camp, thought the opportunity favourable for an invasion of Bengal. At Buxar on the Ganges, he and his army of fifty thousand men were met by Hector Munro with a small force. Shuja-ud-daulah, after a bloody contest, was signally defeated, and his camp and one hundred and sixty guns enriched the victorious troops. It is the battle of Buxar and not the rout at Plassey which laid the foundation of our Empire. It broke the power of the Nawab of Oude ; it led to the Moghul Emperor coming to our camp to negotiate ; and it took our arms across the Ganges into the wide central plain of India. Clive having assumed under a grant from the Emperor of Delhi the direct revenue administration of Bengal, Behar and Orissa, congratulated his masters on " having become the sovereigns of three kingdoms," but to extend their possessions. further would be " a scheme so extravagantly ambitious that no government in its senses would dream of it." He determined to restore to the Nawab Vizier, Oude, Ghazepoor and Benares, and to maintain and strengthen the new state as the buffer state between Bengal and the Mahrattas and the Afghans. The districts of Korah and Allahabad were given to the titular Moghul Emperor, who thus became a dependant of the Bengal Government.

On January 26, 1775, Shuja-ud-daulah died and was succeeded by his son, Asaf-ud-daulah. The majority of the council at Calcutta considered all the treaties made with Shuja-ud-daulah as purely personal, and consequently invalid on the death of one of the contracting parties. They therefore resolved to make a heavier bargain with his successor, and Philip Francis, who had denounced Hastings for " letting out British troops for hire to the Vizier," determined to increase the amount that the Nawab had to pay for them. Hastings expressed an opinion that the present subsidy was sufficient and that it ought not to be increased. " I doubt," he stated, " whether a larger sum would in reality prove a gain to the Company." It was however resolved that an increase of the subsidy be demanded from the Nawab to make it equal to the expenses of the troops. Thus we find the statesman, who has been branded as a violator of treaties and the oppressor of natives

by extortions and exactions, doing his utmost to prevent
his colleagues from extorting any concession from a native
prince inconsistent with a former treaty.[1] A fresh treaty
was extracted from the Nawab : the subsidy was raised ;
all arrears due by his father were to be paid by him, and he
was forced to cede to the Company the province of Benares,
valued at more than two hundred thousand pounds a year.
The burden imposed upon the Nawab by the Francis Junto,
and his own extravagant debauchery, first led to the internal
confusion and financial straits which became chronic in
Oude. To his wild expenditure Lucknow however owes
some of her finest buildings—the Imambara, the Rumi
Darwaza, the Char Bagh, and the Residency. He was an
incompetent ruler, but his liberality and munificence won
the hearts of his subjects. In 1797 Asuf-ud-daulah died
and his putative son being put aside by Sir John Shore,
then Governor-General, his brother, S'adat Ali, was placed
on the *Musnud*. A fresh treaty was made between him and
Sir John Shore. The fort of Allahabad was handed over
to the British Government, and in return the Company
agreed to maintain not less than ten thousand troops in
Oude. If at any time however the force amounted to more
than thirteen thousand or less than eight thousand, an increased subsidy was to be paid or a decrease allowed accordingly. Soon after the treaty was signed, Lord Mornington,
afterwards Marquess Wellesley, became Governor-General.
Among the dangers which threatened India at that time
was the invasion of Zaman Shah, the reigning sovereign of
Afghanistan. The Mahrattas refused to enter into an offensive alliance with the Governor-General. The ruler of Oude—
our buffer state—was totally incapable of resisting an invader.
The English Commander-in-Chief reported that, while the
danger of an invasion was great, the Nawab's army was

---

[1] *The Administration of Warren Hastings*, 1772–85. Reviewed
and illustrated from original documents by G. W. Forrest

not only a heavy drain on his finances but a real and formidable danger to the British Government. "Towards the close of 1799," writes the Duke of Wellington, in a memorandum on his brother's Government of India, "the Governor-General, acting under the treaty of his predecessor, called upon the Nawab of Oude to dismiss his expensive, useless, and dangerous troops and to fill their places by increased numbers of the Company's troops." The King evaded the demand, and delayed, but after many difficulties, arrangements were made for introducing into his territories 3,000 additional troops at his expense. A reform of the Civil administration was also pressed on the Nawab. He now declared that he was not able to pay the subsidy, and Lord Wellesley determined to place it on the basis of territorial security. After a long negotiation a fresh treaty was signed on November 10, 1801, "by which in commutation for subsidy and for the perpetual defence of his country," the Nawab ceded Rohilcund, the Lower Doab, between the Ganges and the Jumna, and a large extent of country between the Ganges and the river Gogra down to Benares. The two former were, as Wellington says, his frontier provinces towards the Mahrattas, the Sikhs and the Afghans; the latter state bordered upon the dominion of the Company. The policy of Wellesley with regard to Oude has been warmly criticized. But a dispassionate study of the State documents clearly shows that while he acted for the safety of India he acted at the same time with due regard to the faith of existing treaties and what was due to the people and sovereign of Oude. It would have been better for the people if he could have annexed the kingdom. The condition of the country rapidly grew worse. Thirty years after Wellesley's treaty the Court of Directors remarked " it was the British Government which, by a systematic suppression of all attempts at resistance, had prolonged the misrule, which became permanent when the short-sightedness and rapacity of a semi-barbarous Government was armed with the military strength of a civilized one." Lord William Bentinck, who had tra-velled through the country and represented to the East India Court its desolation and decay, was authorized to assume at once the government if it were necessary. But the Governor-General was a man of singular moderation, and unfortunately for the people of Oude he did not avail him-self of the permission granted him. He merely informed the King of the instructions he had received, and stated that their execution would be suspended in the hope of his adopting the necessary reforms. It was a vain hope. The character of the Nawab Nasir-ud-din was stained with every vice, and his life was consumed in low debauchery. The King's barber was the greatest man of the court. " His influence was far greater than that of the native Prime Minister." He had come out to Calcutta as a cabin-boy. Having been brought up a hairdresser in London, he had left his ship on arriving in Calcutta to resume his old busi-ness. Making some money he took to going up the river with European merchandise for sale. Arrived at Lucknow he delighted the King by the way he curled his hair. " Honours and wealth were showered upon the lucky coiffeur. He was given a title of nobility. Sofraz Khan (" the illustrious chief ") was his new name, and men bowed to him in Oude. " The power of the barber waxed daily greater. His pride increased with his power ; and no limits were set to the caprices and wild pranks of despotic authority and reckless depravity combined. The scenes which oc-curred in the palace were whispered over India. His majesty might one hour be seen in a state of drunken nudity with his boon companions and the low menial who was his chief confidant ; at another, he would parade the streets of Lucknow, drunk at midday, driving one of his own elephants. All decency and propriety were banished

from the court." On the night of July 7, 1837, Nasir-
ud-din died, and the chief Begum attempted to place on
the *Musnud* his putative son, Munna Jan. "During the
twelve hours' tumult that ensued, the Resident, his suite,
and the rightful heir to the throne, were all in the hands of
an infuriated mob. Armed soldiers with lighted torches
and lighted matchlocks in their hands, held possession of the
palace, stalked throughout its premises, and spared no
threats against the British authorities, if they did not assent
to the installation of their creature, Munna Jan. The
nearest succour had to come five miles from the cantonment.
Five companies of Sepoys, with four guns, however, soon
arrived. The Resident managed to join his friends. He
then gave the insurgents one quarter of an hour's
grace. When that had expired, the guns opened, and a few
rounds of grape were thrown into the disorderly mass, who
thronged the palace and its enclosures. Morning dawned
on an altered scene ; the rioters had succumbed or dispersed ;
the dead were removed ; the palace was cleared out ; and
by ten o'clock in the forenoon, the aged, infirm, and
trembling heir to the crown was seated on the throne that,
at midnight, had been occupied by the usurper. The
Resident placed the crown on the new King's head, and the
event was announced to the people of Lucknow by the very
guns which a few hours before had carried death and con-
sternation among the Oude soldiery." The new sovereign,
Muhammad Ali Khan, was a respectable old man who made
some earnest efforts to improve his kingdom. But the
period of improvement was most brief. He was succeeded
by his son, Amjad Ali, a man of frivolous disposition, who
would not attend to business or to any advice. On his
death in February, 1847, Wajid Ali, "the last and, with the
exception of Nasir-ud-din, perhaps the most despicable of
his line, mounted the throne." In November, 1847, Lord
Hardinge visited Lucknow, and administered to Wajid Ali

the same rebuke and the same warning which had been addressed to his predecessors. He was told that if a marked improvement were not visible in two years the Company would assume the government of Oude. Not two years, but nine years, rolled on, and no improvement was made in the Government. Then on February 13, 1856, the Province of Oude was annexed on the righteous ground that " the British Government would be guilty in the sight of God and man, if it were any longer to aid in sustaining by its countenance an administration fraught with evil to millions." The country was constituted into a chief Commissionership, and the first efforts of British Administration were guided by the tender and generous hands of Sir James Outram. But his health unfortunately broke down under the heavy strain of work, and in April, 1856, he was obliged to resign the rule of the province and return to England. Outram's successor, in attempting with the most laudable intentions to introduce into the new province the Revenue administration of the elder districts, alienated all the great landlords and inspired general discontent and misgiving. Lord Canning, having become to a certain degree aware of the feeling which had spread through the province, sent Henry Lawrence to Oude that he might conciliate the hearts of the inhabitants by his justice and tact ; but it was too late. The object for which he had been sent was in a fair way of accomplishment when the great storm burst, and Henry Lawrence knew that upon his success or failure depended the vital interests of the Empire. And from the first overt act of mutiny on May 3, 1857, to the hour of his death, there was nothing left undone by Henry Lawrence to stem the tide of revolt and to maintain the British authority. It was the courage and steadfastness with which he had inspired all around him, and the wise precautions which he had taken with regard to the supplies and food, which enabled the heroic garrison of Lucknow to baffle all the efforts of their enemy.

The Residency entrenchments, in which Henry Lawrence concentrated his small force, covered almost sixty acres of ground, and consisted of a number of detached houses, public edifices, outhouses, and casual buildings, netted together and welded by ditches, parapets, stockades and batteries into one consentaneous whole of resistance. On the summit of the plateau stood the Residency proper, the official residence of the Chief Commissioner, a lofty building three stories high, not without grace and dignity. A superb portico gave a considerable degree of grandeur to the eastern entrance, and a wide and lofty colonnaded verandah extended along the western front. Near the Residency stood another large pile of building called the Banqueting Hall, where large and spacious apartments had been built for state receptions. Passing through the Bailey Guard Gate, now riddled with bullets, we come to a ruined building, and in one of the rooms a notice informs us, " Here Sir H. Lawrence died." This ruined building was the extensive one-storied house, occupied by Dr. Fayrer, the Residency Surgeon. Here many ladies found a hospitable shelter, and it had the advantage of having underground rooms to which they could retire when the fire of the enemy became heavy. Along the flat roof were placed sandbags, and sheltered by them our men were able to return the fire of the foe. The post was commanded by Captain Weston and Dr. Fayrer, a keen sportsman and a first-rate shot. It was on the second day of the siege, while Henry Lawrence was discussing with Captain Wilson, the Deputy-Assistant Adjutant-General, a memorandum as to how the rations were to be distributed, that a shell entered his apartment in the Residency, burst, and gave him a mortal wound. As the Residency had become a special target for the enemy they removed the wounded man to Dr. Fayrer's house, which was more sheltered from their artillery. They laid him in the northern verandah. A consultation was held, and the medical men decided

THE RESIDENCY, LUCKNOW.

that even amputation at the hip joint offered no hope of saving life ; nothing could be done but to alleviate suffering. The rebels had learned what had occurred, and whither the chief had been removed, and they smote the house with a smashing fire. " As his time drew near, Sir Henry asked to receive the Lord's Supper ; and in the verandah, with the shells hissing through the air, and the pillars crashing to the stroke of the bullets, the holy rite was performed. When it was ended, with a calm fortitude which excited the admiration of those about him, he appointed his successor, and gave detailed instructions as to the conduct of the defence. He earnestly exhorted them to preserve internal tranquillity, to economize their ammunition and the supplies, to protect the women and children from all evil, to exert themselves indefatigably to rouse and sustain the spirit of the garrison, never to treat with the enemy, and on on account to surrender. He expressed his wishes with regard to his children, sending loving messages to them. The children of the British soldiers, who had been the special object of his charity, he recommended to the care of his country. His fancy then reverted to the happy days of his own childhood spent with his mother. He spoke often of the devoted wife who had gone before him, and he repeated the sacred texts which had been their guide and their comfort. In the hour of rebellion there came home to him, whose heart was full of compassion and charity for all humanity, the words inscribed on her tomb : ' To the Lord our God belong mercies and forgivenesses, though we have rebelled against Him.' He expressed a wish to be buried ' without any fuss ' and to be laid in the same grave as the British soldier ; and he desired that no epitaph should be placed on his tomb, but this : ' Here lies Henry Lawrence, who tried to do his duty. May God have mercy on him.' " [1]

[1] *Selections from the Letters, Despatches, and other State Papers*

AITKEN POST, BAILEY GUARD, LUCKNOW.

221

Directly below Fayrer's house we find on the east front a pillar with " Financial Post " written on it. It is the first of a series of pillars which mark the different important posts held by the garrison. Here stood the Financial Commissioner's office, a large two-storied house, the enclosure wall of which formed a part of our line of defence. It was commanded with great ability by Captain Saunders, 18th Native Infantry. A little to the west of the " Financial Post " we come to " Sago's Post," where stood the house of Mrs. Sago, the mistress of a charity school. It was a small ow building, the enclosing walls and grounds of which were abandoned and the defence confined to the house itself. A narrow passage, to traverse which proved fatal to many during the siege, led up to the Judicial Commissioner's office, a large two-storied building situated on high ground. Here the outer wall, owing to the slope of the ground, had to be abandoned, and a strong barricade of fascines and earth constructed. This important position, which was greatly exposed to the enemy's fire from the east, was commanded by Captain Germon, 13th Native Infantry. Next to the Judicial Commissioner's office came " Captain Anderson's Post." This was a small house, situated on rising ground, and formed the south-eastern angle of our position. When the Residency was being put in a state of defence, the wall of the enclosure round the house was thrown down, and a stockade erected in its place. Within the stockade was a ditch; then came a mound about five feet high; then another deep ditch with pointed bamboos placed at the bottom. Having the enemy only a few yards from the house on the left, and in front, it was one of the most exposed outworks of the whole Residency position. Below it, and communicating with it by a hole in the wall, was the Cawnpore Battery. Captain Anderson has left a graphic description

Preserved in the Military Department of the Government of India.
Edited by G. W. Forrest. Vol. ii. Lucknow.

of the desperate assaults which those who held it had to
repel.

" Again and again they made the attempt, but back they had
to go by a steady fire. Their chiefs came to the front, and
shouted out, ' Come on, come on—the place is ours—it is taken.'
And the Sepoys would then rush forward, then hesitate, and
finally got under cover of the stockade, and kept up a fearful
fire. Some hundreds of them got under the Cawnpore Battery,
but found the hand-grenades rather disagreeable, and had to
bolt rather sharp. Poor Major Banks came up, and cheered us
during the hottest fire, and we were glad to see him. Our shells
now began to fall amongst the enemy, and this still further roused
their indignation. You could hear additional yells and horrid
imprecations on the heads of all CHRISTIANS. No less than three
times were we assaulted by enormous odds against us, and each
attack was, thank God, successfully repulsed. There we were,
a little body, probably not eighty men in all (i.e. Cawnpore
Battery, our post, and Captain Germon's), opposed to several
thousands of merciless bloodthirsty fanatics. We well knew
what we had to expect if we were defeated ; and, therefore,
each individual fought, as it were, for his very life ; each loophole
displayed a steady flash of musketry, as defeat would have been
certain death to every soul in the garrison. Had the outposts
fallen, they were in such immense numbers that we could never
have turned the enemy out, and then not a man, woman, or
child would have been spared. It was, indeed, a most anxious
time, and the more so, as we did not know how matters were
progressing at other points. We dreaded that the others might
have been even *further* pressed than we were. At intervals I
heard the cry of ' more men this way ' ; and off would rush two
or three (all we could possibly spare) here and there ; and then
the same cry was repeated in an opposite direction, and then the
men had to rush to support their comrades, who were more
hotly pressed, and so on ; as the pressure became greater at
particular places, men rushed to those spots to give assistance.
During this trying time even the poor wounded men ran out
of the hospitals, and those who had wounds in the legs threw
away their crutches, and deliberately knelt down, and fired as
fast as they could out of the loopholes. Others, who could do
little else, loaded the muskets, whilst the able-bodied soldiers

223

fired ; and in this odd manner these brave men of her Majesty's 32nd upheld the honour of their nation, and strained every nerve to repel the furious attacks of the enemy."

Leaving the Cawnpore Battery we pursue our walk past Duprat's Post, where a gallant Frenchman did right good service for us, till we come to a pillar which marks Gubbin's house. This was two stories in height and solidly built of masonry. " On the southern side a spacious and handsome portico marked the principal front, and beyond it soared a lofty forest tree, covered in spring with pale yellow blossoms. During the siege its colossal trunk and massive branches interrupted many a round shot : day by day the boughs were shot away till little but the stem remained. As a huge branch came crashing down, an old Sikh soldier remarked, 'It has repaid all the Company's salt.' The battered trunk of the old tree still stands before the ruins of the house, a striking memorial of the great siege." [1]

From Gubbin's Post we walk to the Begum's Khote and descend to the subterranean apartments where the ladies passed their days during the siege. One of them has given us a description of their daily life :—

" We all sleep (that is, eleven ladies and seven children) on the floor of the Tye Khana, where we spread mattresses and fit into each other like bits in a puzzle, so as best to feel the punkah. The gentlemen sleep upstairs in a long verandah sort of room on the side of the house least exposed to fire. My bed consists of a purdah and a pillow. In the morning we all roll up our bedding, and pile them in heaps against the wall. We have only room for very few chairs down there, which are assigned to invalids, and most of us take our meals seated on the floor, with our plates on our knees. We are always obliged to light a candle for break-fast and dinner as the room is perfectly dark. Our usual fare consists of stew, as being easiest to cook ; it is brought up in a large deckger (copper stew-pan), so as not to dirty a dish, and

---

[1] *Selections from the Letters, Despatches, and other State Papers Preserved in the Military Department of the Government of India,* edited by George W. Forrest. Vol. ii., Lucknow (Introduction).

a portion ladled out to each person. Of course we can get no bread or butter, so chapathies (unleavened cakes) are the disagreeable substitute."

For about half an hour in the evening the women were permitted to sit in the portico and breathe a little fresh air. This was in the fiery month of July. Even in December we are glad to escape from the dark dungeon and find our-selves in the sunlight. Calm and beautiful is the scene. The sky is as blue as in Italy ; the sward is as trim and green as in England, and glorious red roses are in full bloom. We mount the steps which lead to the handsome marble cross erected in memory of " Henry Lawrence and the brave men who fell in defence of the Residency." From the topmost step we see in the far distance the city with its cupolas and domes ; at the foot of the garden flows the Goomtee, whose banks are lined with cornfields and groves of noble trees. Yet this spot is the scene of a great agony. Here men, women and children dwindled away, worn out by wounds and disease. Here often must they have watched for signs of relief, but for three months the weary eyes saw the dawn burst forth over the city and the burning sun set, and no succour came to them. Then one day as a flight of bullets swept over their heads a whistling sound was heard and a cry arose from the soldiers, " It is the Miniè ! " the bullet of the Miniè rifle. At once they understood that friends were near, and they gazed searchingly about the lines, but they could only see the enemy firing swiftly and heavily from the flat roofs of the houses. Then, after the lapse of five long minutes they beheld our soldiers fighting their way through one of the main streets. From the Memorial Cross we make our way to the churchyard which lies below. Beneath the shade of some wide-spreading trees there are a multitude of graves, around which are growing bright flowers, and the paths are radiant with roses. The inscriptions tell us the spot contains the sacred dust of heroes. We walk to a plain tomb and slowly read, " Here lies Henry Lawrence, who tried to do his duty. May the Lord have mercy on his soul."

After leaving the Residency, we drive to the great Imambara, or largest room in the world which has an arched roof without supports. The historian of Indian Architecture writes :

" This immense building is covered with vaults of very simple form and still simpler construction, being of a rubble or coarse concrete several feet in thickness, which is laid on a rude mould or centreing of bricks and mud, and allowed to stand a year or two to set and dry. The centreing is then removed, and the vault, being in one piece, stands without abutment or thrust, apparently a better and more durable form of roof than our most scientific Gothic vaulting, certainly far cheaper and far more easily made, since it is literally cast on a mud form, which may be moulded into any shape the fancy of the architect may dictate."

The Imambara was built by the Nawab Asuf-ud-daulah, in the year of the great famine, 1784, in order to afford relief to the famine-stricken people. Legend relates that many of high rank were driven by hunger to join in the work, and that to spare their feelings their names were called out at night and their wages paid to them. The monarch invited the architects to submit their plans to competition, and only stipulated that the building should be no mere copy, and that it should surpass all other buildings in beauty and magnificence. The magnificent ornaments and decorations which adorned the building have perished, but the Imambara stands a graceful monument of the monarch who erected it and who lies buried in it. It was after the reign of Asuf-ud-daulah that buildings began to be erected in Lucknow which are the most debased example of architecture in India. A court steeped in luxury and vice sought only to erect palaces bastard in style and of tawdry splendour.

THE KAISAR BAGH, LUCKNOW.

From the Imambara we drive past the Residency to the Kaisar Bagh, or Garden of Cæsar, built by the ex-King, Waji Ali Shah, at a cost of eighty lakhs, and, entering the gateway, pass up an open court in front of the gateway, called the Jilarkhana or place from which the royal procession used to start. An old traveller, who wrote an interesting account of a " Tour along the Ganges and Jumna," has given a graphic description of a royal procession in Lucknow :

" As we approach the grand gateway the massive folding doors flew open, and the Nawab advanced surrounded and followed by his principal courtiers, all on elephants richly caparisoned, and they in their most splendid and costly costumes. This spectacle was uncommonly grand and impressive, the richness of the housings of the elephants, fifty in number, the immense and gaudy banners, the spirited and beautiful Arab horses : all this splendid pageant, bursting at once from a noble gateway embosomed in a wood, had an effect at once magnificent and highly picturesque."

Passing through a gateway covered by a screen, we cross the Chini Bagh (so called from the large China vessels with which it was decorated), and passing under a gate flanked by green mermaids, we reach the Hazrat Bagh. On the right is the Chandiwali Barahdari, which used to be paved with silver, and the Badshah Manzil which used to be the special residence of the King. On the left is a file of buildings called the Chaulakhi, built by the royal barber and sold to his sovereign for four lakhs. Here resided the Begum and her chief ladies, and in the days of the Mutiny the rebel Queen here held her court. In one of the stables nigh at hand were confined the British captives who were taken from hence to be cruelly murdered. Passing onward, we come to another great gateway which leads to a fine open square, the buildings round which were occupied chiefly by ladies of the harem. A little beyond this we reach a building known as Kaiser Pasand, or Cæsar's Pleasure, surmounted

by a gilt semi-circle and hemisphere : in it three English
ladies and two Englishmen were confined during the Mutiny,
and from it led to be brutally massacred with the other captives. Opposite the door of the Kaisar Bagh is the monument which marks the spot where the foul deed was perpetrated. Raja Lal Singh, a great and influential landlord,
followed the prisoners to the fatal scene and mounted one
of the gates of the Kaisar Bagh, since destroyed, in order to
better feast his eyes on the dying agonies of the victims.
After the Mutiny he had been received back into favour,
his rebellion was condoned by the amnesty, and he must
have persuaded himself that the memory of his deed had
faded away, when justice overtook him. His confidential
servants turned against him, and thus link after link, a
wonderful chain of circumstantial evidence developed
itself and brought home his guilt. Two years after the commission of his crime, on the very spot on which it was committed, he was hanged.

From the Kaisar Bagh we drove to the Farad Bakhsh
Palace, which was for many years the Royal residence.
S'adat Ali Khan, the half brother to Asuf-ud-daulah, purchased the part which overhangs the river from the French
adventurer, Claude Martin, and added the rest. A spacious
throne-room was set apart for Royal Durbars. At the
accession of a new King the Resident used to place him on
the throne, and then present to him a *nazar* to show that the
British acknowledged his Government. A fair pilgrim who
visited Lucknow half a century ago has described the ceremony :

" The King went into the next apartment, where the Resident,
with all due form, having taken off the King's turban, placed the
crown upon his head, and he ascended the *musnud*."

" I was standing next to the Resident and the Prime Minister,
when, during a part of the ceremony, a shower of precious stones
was thrown over us. I looked at the Resident and saw him move

his arm to allow the valuables that had fallen upon him to drop to the ground ; I imitated his example by moving my scarf, on which some were caught ; it would have been *infra dig.* to have retained them ; they fell to the ground and were scrambled for by the natives ; the shower consisted of emeralds, rubies, pearls, etc., etc."

After the ceremony was over, the lady visited the zenana of the King, and writes thus to a lady friend :

" But the present King's wives were superbly dressed and looked like creatures of the Arabian Tales. Indeed, one (Taj Mahal) was so beautiful, that I could think of nothing but Lalla Rookh in her bridal attire. I never saw any one so lovely, either black or white. Her features were perfect, and such eyes and eyelashes I never beheld before. She is the favourite Queen at present, and has only been married a month or two ; her age, about fourteen ; and such a little creature, with the smallest hands and feet, and the most timid, modest look imaginable. You would have been charmed with her, she was so graceful and fawn-like. Her dress was of gold and scarlet brocade, and her hair was literally strewed with pearls, which hung down upon her neck in long single strings, terminating in large pearls, which mixed with and hung as low as her hair, which was curled on each side her head in long ringlets, like Charles the Second's beauties. On her forehead she wore a small gold circlet, from which depended and hung, half way down, large pearls interspersed with emeralds. Above this was a paradise plume, from which strings of pearls were carried over the head, as we turn our hair. Her earrings were immense gold rings, with pearls and emeralds suspended all round in large strings, the pearls increasing in size. She had a nose-ring also with large round pearls and emeralds ; and her necklaces, etc., were too numerous to be described. She wore long sleeves, open at the elbow ; and her dress was a full petticoat with a tight body attached, and open only at the throat. She had several persons to bear her train when she walked ; and her women stood behind her couch to arrange her head-dress, when, in moving, her pearls got entangled in the immense robe of scarlet and gold she had thrown around her. This beautiful creature is the envy of all the other wives, and the favourite at present of both the king and his mother, both of whom have given her titles."

LUCKNOW

From the Farad Bakhsh we drive to the Shah Najif, which was built in 1814 by Ghazi-ud-din Haidar, and it is now his mausoleum. It is a white mosque, with an immense dome, of no architectural worth. Inside are some quaint interesting pictures of the Nawabs of Oude and the lights of their harem. The Shah Najif is chiefly interesting to the traveller on account of its being the scene of a most stubborn and critical struggle in Sir Colin Campbell's first relief of Lucknow. After fighting every inch of ground from the first streak of dawn, our troops reached it as the afternoon was waning. It barred the way to the Residency. Sir Colin Campbell determined to carry it before nightfall, and Peel, who has won a high place in the bead-roll of England's heroes, brought up his Naval brigade and placed his 24-pounders, mortars and battery before the mosque. " For three hours the bombardment lasted, and no impression was made on the stout walls. For three hours the Shah Najif sent forth a perennial stream of fire but to be checked by our heavy guns. To remain was sheer death. To retreat by the narrow defile blocked by troops was out of the question. The moment was decisive. Colin Campbell collecting the 93rd around him said unto them, ' I had no intention of employing you again to-day, but the Shah Najif must be taken. The artillery cannot drive the enemy out, so you must with the bayonet.' " [1] Thus spoke the old chief, and he stirred the spirit and soul of every man by telling them that he would lead them himself. Peel, manning again all his guns, redoubled his fire. Under cover of this heavy cannonade the 93rd advanced, and " the grey-haired veteran of many fights rode, with his sword drawn, at their head. Keen was his eye as when in the pride of youth he led the stormers at Sebastian. They went

[1] *Selections from the Letters, Despatches, and other State Papers preserved in the Military Department of the Government of India,* Edited by George W. Forrest. Vol. ii., Lucknow (Introduction, p. 303).

on steadily till before them towered a wall twenty feet high, from whose parapet and countless loopholes came in blasts a storm of musket balls. Many fell. The assailants replied to their slayers with musketry yet with little effect, and no ladders were available for escalading the ramparts. Nothing to be done but to break them. Peel poured his broadsides into the stout massive walls. But no impression was made on the solid masonry. Never did English soldiers and sailors distinguish themselves more than on this afternoon. They worked the guns, though every moment many were killed and more were wounded. But while their own losses were terrible, they could inflict but little in return. They were being destroyed by bullets and that was all. Day was fast turning into night. The rocket tubes were brought up, and while they discharged their fiery missiles into the building, Peel, with the reluctance of a brave man, slowly withdrew his guns. At this moment fifty Highlanders, creeping stealthily through the brushwood, guided by Sergeant Paton of the regiment, reached a rent in the wall which Paton had discovered. A soldier was pushed up with some difficulty. He reported that no enemy could be seen. Several men immediately followed. A company of sappers were sent for, who quickly arriving enlarged the opening and more Highlanders entered. The small party pushing on gained the main gateway and threw it open for their comrades. The white dresses of the last of the garrison were just seen gliding away amidst the rolling smoke in the dark shadows of the night." [1]

Midway between the Shah Najif and the Kaisar Bagh is the mess house, a strongly built plain house which at the time of Sir Colin's advance was defended by a ditch twelve feet broad and scarped with masonry; beyond that there

---

[1] *Selections from the Letters, Despatches and other State Papers preserved in the Military Department of the Government of India.* Edited by George W. Forrest Vol. ii., Lucknow (Introduction, p. 303).

was a loopholed wall. Sir Colin, in order to save his infantry, had determined to use his guns as much as possible,
and it was after the building had been battered for about
three hours, and the musketry fire of the enemy had begun to
slacken, that the Chief, thinking it might be stormed " without much risk," gave the order to advance. The storming
party consisted of a company of the 90th Foot, under
Captain Wolseley and a picquet of her Majesty's 53rd under
Captain Hopkins, supported by Major Barnston's battalion
of detachments, under Captain Guise, Her Majesty's 83rd
Foot, and some of the Punjab Infantry under Lieutenant
Powell. The mess house was carried immediately with a
rush, and by order of the chief, Lieutenant Roberts,
assisted by Sir David Baird and Captain Hopkins, planted,
under a shower of bullets, a regimental colour on one of its
turrets to show Outram and Havelock how far they had
advanced. Twice was it shot down. " Notwithstanding,
I managed," writes Lord Roberts, " to prop it up a third
time on the turret, and it was not again hit, though the
enemy continued to fire at it for some time." The troops
then pressed forward with great vigour and lined the wall
separating the mess house from the Moti Mahal. Here the
enemy made their last stand. Captain Wolseley sent for
some sappers, who coming up made openings in the wall
through which the troops poured and attacked the network
of buildings within. The rebels fought stubbornly, but they
were driven at the point of the bayonet from room to room,
and after the lapse of some time thrust forth from the vast
enclosure. " The relieving forces and garrison were now
separated by only twenty-five yards, but an iron tempest
swept across the open road." Colonel Napier and Lieutenant
Sitwell were wounded in running the gauntlet of fire, but
Outram and Havelock crossed over unhurt to the outside
wall of the mess house enclosure. An opening was quickly
made by the sappers through which they entered. On the

sward sloping down from the mess house stood Colin Campbell, and a blaze of shot and musketry from the Kaisar Bagh rose upon them as the three veterans met. " This was a very cordial meeting," wrote Hope Grant, " and a cordial shaking of hands took place. On Outram privation had not told so heavily, but the hand of death was on Havelock, though he lighted up a little on being told for the first time that he was Sir Henry." Loud rang the cheers as the news spread along from post to post that the three Generals had met. " The relief of the besieged garrison had been accomplished." In these few terse words their Commander-in-Chief announced the accomplishment of a brilliant achievement, guided by a master hand, and brought to a successful close by the pluck of the British soldier. " Every man in the force," wrote Sir Colin, " had exerted himself to the utmost, and now met with his reward."

After leaving the Shah Najif we drove to the Secunder Bagh (Alexander Garden), which was the scene of one of the most stubborn and sanguinary contests during the mutiny. It is a high-walled enclosure about one hundred yards square, with bastions at the angles and carefully loopholed. In the centre was a two-storied house which Wajid Ali built for one of his ladies, Sikandar Mahal. Sir Colin Campbell did not use the language of exaggeration when he wrote, " There never was a bolder feat of arms than the storming of Secunder Bagh." The enemy finding escape impossible, fought with the courage of despair and the fury of religious hate. " A din of hideous noises rose into the air, the rattle of musketry : the curses, and yells of sepoys, the fierce cry of the British soldier : ' Remember Cawnpore, boys ! ' " Next morning the bodies of two thousand sepoys, dressed in their old uniforms, lay in heaps. And now where curses and yells and the rattle of musketry and cries of death sounded : silence.

LUCKNOW

From the Secunder Bagh we proceed to the fantastic pile of buildings which the French adventurer, Claude Martin, erected as a residence for himself. Martin was a native of the city of Lyons, and served under Lally in the regiment of Loraine. After Chandernagore was taken by Clive he entered the service of the East India Company, and rose to the rank of Captain. He then entered the service of the Nawab of Oude, but was allowed by the Company to retain his rank and enjoy promotion. The Marquis of Hastings, who, when Governor-General, visited Lucknow (October, 1814), writes :

" The house, built in the English style, stands upon a gentle elevation with some extent of lawn about it. On returning to Constantia I had the opportunity of considering that mansion. It was erected by General Martyn, a native of Lyons in France, who came to India as a private soldier. Having got into the service of Asoph-oo-Dowlah, he distinguished himself by his talents so as to obtain rapid promotion ; but his strict accuracy to punctuality in all pecuniary concerns was more beneficial to him. His character in that respect became so established that the natives who had amassed money and dreaded the rapacious gripe of the sovereign, entrusted their riches to the care of General Martyn. Such amplitude of funds enabled him to take advantage of many favourable opportunities, and to make many advantageous speculations, so that he gathered extraordinary wealth. He expended some of it in erecting this house on a plan entirely his own. The idea of it was probably taken from those castles of pastry which used to adorn desserts in former days. The mansion consisted of three stories gradu-ally diminishing in the size of the square, so as to leave to the two upper stories a broad space between the apartments and the parapet which covered the wall of the story below it. This was for the purpose of defence, with a view to which the building was constructed. The doors of the principal floor were plated with iron, and each window was protected by an iron grate. Loopholes from passages above gave the means of firing in perfect security upon any persons who should force their way into these lower apartments. The spiral stone staircases were blocked

235

at intervals with iron doors ; in short, the whole was framed for protracted and desperate resistance. The parapets and pinnacles were decorated with a profusion of plaster lions, Grecian gods, and Chinese figures, forming the most whimsical assemblage imaginable. Still, the magnitude of the building, with its cupolas and spires, gave it a certain magnificence."

Leaving the Martinière, there is yet one spot sacred to Englishmen to be visited before quitting Lucknow. It is the tomb of Havelock. A lofty obelisk marks his resting-place :

" On the low plain by the Alum Bagh," wrote a gallant soldier, " they made his humble grave ; and Campbell and Outram, and Inglis, and many a stout soldier who had followed him in all his headlong march, and through the long fatal street, were gathered there to perform the last rites to one of England's noblest dead. As long as the memory of great deeds, and high courage, and spotless self-devotion is cherished amongst his countrymen, so long will Havelock's lonely tomb in the grove beneath the scorching Eastern sky, hard by the vast city, the scene alike of his toil, his triumph and his death, be regarded as one of the most holy of the many holy spots where her patriot soldiers lie."

X

CAWNPORE

THE story of Cawnpore is as tragic as the tale of the last agonies of the Athenian host in Sicily, and it will be of interest to Englishmen as long as we care to remember the story of our people. Some of our Indian administrators would like to destroy all memory of that great agony.of our race, the Indian Mutiny. But time cannot utterly destroy the written records of great events or the theatre of their enactment. The ridge at Delhi, the Lucknow Residency, and the Ghat at Cawnpore are the witnesses of that world-wide tragedy which the flow of centuries will not wipe from memory. And it would not be well they should be effaced. The story of the Mutiny is the prose epic of our Indian Empire, and those who read it in the right spirit will find something beyond cruel atrocities, exciting adventures, or battle scenes. And nowhere surely do the lessons which the Indian Mutiny convey speak with a clearer and nobler voice than they speak at the Residency at Lucknow and the ill-fated Ghat at Cawnpore.

The city of Cawnpore, forty miles south-west of Lucknow, lies on the south bank of the Ganges which formed from very ancient times the frontier defence of the people of Oude and Bengal against their northern neighbours. When Clive decided to maintain and strengthen Oude as a friendly state interposed between Bengal and Northern India, he selected Cawnpore on account of its advanced and com-

manding position as the best station in the Nawab of
Oude's dominions to canton the brigade lent to him subject
to a subsidy for the protection of the frontier. In 1801,
when Cawnpore was comprehended within the limits of the
Company's powers, it became the frontier station of the time,
and attained the prominent military position of being the
headquarters of the field command of Bengal, a command
which, while including the King's and Company's troops,
artillery, cavalry and infantry, amounted to 40,000 effectives.
The advance of our frontier to the north, however, occasioned
a revisal of our military position, and Cawnpore was most
unwisely denuded of its European troops. In the spring of
1857 sixty-one European artillerymen with six guns were the
only representatives of the English army at Cawnpore. And at
Cawnpore resided the pretender to the honours of the Mahratta Peshwa. The native troops consisted of the 1st, 53rd
and 56th Native Infantry, the 2nd Cavalry, and the native
gunners attached to the battery, about 3,000 in number.
Most of these men had been recruited from the neighbouring
province of Oude, whose annexation had touched their
pride and affected their interests. It only required a single
act of imprudence—the greased cartridges which roused
their caste prejudices—to drive them to mutiny. In May,
1857, the officer in command of the Cawnpore division was
Major-General Sir Hugh Wheeler, K.C.B., who had for upwards of fifty years been attached to the Bengal army,
had served with it in quarters and on the field : who had
fought and bled in its ranks, who had a pride in the courage
and devotion of the sepoy and a thorough knowledge of his
language and mode of life. But no European can completely gauge the feelings and passions of an Oriental.
General Wheeler visited the lines daily and had long con-
versations with the men in the hope of maintaining their
confidence and of allaying the feverish excitability which had
arisen on account of the belief that their religion was being en-

dangered by the use of defiled cartridges. The men conversed with the General and his son, his *aide-de-camp*, without reserve and without any sign of sullenness, but their fears were not allayed nor their anxiety lessened. On June 3 General Wheeler reported to the Governor-General— "All quiet, but subject to constant fits of excitement." At a late hour that evening he despatched another message to Lord Canning. "Sir Henry Lawrence having expressed some uneasiness, I have just sent him by *dâk gharries* out of my small force two officers and fifty men, Her Majesty's 84th foot; any conveyance for more not available. This leaves me weak, but I trust holding my own until more Europeans arrive."

This was the last message that reached Lord Canning from Sir Hugh Wheeler and it was worthy of the gallant soldier. He had at a comrade's call denuded his own scanty command, though every day brought him fresh reports of the mutineers' intentions to surround him. The very evening that he sent forth fifty men to the aid of Henry Lawrence news reached him that an outbreak of the cavalry was imminent, so he issued orders that the women and non-combatants should assemble within the entrenchment, and that night about eight hundred souls went to their prison-grave. Of these about four hundred were women and children. To guard them there were about two hundred English soldiers of all arms, eighty officers, a few civilians and a small body of loyal sepoys.[1]

The places where the women and children assembled were two large barracks, formerly the hospital barracks of a dragoon regiment, and at the time occupied by the depôt of Her Majesty's 32nd Regiment consisting of the invalids, and women and children of the regiment. They were single-

---

[1] *Selections from the Letters, Despatches and other State Papers preserved in the Military Department of the Government of India*, Edited by George W. Forrest. Vol. ii., Lucknow (Introduction, p. 154).

storied buildings, intended each for the accommodation of a company of one hundred men ; one of them was thatched and both were surrounded by a flat-roofed arcade or verandah. The walls were of brick, and the usual out-offices were attached to the building. In order that they might resist a sudden attack a trench was dug around these barracks and the earth thrown up on the outside so as to form a parapet about five feet high, and they were armed at their principal points by artillery. Ten guns constituted the sole defence by artillery of the entrenchment, and a mud wall, not even bullet proof at the crest, was its sole bulwark. A stately church now marks the site where the hospital stood, and a row of pillars indicate what may be called the line of fortifications. As we stood at the door of the church one December morning, we saw in the plain beyond the thin red line of the British soldiers, and the drums and fifes sent forth a lively tune. Looking out in the early morning —the morning of Sunday, June 7,—the besieged saw the enemy busy erecting batteries. Some hours after sunrise they opened fire. Hour by hour the fire grew more severe and dangerous as the enemy got their guns into position. " All through this first weary day the shrieks of the women and children were terrific ; as often as the balls struck the walls of the barracks, their wailings were heart-breaking, but after the initiation of that first day they had learnt silence, and never uttered a sound except when groaning from the horrible mutilations they had to endure. When night sheltered them, our cowardly assailants closed in upon the entrenchments, and harassed us with incessant volleys of musketry." Men, women, and children fell victims to the enemy's fire. But the survivors were more to be pitied than the dead. The pressure of famine became every day more severe. " All were reduced to the monotonous and scanty allowance of one meal a day, consisting of a handful of split peas and a handful of flour, certainly not more than half a pint together, for the daily ration." Now and then the scanty fare was increased by some horse-soup, and it became a more cherished object to shoot a horse than its rider. " One day a strange dog approached the entrench-ment. The cur had wandered from the sepoy barrack, and every possible blandishment was employed by my men to tempt the canine adventurer into the soup-kettle. Two or three minutes subsequently to my seeing him doubtfully trotting across the open, I was offered some of his semi-roasted fabric, but that, more scrupulous than others, I was obliged to decline." Not far from the church is the only well from which the besieged could procure water. The masonry bears marks of the innumerable bullets which struck it—for the enemy invariably fired grape upon the spot as soon as any person made his appearance, or at night if they heard the creaking of the tackle. The frame work of beam and brick which protected the drawers was soon shot away. The machinery went next, and the buckets were thenceforward hauled up hand over hand from a depth of more than sixty feet. As we stood at the well, we thought of John Mackillop of the Civil Service, one of England's authentic heroes. Veiling devotion under a jocose pretence of self-depreciation, he told his friends that, though no fight-ing man, he was willing to make himself useful where he could, and accordingly he took his post at the well. He drew water for the women and children as often as he could, but his tenure of office was of short duration. It was less than a week after he had undertaken this self-denying ser-vice, when his numerous escapes were followed by a grape-shot wound in the groin, and speedy death. Disinterested even in death, his last words were an earnest entreaty that " somebody would go and draw water for a lady to whom he had promised it." The soldiers could not bear to hear the cry of the thirsty children, and at the cost of many heroic lives it was procured. Captain Thomson, one of the survivors of the siege, writes : " I have seen the children of my brother officers sucking the pieces of old water-bags, putting scraps of canvas and leather straps into the mouth to try and get a single drop of moisture upon their parched lips." On the eighth day of the siege a shell filled with combustible materials settled in the thatch of the hospital, and the whole structure was burnt. Then two hundred women and children had to pass twelve days and nights in the trenches upon the bare ground. Many of them were delicately nurtured ladies, who had never known what privation was. But the hour of danger proved their heroic worth. They uttered no cry of despair. They handed round the ammunition, encouraged the men to the uttermost, and with tender solicitude attended to the wounded. Kindly death came to some, and put an end to their toil and sorrow. A single shell killed and wounded several of them who were seated in the ditch. Mistress White was walking with a twin child at either shoulder, and her husband by her side. The same ball slew the father, broke both elbows of the mother, and severely injured one of the orphans. " I saw her afterwards," writes Captain Thomson, " in the mainguard lying upon her back, with the two children, twins, laid one at each breast, while the mother's bosom refused not what her arms had no power to administer." Day by day the number of the garrison grew less while the number of the enemy increased. The rebels made a determined assault on the entrenchments, and were driven back by the heroic defenders. They then determined to treat with the English. Reduced to the last extremity, the small remnant of British troops made terms securing a safe passage down the river for the women and children and their companions. It was the only resource. The treaty was made with Nana Sahib, the adopted son of the last Peshwa, whose claim to the pension settled on the Sovereign of the Mahrattas Lord Dalhousie rightly disallowed. No suspicion of treachery crossed the minds of the troops, because the Nana had cultivated the society of Englishmen and had showered his civilities upon them. It was to him that Sir Hugh Wheeler in the hour of

TEMPLE OF ŚIVA—CAWNPORE.

distress applied for assistance, but at the moment of the Mutiny he put himself at the head of the rebels.

Leaving the church we pass the ground traversed by that body of men, women and children in their march to the

243

ghat, where took place the foul massacre. Above the ghat is a temple dedicated to cruel Śiva. But his fane is fast falling into ruins. Seated on the steps of the temple it is hard to realize that historical tragedy. All around is so calm and peaceful. No sound breaks the stillness of the air. Not a breath of air ruffles the broad waters of the Ganges. A country boat is floating down the stream, and the wide white sails catch the golden rays of the sun as it rises above the horizon this fresh December morning. It was the fiery month of June forty-five years ago, when the small band who had so heroically defended the entrenchments embarked on the boats drawn up on the long sandbank which stretches below us. As soon as the last man was on board, the word " Off " was given—a welcome sound after a weary month of hardship and imprisonment. But the command fell on traitorous ears. A blast of a bugle was heard, and at the signal the crew leaped into the water and waded towards dry ground. Before they quitted the boats, they had secreted burning charcoal in the straw roofs, and now they burst forth into a flame. From every bush that lined the bank came forth a deadly shower of bullets, and from the house to our left, where we see an English child playing, two guns poured forth a storm of grape. The men tried to push the boats into mid-current, but all in vain. Then was witnessed a scene without its parallel in history or fiction. " Some of the boats presented a broadside to the guns, others were raked from stern to stem by the shot. Volumes of smoke from the thatch somewhat veiled the full extent of the horrors of that morning. All who could move were speedily expelled from the boats by the heat of the flames. Alas ! the wounded were burnt to death : one mitigation only there was to their horrible fate—the flames were terribly fierce, and their intense sufferings were not protracted. Wretched multitudes of women and children crouched behind the boats, or waded out into the deeper

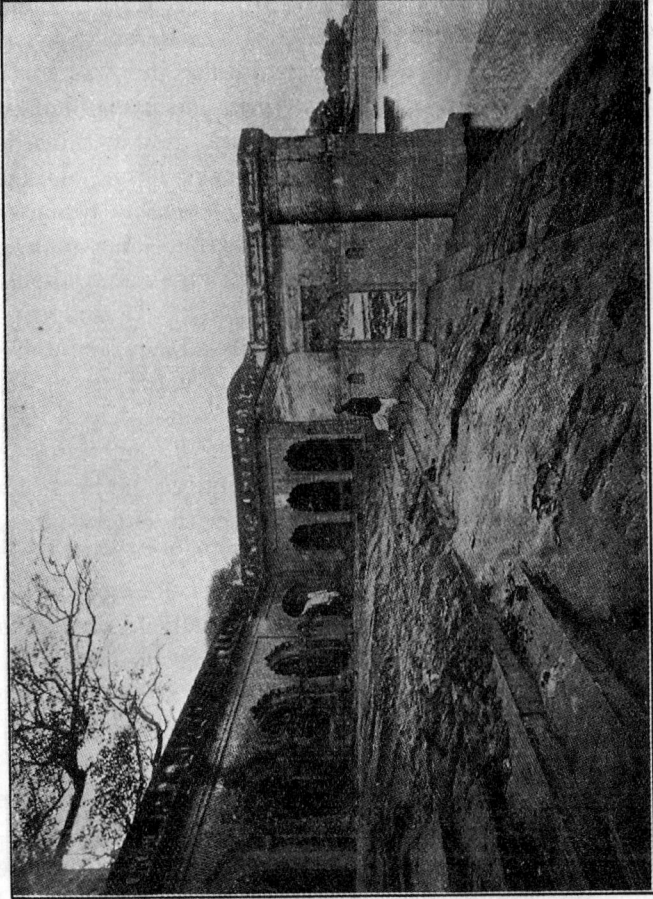

THE MASSACRE GHAT, CAWNPORE.

245

water, and stood up to their chins in the river to lessen the probability of being shot." The troopers drawn up near the temple then plunged into the water, and sabred those whom the bullets spared. At length two hundred women and children were all that were left of the heroic garrison. And they were led back along the road which they had come, past the entrenchments which their husbands had so valiantly defended, past their old homes, now in ruins, to the pavilion of the Maharajah, who, after reviewing his captives, ordered them to be taken to the Assembly Rooms—the scene of many a former festive gathering—and confined there. On July 1 he ordered them to be removed to a house which had been occupied by a native clerk. It comprised two rooms twenty feet long and ten broad, and a number of dark closets which had been intended for the use of servants, and an open court some fifteen feet square. Here for a fortnight in July were confined these tender women and delicate children. They had no furniture, no beds, not even straw to lie upon. They were fed with only one meal a day, consisting of coarse bread and dhall. On July 15 news reached Cawnpore that Havelock's victorious army was within a day's march of the city. A Council, over which the Nana presided, was held and it was resolved that the prisoners must be slain. A stern retribution the leading rebels knew would be exacted by the British troops for the innocent blood already shed, and many who had aided and abetted their chief dreaded their recognition by some of the prisoners who had long resided at Cawnpore. Having decided that all the captives should be put to death the assembly dispersed. That evening at 6 p.m. the women and children were hacked to pieces by five ruffians of the Nana's guard. When darkness, as darkness itself and as the shadow of death, fell, the groans ceased and " the doors of the buildings were closed." Over the events of that wicked night a gloomy mist still hangs, unpenetrated and for ever

VIEW FROM THE RIVER, BENARES.

247

unpenetrable. Three hours after the break of day the doors were opened and the bodies removed and thrown into a well hard by.[1]

From the ghat we drive to the Memorial Gardens. We enter the iron gates, and walk up the broad path lined with noble trees. The grass is as trim and green as an English lawn, and the beds are bright with flowers, and the road is lined with bushes of yellow and dark crimson roses. The air is sweet with scent of orange flowers. Slowly we mount the steps, and read the solemn words engraved on the marble pedestal which covers the fatal well :—" Sacred to the Perpetual Memory of a Great Company of Christian People, chiefly Women and Children." The ugly Gothic memorial and the somewhat meretricious figure of an angel in white marble mars the solemnity of the spot. As in the Coliseum at Rome, the only symbol above that well should have been the symbol of a great agony, the symbol of the Cross, the symbol of the faith in which these women who lie quiet and undisturbed in the well beneath lived and died. " And it was said unto them that they should rest yet for a little season."

---

[1] *Selections from the Letters, Despatches, and other State Papers preserved in the Military Department of the Government of India.* Edited by George W. Forrest. Vol. ii., Lucknow (Introduction).

XI

BENARES

IN India, far more than in any part of Europe, even
Italy, the life of the present is imposed upon the
strata of successive past generations. Vedic, Brahminic,
Buddhist, and Muslim civilizations have flourished and decayed on nearly the same spot, and we find a city like
Benares surviving all revolutions, and remaining a centre
of commercial and religious life. It is impossible to tell
when the Hindus began to build temples and tanks and
ghats by the broad waters of the Ganges, and Benares became the centre of Hindoo religious life. It was at an early
stage in the world's history when men began to worship the
fertilising power of a stream and to deify the beneficent gifts
of nature. The beautiful goddess Ganga is the heroine of
many a Hindu mythological legend. She is intimately
connected with Śiva, the chief deity of Benares, and the
River Ganga is represented falling from his head. Śiva is
Time, the Sun, Fire, the destroyer, the generator. But it is
as the generator he is worshipped at Benares. The temple
which attracts the most worshippers and receives the highest
meed of honour is dedicated to him, and his image is a plain
lingam. Before it is the kneeling Bull, Nandin the gladdener.
Moore, in his Hindu Pantheon, writes :—" As the God of
Justice, which character he shares with Yama and other
deities, he rides a bull, the symbol of divine justice." It is,
however, the common symbol of the Phallic worship, as re-

presented in the legend of Europa. It was for this reason that the Jews regarded the making of a golden calf as a deadly sin. The worship of the Bull was a part of the fetish worship of the Egyptians, and to make a calf was to relapse into the foul rites of their old masters. And the Lord said unto Moses, " Go, get thee down ; for thy people which thou broughtest out of the land of Egypt have corrupted *themselves*. They have turned aside quickly out of the way which I commanded them ; they have made them a molten calf, and have worshipped it, and have sacrificed thereunto, and said, these *be* thy gods, O Israel, which have brought thee up out of the land of Egypt." Serpents are bound in Śiva's hair, are round his neck, wrists, waist, arms, and legs. A crescent on his forehead or his hair is common in images or pictures of him. The male creator has from the earliest times been identified with the Sun, and the female with the crescent Moon ; and one of the symbols of this celestial union of the sexes was a Sun lying within the Moon's crescent. The crescent is the prominent symbol in all the lingam temples in India. It was the chief symbol of the Kaaba at Mecca, where the obscene worship of the black stone roused the sensitive mind of Muhammad. The Muhammadans adopted the symbol of the old cult, but against the cult like their founder they have waged ruthless war. Mahmud of Ghazni broke to pieces the lingam at Somnath, one of the most sacred shrines belonging to the worship : Aurangzeb at Benares destroyed the old temple of Śiva, and built upon its site a mosque.

The rays of the setting sun fall on the gilded tower of the temple of Visvesvara, the Lord of all, as we approach the shrine. Over the narrow doorway which leads to the temple is a small figure of Ganeśa, the God of Prudence and Policy, first-born of Śiva and Parvati. " He is represented with an elephant's head, an emblem of sagacity ; and is frequently attended by a rat, sometimes riding on one, the conduct of that animal being esteemed by the Hindus as peculiarly marked by wisdom and foresight : he has generally four hands, but sometimes six or eight or only two. He is invoked by a Hindu, I believe, of all sects, in the outset of any business ; if he build a house, an image of Ganesa is previously propitiated and set upon or near the spot ; if he write a book, Ganeśa is saluted at its commencement, as he is also at the top of a letter ; beginning a journey Ganeśa is implored to protect him, and for the accommoda-

GOLDEN TEMPLE.

tion of travellers his image is occasionally seen on the roadside, especially where two roads cross ; but sometimes it is little else than a stone rudely chiseled into something like an elephant's head, with oil and red ochre daubed over it, decorated perhaps with a chaplet of flowers by some pious neighbour or traveller." Over the shops of bankers and other tradesmen the figure of Ganeśa is often seen. There is no deity so often addressed as the God of Wisdom and Prudence. He bears a resemblance to Janus, " the god who presided over the beginning of all undertakings , the first libations of wine and wheat were offered to him and a preface of all prayers was addressed to him." Passing through the doorway we enter an enclosure, where several shrines are visible. Worshippers, male and female, are paying their devotions at them. A half-naked Brahman, with clear-cut intellectual features and a bearing which denotes the breeding of centuries, pauses a few moments before one of the minor shrines, and then proceeds to the symbol of Śiva, and bows with deep reverence before it. He then rises and gives to the priest his offering, a few pieces of silver, some grain and rice, and he rings one of the bells suspended from the roof to attract the attention of the god. Then comes a woman with a bright graceful robe thrown round her almond-coloured body so as to reveal its graceful contour, her jet black hair is tightly fastened by a roughly ornamented comb, and ornaments of gold and silver are on her wrists. With wonderful grace she carries a large plate containing bright flowers and rice and grain as emblems of fertility. Her whole soul seems overawed as she prostrates herself before the deity and invokes him for the blessing of fruitfulness. The temples of Visvesvara are not attractive from a purely architectural point of view. The carving upon them is poor, but the dome and tower glittering in the sun is effective. Leaving the enclosure we come to a large collection of lingams raised upon a platform, and into the wall are built many small idols. They are supposed to have been taken from the old temple which Aurangzeb destroyed, whose remains form a large portion of the western wall of the mosque. The mosque itself is chiefly interesting on account of the Muhammadans having done what they had so often done in other parts of India— used the pillars of the Hindoo fane for their own shrine.

Between the mosque and the temple of Visvesvar, situated in a quadrangle surrounded by a handsome colonnade is the Gyan Kup, or well of knowledge. Here Śiva is supposed to reside. The quadrangle is filled with mendicants, pilgrims, aristocratic Brahmans, women and children, and

A FAKIR OF BENARES.

cows, all huddled together. There is the Vairagi, with his necklaces and beads, the revolting looking Naga with long curls on his head, a *lungoti* round the waist, and his body coloured to an ashy tint. A crowd is gathered around a sleek looking man in a red dress, who is accompanied by a bull covered with a long shift adorned with shells. A picture of Mahadev on the turban marks the Jokri sect, and he is singing an account of the wars of Mahadev to extract alms from the faithful. Near the platform of the well stands a man, shaven from head to foot, with his body rubbed with ashes. A piece of red cloth is round his waist, and in one hand he carries a vessel with a spout, in the other a bamboo at the top of which a piece of red cloth is tied. This is the *danda* or one who keeps a *dand* (bamboo stick) with him. The vessel is his sole possession in the world. He uses it for bathing, drinking, and eating. Silver and gold he scorns. He buys cooked food from Brahmans ; for to cook it himself would deprive him of a fragment of time which must be wholly spent in the contemplation of the deity. The well is surrounded by a colonnade with handsome pillars, and crowds of pilgrims are pushing forward in order to throw into the stagnant greenish water offerings of flowers. A Brahman draws a silver goblet full of the liquid, and with a look of rapt ecstasy a woman drains the fluid which exhales a foetid smell. The sight is too much for the nerves ; and we move away glad to escape from the greasy men and women and the deafening din of gongs and voices. We come to the figure of a large bull, about seven feet high, cut in stone, dedicated to the God Mahadev, and a little further is a temple dedicated to the same deity. All around are small fanes of no great architectural beauty, but the rich carving, full of life and originality, which adorns them from base to summit well repays study. Leaving these Eastern caskets we come to a small shrine dedicated to Saniscara, or the planet Saturn. The image is a round silver disc, from which hangs an apron to conceal the absence of a body. For seven years Saturn troubles the life of every man who does not worship at his shrine. Near Saturn is a shrine of the good Anapurna, who takes care that none suffer from hunger. She is a very common household deity, and in the Deccan most families include her among their *Dii Penates*. She is represented usually with a ladle in her hand, in the company of Ganeśa, with the lingam of Śiva before him, and the kneeling bull on the other side. The Mahratta matron prays for children to the lingam, to Ganeśa for prudence and propriety of conduct, and to Anapurna for daily bread. Her shrine at Benares was built by one of the Peshwas. It consists of a tower and a dome supported by pillars, between which a bell is hung, which is constantly kept sounding by devout worshippers. The goddess has silver eyes and a necklace of jewels, and wears a mask of gold or burnished copper. The temple stands in the centre of a quadrangle, in each corner of which is a shrine respectively dedicated to the Sun, Ganeśa, Gauri (sankara), and Hanuman, the monkey god; the last being an immediate offspring of the favour of the sun, is regarded as the son of Śiva. The idol representing the sun is seated in a chariot drawn by seven horses, and is surrounded by a halo indicative of the rays of light which he emits from his person in all directions. Near the shrine of Gauri is a stone box meant to contain all the gifts of rice and grain of the pilgrims. Hundreds of the poor are thus daily supplied with food. At the threshold of the temple are seated beggars, with cups in their hands, into which the worshippers, as they enter or depart from the temple, throw small quantities of grain.

Benares is bounded by a road which, though fifty miles in circuit, is never distant from the city more than five kos ($1\frac{1}{2}$ miles) : hence its name Panch-kos Road. All who die within this boundary, be they Brahman or low caste, Muslim or Christian, be they liars, thieves or murderers, are sure of admittance into Śiva's heaven. To tread the Panch-kos Road is one of the great ambitions of a Hindu's life. Even if he be an inhabitant of the sacred

city he must traverse it once in the year to free himself
from the impurities and sins contracted within the holy
precincts. Thousands from all parts of India make the
pilgrimage every year. By the roadside, lined with noble
trees, there are tanks where the pilgrim must perform the
sacred ablutions, and there are numerous shrines to which
he may offer his prayers. The journey must be made on
foot, and the luxury of shoes is not permitted. On the
way the pilgrim must not quarrel or use harsh language,
and he must not give or receive any gift from a friend—
nay, not even a handful of grain nor a cup of water. But
along the last stage he scatters barley on the ground in
honour of Śiva, the emblem of creation. Arrived at the
Manikaranika Ghat, from whence he started, he bathes
in the river, makes an offering of money to the priest in
attendance, and then goes to the temple of Sakshi-Binark,
or the witness-bearing Ganeśa, to have his pilgrimage
attested·and recorded by the deity. The temple stands in
a square, and was built by a Mahratta a little more than a
century ago. Near it is a small shrine dedicated to the
planet Venus, or Sukresvara, where persons come to pray
who wish to have handsome sons. Even on the barren
a fine son is bestowed, and so long as he lives in the sacred
city he passes a happy life, and at death he departs to
Śiva. Aphrodite also had a similar power of granting
beauty. Darkness had begun to fall as we reached the
temple of Venus. Lamps are lit in the shrines, and the
priests sound the bells, not to invite worshippers, but to
inform the world that the deity was about to retire to
rest. We, too, are glad to escape from the filthy smells
and noises and the weird idols of the dark worship of Śiva.
Here are no sensuous charms united to spiritual life, but
all is revolting and material.

At the break of dawn we find ourselves at the Observatory by the riverside, the sun has begun to shine brightly

on the blue waters of the Ganges, and a clear cold wind to blow away the mist which enveloped the city. A broad flight of steps leads to the summit of a huge massive building, a terraced height well suited to the watchers of the stars. The apparatus does credit to the zeal and knowledge of science possessed by the Hindus two centuries ago. There is a mural quadrant, by means of which the sun's greatest declination and the latitude of the place can be ascertained. There is a gigantic gnomon, thirty-six feet long, sloping and pointing to the north pole, which is rightly termed *Yantra-Samrat*, or prince of instruments. On each side of it are arcs of a circle so divided as to act as a sun-dial. Near to the dial is a small mural quadrant, and to the east is a gigantic equinoctial circle made of stone. Then we come to an instrument called *Chakrajantra*. It consists of a circle of iron turning on an axis fastened to two walls, and pointing to the north pole. It was intended to show the declination of any star or planet. Not far from it is an azimuth compass, consisting of an outer and inner wall surrounding a broad pillar. The upper part of both walls is graduated into 360 degrees, and shows the points of the compass with iron spikes to mark the cardinal points. The Observatory at Benares has fallen into neglect and disuse, and we could find no one to explain the use of the instruments. At one time the cool cloisters were thronged with sages, who strove to read the destinies of man in the books of the heavens, and calculated the celestial changes on which the Hindu festivals depend. Tavernier has given us a description of the Observatory in its palmy days, when two of the young princes of Jeypore were pupils there, studying astronomy under skilful pundits. He writes :

" I saw two of the children of that prince there at school, who had for their masters several Brahmins, who taught them to write and read in a language peculiar to the idolaters' priests, and far different from the speech of the common people. Enter-

257   S

ing the court of that Colledge, and casting my eyes up, I discovered two galleries that went round the court, where I saw the
two princes sitting, attended by several petty lords and Brahmins,
who made several mathematical figures upon the ground with
chalk. The two princes, seeing me, sent to know who I was ;
and understanding I was a Frank, they sent for me up, and asked
me several questions touching Europe and particularly touching
France. Whereupon there being two globes in the room which
the Hollanders had given the Brahmins, I showed the princes
where France lay upon one of them."

After leaving the Observatory we entered a boat to float
down the stream. We had often read and heard of the
delights of seeing Benares from the river, but we had no
conception of the beauty and infinite variety of the views
which unfold themselves to the eye. We see the large stone
azimuth circle towering above the centre of the Observatory,
and a lovely balcony overhangs the river. With wonderful
skill the projection is covered, as the height increases, with
massive ornaments, and so all sense of instability is avoided.
The sun lights up a long, red sandstone frontage with a
massive gateway flanked by flowers. Near is a picturesque
old temple with a tamarind tree hanging overhead, and a
priest in yellow is seated near telling his beads. Then we
float by a ghat crowded with women and children. How
picturesque they look in their close bodices and pink, purple,
and yellow robes ? The clinging garments reveal their
supple charms as they emerge from the waters, but with
wonderful dexterity their wet garments are swiftly changed
under a large wrapper. It is only the fat and forty who are
awkward. The garments changed, the Brahman priest fixes
the frontal mark, and pronounces a mantra, or sacred
text, for his spiritual daughters. Then we slowly drop
by a long ghat backed by a picturesque terrace, which is
crowded with priests, old and young, dressed in green and
yellow, seated under kiosks and parasols, all busily engaged
retailing chaplets and armlets, and certificates of purifica-

BATHING GHAT, BENARES.

tion to the throngs of pilgrims which crowd the steps. We watch father, wife and little boy being led by two contending priests to the river's brink. The woman throws off the greater part of her clothing as she approaches the water's edge, and hands it to the sleek young Brahman who has got the better of his rival. Then she plunges into the sacred stream. The fat copper urchin is stripped of his gaudy clothes by his stern parent, and handed to the dame, who plunges him, unwilling to be cleansed of his sins, in the sacred waters. Then with considerable dignity the head of the house enters the stream. After thoroughly washing away the sins of years, the family return to the sleek Brahman, who marks their foreheads. The father returns to the water's edge and fills a bottle, which he carries to an aged priest dressed in bright green, seated near, and he, with great solemnity, sets a seal to mark its genuineness. The great object of hope is realized. The pilgrimage to Benares has been made. In some remote village will that bottle be carefully preserved; and round the fire at night will often be told the tale of the wondrous sights seen in the sacred city. Happy is he who makes a pilgrimage to Benares, but thrice happy is he whose soul ebbs away at its sacred stream, and whose body becomes a prey to the flames at the sacred ghat. As we pass it we see the funeral piles and a body by the water's edge ready to be placed on one of them. The rays of the sun light up the graceful spire of the golden temple, and glitter on the stream, and fill the white sails of the small shallops which are swiftly skimming over the water. At the Manikaranika, one of the most sacred of all the ghats, our water pilgrimage comes to an end.

We mount the steps and watch the women bathing in the sacred tank : its fetid water is regarded as a healing balm which will wash away all the sins of the soul. A poor creature whose leprous limbs are fast falling away totters

down the steps. Then he descends into the water and laves
his head and body with the liquid. By the tank are lying
two or three other stricken creatures. Then across the
mind rises a vision of that scene enacted nineteen centuries
ago at the pool of Bethesda. In a niche upon the stairs
is a figure of Vishnu, the preserver—the second person of
the Hindu Trimurti or Triad. Legend states :

" The god Vishnu dug this well with his *discus*, and in the
place of water filled it with perspiration from his own body,
and gave it the name of *chakra pushkarini*. He then proceeded
to its north side and began to practise asceticism. In the meantime, the god Mahadeva arrived, and looking into the well
beheld in it the beauty of a hundred millions of suns, with which
he was so enraptured that he at once broke out into loud praise
of Vishnu ; and in his joy declared that whatever gifts he might
ask of him he would grant. Gratified at the offer Vishnu replied
that his request was that Mahadeva should always reside with
him. Mahadeva, hearing this, felt greatly flattered by it, and
his body shook with delight. From the violence of the motion,
an earring, called, *manikarnika*, fell from his ear into the well.
From this circumstance Mahadeva gave the well the name of
Manckarancka, and endowed it with two properties—the first,
muktikshetra (salvation field), that of bestowing salvation on its
worshippers ; and the second, *turansubhakarni*, that of granting
accomplishment to every good work ; and commanded that it
should be the chief and most efficacious of pilgrimages."

In front of the tank is the temple of Tarkeshwar, or the
god of salvation. If this deity has been propitiated, he
can pour into the ear of the dying Hindu a charm of such
efficacy that it delivers him from misery, and secures for
him an eternity of happiness and joy. The idol is invisible
because it is kept in a cistern filled with water. Above
this temple is a large round slab, called *charan-paduka*,
which projects slightly from the pavement, and in the middle
of it stands a stone pedestal, the top of which is inlaid with
marble. In the centre of the marble are two small flat

objects which are supposed to represent the two feet of Vishnu, and mark the exact spot where he

" Down right into the world's first region threw
His flight precipitant."

The spot is held in great veneration, and multitudes flock to the feet of Vishnu, in the sure hope that it will give them a certain introduction into heaven. Near the sacred spot is a temple containing a hideous figure of Ganeśa, having three eyes, a silver-plated scalp ornamented with a garland of flowers, and an elephant's trunk partially concealed behind a cloth. At the foot of the idol is the figure of a rat, and a small fountain. Leaving this temple we proceed to tread our way homewards through the narrow streets. It is a difficult task on account of the men, women, children, beggars, and bulls sacred to Śiva, which throng the narrow way. The lofty houses richly embellished with galleries, projecting oriel windows, and broad and overhanging eaves keep out the rays of the sun. Under the shadow of the houses, and at the angles of the streets, are shrines covered with flowers, animals, and palm branches, all wrought with sharpness and delicacy, and displaying a wealth of imagination. They were evidently done by men who enjoyed giving play to their genius. · Wide spaces of the houses are covered with deep and rich colour ; no attempt is made at design ; but the pleasure must be derived from the hues alone. The whole street is life, movement, and colour. The shops are bright with brass and copper vessels of all kinds and shapes, some intended for domestic use and others for that of the temple. From the shops of the dyers hang cloths of all colours : brilliant green and rich blue, deep red, and superb yellow. In the cloth merchant's we gaze at bales of costly tissues, and scarves of gold and silver stuff with deep fringed borders beautifully wrought. A little urchin with yellow silk trousers and scarlet coat is trying on a velvet cap largely ornamented with tinsel. After much haggling it is purchased, and the proud parents carry him away. Then a halt is made at a confectioner's. In the front the senior partner is engaged in selling the delicacies ; at the back a very greasy assistant with a black cloth round him is engaged in pouring from huge ladles upon an iron plate a very black mixture, upon which the flies are sitting in myriads. One more dream of life is dispelled. The dainty cookshops, of which one as a boy used to read with hungry delight in the " Arabian Nights," do not exist. Thus observing, we pass through the most unique city in the East.

At evening we drove to the Ashi Ghat and were slowly towed up the river, past the palace of Ramnagar, which crowns the water's edge. Then we set sail and tacked across the stream, narrowly escaping collision with a cotton boat which was swiftly sailing down the stream with her wide saffron sail full set. At the wharf we were courteously met by the secretary of the Maharaja, who escorted us to the Castle. In a fine room paved with marble we met the son of the rajah, who was most courteous. He led us to a marble balcony, which commands a view of surpassing beauty. Below us are the broad blue waters of the Ganges, opposite are the green corn-fields and groves of trees of the most luxuriant kind. Down the stream we see the temples overhanging the waters glowing in the sunlight, and the graceful minarets of the mosque towering to the sky. The sun had set when we re-embarked ; and a thick mist had fallen over the river, but through the mist shone the lights on the Ghats, and seen through the veil of night the houses looked dark and grim. Then suddenly we turn a bend of the stream, and we see vast tongues of fire shooting forth from a pyre. The crackling of the wood breaks the stillness around, and through the red light, perched on some steps are seen the mourners. And

"I felt the wind soft from the land of souls ;
  The old miraculous mountains heaved in sight
  One straining past another, along the shore,
  The way of grand dull Odyssean ghosts
  Athirst to drink the cool blue wine of the seas
  And stare on voyagers."

At dawn we left Benares and drove across a vast green plain of corn covered with fine groves of trees, to Sarnath, to see the old Buddhist relics. This small insignificant village, with its brick houses and squalid huts, is one of the most sacred spots in the world. It is the Jerusalem of millions of beings, for the great tower which rises near it marks the spot where Buddha for the first time "turned the wheel of the law"—that is, where he first preached the doctrines which have supplied spiritual life to millions. "Be pure, be good ; this is the foundation of wisdom ; to restrain desire, to be satisfied with little. He is a holy man who doeth this. Knowledge follows this." Here is the essence of Buddhism, here is its power : and Buddha added : "Go into all lands and preach this gospel ; tell them that the poor and lowly, the rich and high, are all one, and that all castes unite in this religion, as unite the rivers to the sea."[1] Thus the lowest Sudvas or aboriginal was placed on an equal rank and received equal rank with the Brahman and Kshatrya, and the teaching of Buddha, like the teaching of Christ, won the hearts of the people. But as the author of *The Religions of India* points out, the significance of the Church organization in the development of Buddhism should not be under-estimated. "Contrasted with the lack of an organized ecclesiastical corporation among the Brahmans, the Buddhistic Synod, or congregation Sangha exerted a great influence. In different places there would be a spot set apart for the Buddhist Monks. Here they had their monastery buildings, here they lived during the rainy season, from out this place as a

[1] *The Religions of India.* By Edward Washburn Hopkins, 319.

centre the monks radiated through the country, not as lone
mendicants, but as members of a powerful fraternity." At
Sarnath existed a monastery which Hiouen-Thsang, the

DHAMEK TOPE, SARNATH.

Chinese traveller, who visited India about the middle of the
seventh century, has described. He writes :

265

" To the north-east of the river Varana about ten li or so, we come to the *Sangharama* or Lu-ye (stag-desert). Its precincts are divided into eight portions (sections) connected by a surrounding wall. The storied towers with projecting eaves and the balconies are of very superior work. There are fifteen hundred priests in this convent. In the great enclosure is a *vihara* (monastery), about 200 feet high; above the roof is a golden covered figure of the Amra (*An-mo-lo-mango*) fruit. The foundations of the buildings are of stone, and the stairs also; but the towers and niches are of brick. The niches are arranged in the four sides in a hundred successive lines, and in each niche is a golden figure of Buddha. In the middle of the *vihara* is a figure of Buddha made of native copper. It is the size of life, and he is represented as turning the wheel of the law (*preaching*)."

Hiouen-Thsang proceeds to tell us that to the south-west of the monastery was a stone *stupa* or tope, and in front of it a lofty pillar. " The stone is altogether as bright as jade. It is glistening, and sparkles like light; and all those who pray fervently before it see from time to time, according to their petitions, figures with good and bad signs. It was here that Tathâgata, having arrived at enlightenment, began to turn the wheel of the law." A vast tower, called Dhamek, a hundred and ten feet high and ninety feet in diameter at its base, still marks the spot where Buddha first turned the wheel of the law. The lower part up to a height of about forty-three feet, is built of enormous blocks of sandstone, connected together by cramp-irons; but the remainder of the tower is a massive cylinder of brick, which in former times was probably encased in a layer of stucco or stone. The lower part has eight projecting faces, in each of which is a small niche, evidently intended to hold a figure of Buddha. Each niche is encircled with exquisitely carved flowering foliage.[1] Below the niches a triple band of ornament encircles the tower. The broad middle band consists

[1] *History of Indian and Eastern Architecture.* By James Fergusson, p. 67.

entirely of various geometrical figures, the main lines being finely and deeply cut, and the intervening spaces filled with various patterns. The upper band consists of a richly wrought scroll of the lotus plant with only leaves and buds, but the lower bands contain the full-blown flowers, as well as the buds. On one side in the middle of the ornament there is a human figure seated on a lotus flower, and holding two branches of the lotus in his hand. " On each side of him there are three lotus flowers, of which the four nearer ones support pairs of Bahmani geese, while the two farther ones carry only single birds. Over the nearest pair of geese on the right hand of the figure there is a frog. The attitudes of the birds are all good, and even that of the human figure is easy, although formal. The lotus scroll, with its glowing lines of graceful stalk, mingled with tender buds and full blown flowers and delicate leaves, is very rich and very beautiful." [1]

South of the great tower of Dhamek is a lofty ruined mound of solid brickwork. This is the ruin of the *stupa* described by Hiouen-Thsang as " being about three hundred feet high. The foundations are broad, and the buildings high and adorned with all sorts of carved work and with precious substances." Round the tower are small mounds in which excavations made according to the indications of Hiouen-Thsang led to the discovery of the ruin of the celebrated monastery. The excavations also revealed the similarity between the plans of the *viharas* which were erected and those hewn in the rock as at Ajanta. In the former, however, the cells and chapels were arranged round a square court, while in the caves they surrounded a chamber of the same form. It was also discovered that the monastery must have been pulled down after the lapse of several centuries, and rebuilt on the ruins. The final destruction of the large monastery, which took place towards

---

[1] *Archæological Survey of India.* Vol. i. p. 110.

the ninth or tenth century, was, no doubt, sudden and unexpected, for among the calcined beams of the roofs and beneath the ashes have been found, as in Pompeii, household utensils, corn, and remains of wheaten cakes. The monks must have been surprised by their foes, and the conflagration so swift that they had to fly for life as they were preparing their daily food. Many must have perished in the flames. The old tower is all that remains to remind the traveller of the former greatness of the monastery.

The rapid growth and untimely disappearance of Buddhism is a startling religious fact. It lingered in India till the twelfth or thirteenth century and then it vanished from its old home. Just as the faith of Jesus now meets with bare toleration in the sacred city of his Passion, so in nearly every district of India which once the disciples of Sakya Muni visited with the most intense devotion, his very name is now forgotten. At the very spot where he first preached his purer faith, his title the "best Lord," Sárnath, is applied to the God Mahadeva, whose symbol, the *lingam*, is enshrined in the small temple on the bank of the lake, where the Master used to come to wash his beggar's bowl. The cause of its extinction, writes the author of *The Religions of India*, is obvious. "The Buddhist victorious was not the modest and devout mendicant of the early church. The fire of hate, lighted if at all by Buddhism, smouldered till Brahminism, in the form of Hinduism, had begotten a religion as popular as Buddhism, or rather far more popular, for two reasons. Buddhism had no such picturesque tales as those that enveloped with poetry the history of the man-god Krishna. . . . Again, Buddhism in its monastic development had separated itself more and more from the people. Not mendicant monks, urging to a purer life, but opulent churches with fat priests; not simple discourses calculated to awaken the moral and religious consciousness, but subtle arguments on discipline and metaphysics were now what Buddhism represented."

The love of man, the spirit of Buddhism, was dead, and Buddhism crumbled to pieces.

As we drive back to Benares, we skirt the Mrigadava, or Deer Park, which is connected with a poetic legend concerning the great teacher. When Buddha was passing through the innumerable existences which were preparing him for the conditions of human life, he was alone on earth as a king of a herd of deer. The Raja of Benares, who was fond of sport, slaughtered so many of them that Buddha, the king of the deer, remonstrated with him, and engaged to provide the Raja with an antelope daily for his table. The Raja agreed to the proposal, and chance daily decided which animal should be sacrificed for the public good. The lot one day fell upon a hind big with young, but she refused to yield herself to her fate, protesting that her offspring's hour to die could not in common justice have come before it had seen the light of day. She told her sorrow to Buddha. He replied, " Sad indeed ; the heart of the loving mother grieves (*is moved*) for that which is not yet alive (*has no body*). I to-day will take your place and die." Going to the Royal gate (i.e. *the palace*), the people who travelled along the road passed the news along, and said in a loud voice, " That great king of the deer is going now towards the town." The people of the capital, the magistrates and others, hastened to see. The king, hearing of it, was unwilling to believe the news ; but when the gate-keeper assured him of the truth then the king believed it. Then, addressing the deer-king, he said, " Why have you come here ? " The deer-(*king*) replied, " There is a female in the herd big with young, whose turn it was to die ; but my heart could not bear to think that the young, not yet born, should perish so. I have therefore come in her place." The king, hearing it, sighed and said, " I have indeed the body of a man, but am as a deer. You have the body of a deer, but are as a man." Then for pity's sake he released the deer, and no longer required a daily sacrifice. Then he gave up that forest for the use of the deer, and so it was called " the forest given to the deer," and hence its name the " deer-plain " (*or*, wild).

The story of Buddha being the king of the deer represents the spirit of gentleness and love which ran like a golden web through the teaching of the Master " who was so kind." Buddha died in the fifth century. When life was fast ebbing away he said to his disciples weeping around him : " Behold, brethren, I exhort you, saying, transitory are all component things : toil without ceasing." And these were the last words of Buddha. Though dead he yet speaketh. " Better than going to heaven, better than lordship over all the world is the reward of entering the stream of holiness." Great is the contrast between Benares with its shrines dedicated to gods endowed with human lusts and passions, and the ruined mound at Sárnath around which lingers the memory of a pure and noble life, and the echo of sweet and earnest words.

XII

CALCUTTA

THREE days after leaving Madras, about dusk, we came to a low bank running into the sea—such a place as that to which the wounded Arthur was borne in his rent armour.

> " A dark strait of barren land :
> On one side lay the ocean, and on one
> Lay a great water, and the moon was full."

We anchored for the night off the Sunderbunds—those dreary swamps where malaria and tigers reign supreme. Lord Valentia, who visited India at the beginning of last century, wrote :

" To these Sunderbunds the Hindoos resort at this season in immense numbers to perform their ablutions in the Ganges, and many to sacrifice themselves to the alligators, which they effect by walking into the river and waiting till the ferocious animals approach and draw them under ; others perish by the tigers every season, yet the powerful influence of superstition still draws them to the spot."

The next morning we resume our voyage. The low shore stretches before us, steaming and glistening in the rising sun ; and the vast inland sea, covered with native boats whose broad brown sails are filling with light and breeze as they swiftly skim over the waters. The river narrows as we go steaming up it, guided and directed along our tortuous and difficult course by the experienced hand and eye of one of the famous Hooghly pilots. It was in the year

1675 that the Worshipful East India Company wrote to Fort St. George, at Madras, as follows :

"We enorder you to write effectually to your Chief and Councell at the Bay to provide careful young men of about twenty years of age, out of any of the ships in the Companies' Service, with the concent of the comandants, to be trained up as pylotts, but not to be imployed as writers, or on any other marcantile affairs, that thereby the Companies' shipping may with safety be carried up the River Ganges, and send news yearly what you doe therein, and an account of their proficiency and their journalls."

In considerable respect was the Hooghly pilot held, for it was ordered that he "should rank next to our covenanted servants."

Much interest is excited on board as we approach the famous shoal, " James and Mary," so dreaded by mariners in days of old. A good deal of literary and philological ingenuity has been spent in accounting for the name, and many subtle derivations have lost their value by Sir George Birdwood discovering a few years ago, among the ancient records of the India Office, the following entry :

" *The Royal James and Mary* (James II. and Mary of Modena) arrived in Balasore Roads, from the West Coast, in August, with a cargo of red wood, candy, and pepper, which she had taken up in Madras. Coming up the river Hooghly on September 24, 1692, she fell on a bank on this side Tumbolie Point, and was unfortunately lost, being immediately overset and broke her back, with the loss of four or five men's lives." "This ship-wreck "—writes Sir George Birdwood—" of *The Royal James and Mary* is the origin of the name which, I believe, is still a puzzle to some in Calcutta, of the James and Mary Sands."

After leaving the " James and Mary " we steer close to the shore, and pass the fortification of Fulta. A little more than a century ago, when the French fleet was hourly expected at Calcutta, orders were given that at Fulta the chain should every evening be laid across the river—a delightfully primitive state of existence. In the present day large sums of money have to be spent on batteries, heavy guns, and torpedoes, and when the fortifications have been completed, military experts of a new school arise and prove that the whole plan of defence is worthless. It was on December 15, 1756, that Clive arrived at Fulta from Madras, and found Drake and his fellow-fugitives in the ships on board which they had taken refuge when Suraja Dowla besieged and took Fort William.

After leaving Fulta the river again broadens till we come to a broad expanse of water, with some large vessels anchored by the river's bank. This is Budge-Budge, or Buz-Buzia, as it was called in the old days. Those who have studied Orme's great History—the favourite work of that good and brave soldier, Colonel Newcombe—will remember how the English force was surprised at night at Buz-Buzia, and how it was saved from destruction by the gallantry and presence of mind of Clive.

As we advance up the river we find huge mills erected on the river banks—witnesses of the growing prosperity of Calcutta, and we pass some of the stately mansions at Garden Reach, which used, in bygone times, before they were shorn of their splendour, to surprise and delight the eye of the stranger, as he approached the " City of Palaces." When these country seats were first erected it is difficult to decide. Mrs. Fay, whose letters throw much light on Calcutta in the olden days, writes (May 22, 1780) as follows :—

" As you enter Garden Reach, which extends about nine miles below the town, the most interesting views that can possibly be imagined greet the eye. The banks of the river are, as one may say, absolutely studded with elegant mansions, called here, as at Madras, ' garden-houses.' These houses are surrounded by groves and lawns, which descend to the water's edge, and present a constant succession of whatever can delight the eye, or bespeak wealth and elegance in the owners. The noble appearance of the river also, which is much wider than the Thames at London Bridge, together with the amazing variety of vessels continually passing along its surface, add to the beauty of the scene."

When the ex-Nawab of Oude was allowed to settle at Garden Reach, the wealthy owners deserted their noble mansions, and Garden Reach ceased to be a fashionable suburb. The fantastic palace, which that monarch erected on the river side, is fast being pulled down by the syndicate which purchased it, and the land is to be let as sites for mills. Opposite the King of Oude's palace is that lovely park of lawns and walks and noble trees—the Botanical Gardens of Calcutta. A century ago they were founded by Colonel Alexander Kyd, for " the collection of plants indigenous to the country, and for the introduction and acclimatisation of plants from foreign parts." The object of the founder has been fully realized. Trees of the rarest kinds, from Nepal and the Cape, Brazil and Penang, Java and Sumatra, are gathered together in that spot. The mahogany towers there, and the Cuba palms form an avenue like the aisle of some lofty cathedral. Noble mango trees and tamarinds are dotted about the grassy lawns ; and there are stately casuarinas around whose stems are trained climbing plants. There are plantains of vast size and beauty from the Malay Archipelago, and giant creepers from South America. The crimson hibiscus and scarlet passion-flower dazzle the eye, and the odour of the champak and innumerable jessamines float upon the breeze. As Bishop Heber remarked, " The Botanic Gardens would perfectly answer to Milton's idea of Paradise, if they were on a hill instead of a dead flat."

North of the gardens lies Bishop's College, and its smooth green lawns and Gothic buildings recall to mind bright days spent on the banks of the Cam. The college was founded by Bishop Middleton, the first of the Metropolitans of India

—prelates who, by their learning, their devotion and their zeal, would do credit to any Church in the world. The object of this institution was " the education of Christian youth in sacred knowledge, in sound learning, and in the principal language used in the country, in habits of piety and devotion to their calling, that they may be qualified to preach among the heathen."

The College owes its Gothic style to William Jones, one of the most remarkable men who ever came to India, and who, by the discovery of coal in Burdwan, has done more than any other man to develop the material wealth of the land. In 1800 he landed at Calcutta, and for ten years followed the trade of a working mechanic. He then became the proprietor of a canvas manufactory at Howrah, and was the founder of that prosperous suburb. In 1811, when an expedition was about to start for Java, the Government found themselves in want of cartridges, and Jones exercised his mechanical skill in establishing a small paper manufactory from which he supplied the Government with all the paper they required. When the expedition was over the factory was closed. Jones was not only a mechanic, but a successful builder. He contracted for the building of the College, because he had a great desire to erect the first Gothic edifice in India. But he was not destined to see the fulfilment of his great ambition. While superintending the erection of the building he caught a fever, which proved fatal in three days.

As we steam past Bishop's College a forest of masts bursts upon our view, and before us, enveloped in a grey mist, lies the port of Calcutta. After passing the entrance of the new docks, the eye is arrested by the vast outlines of the parapets of Fort William, the picturesque gateways and a long row of white barracks half visible above the green fortifications. In 1775, shortly after the battle of Plassey, the fort was commenced by Clive. Captain John Brohier was brought over from Madras to design it. At a consultation held on July 25, 1757—two months before Plassey was fought—a letter was read from Captain Brohier, in which he states :

" The works I propose to erect, with your Honour's approbation, are to form an hexagon, as a citadel to the town from the old dock southwards, as the bank of the river projects in this part, and admits that three of the sides of this citadel flank the current of the river, which I propose to strengthen with proper outworks before them, to multiply the defences of these fronts ; for, as the channel is on this side, a naval force will thereby be exposed to the fire of 100 pieces of cannon, which I conceive must effectually prevent any squadron from passing further up."

In order to " accomplish this great undertaking with all the frugality and diligence which the present state of the Company's affairs and that of Europe demands," Captain Brohier requests that he should employ his own overseers and be allowed to keep the accounts of the expense. But there .was neither frugality nor diligence displayed in the erection of Fort William, and it cost two millions of money —of which fifty thousand pounds were spent in keeping off the encroachments of the river. At the south-west angle of the fort stands an ugly yellow structure, which, the makers of guide-books are pleased to state, is in the " Grecian Ionic style of architecture." It was erected by the citizens of Calcutta—European and Native--to perpetuate the memory of James Prinsep, who founded the science of Indian numismatics and chronology, and who rescued from the dark oblivion of two thousand years the name and history of the great Buddhist Emperor, Asoka, the Constantine of the East. It was the genius of Prinsep which brought to light the long-hidden secrets of the inscriptions incised on pillars and rocks. Like most Anglo-Indian workers in the field of knowledge he was a busy official, and the periods during which he won his laurels were stolen from repose earned by long and

monotonous drudgery in the Assay Master's office at the Calcutta Mint. " My whole day," wrote Prinsep, " is consumed
at the scales. What a waste of precious moments ! " His
short life comprised in all but forty years, and five of these
sufficed for all his splendid discoveries. A road now separates the building from the river, and as it can no longer be
used as a landing-stage it might be pulled down and a more
suitable monument erected in honour of James Prinsep.

As we pass Prinsep's Ghat we notice a Muslim shrine,
whose copper dome glistens in the sun. It is, however, no
shrine, but the monument erected by Lord Ellenborough in
memory of the battles of Maharajpoor and Punniar, which
crushed the rebellion of the overgrown Gwalior army. On
December 28, 1843, at Maharajpoor, the English once more
encountered the Mahrattas. They fought with all their
ancient valour, but had, after a desperate resistance, to
yield to British bayonets. Three thousand of the enemy lay
dead upon the field, and fifty-six superb bronze guns were
the spoils of the victors, and it is these guns which supplied
the metal for the cupola and the pillars which support it.
The same day another British force encountered another
portion of the Mahratta army at Punniar, twelve miles
from Gwalior, and gained a complete victory. Lord Ellenborough, whose vanity prevented his great energy and un-
doubted ability being sufficiently appreciated, was present
at Maharajpoor, and showed much humane attention to
the wounded. His prompt action regarding the mutinous
army of Gwalior was one of the most creditable events in his
administration, but owing to his love of theatrical display
he could not help detracting from its merit by issuing high-
sounding proclamations about the glory of British arms on
the Plains of Scindia.

Leaving the Gwalior monument we pass Rajchunder Das
Ghat, almost abreast of the Eden Gardens, which Calcutta
owes to the generosity of the sisters of Lord Auckland ;

and then we come to the Chandpal Ghat, where in old days governors-general, commanders-in-chief, judges, and bishops used to land in state. Soon after passing Chandpal Ghat we are anchored at a jetty, not far from the spot where stood the old fort, and where " the illustrous Job Charnock, the first conspicuous Englishman on this side of the world," established the English factory.

Captain Hamilton, who " left England before King William came into it as king," in his *New Account of the East Indies*, states :

" The English settled there about the year 1690, after the Moghul had pardoned all the robberies and murders committed on his subjects. Mr. Job Charnock being then the Company's agent in Bengal, he had liberty to settle an emporium in any part on the river's side below Hooghly, and for the sake of a large shady tree chose that place, though he could not have chosen a more unhealthful spot on the whole river."

Hamilton proceeds to relate :

" One year he was there, and there were reckoned in August about twelve hundred English, some military, some servants to the Company, some private merchants residing in the town, and some seamen belonging to shipping lying at the town, and before the beginning of January there were four hundred and fifty burials registered in the clerk's book of mortality."

He adds :

" The Company has a pretty good hospital at Calcutta, where many go in to undergo the penance of physic, but few come out to give an account of its operations."

It is Captain Hamilton who relates the story how the founder of Calcutta rescued his wife from a funeral pyre. He writes :

" The country being overspread with paganism, the custom of wives burning with their deceased husbands is also practised here. Before the Moghul's war Mr. Channock went one time with his ordinary guard of soldiers to see a young widow at that

278

tragical catastrophe ; but he was so smitten with the widow's beauty that he sent his guards to take her by force from her executioners and conduct her to his own lodgings. They lived lovingly many years, and had several children. At length she died, after he had settled in Calcutta ; but instead of converting her to Christianity she made him a proselyte to paganism, and the only part of Christianity that was remarkable in him was burying her decently ; and he built a tomb over her, where all his life after her death he kept the anniversary day of her death by sacrificing a cock on her tomb after the pagan manner. This was and is the common report, and I have been credibly informed, both by Christians and pagans who lived at Calcutta under his agency, that the story was really matter of fact."

In spite, however, of Christian and pagan testimony, it would, as Colonel Yule points out, be hard to reconcile with " the pagan manner " or Hindu rites the sacrifice of an unclean bird. In the churchyard of St. John's beneath a massive mausoleum, octagonal in form with a double dome, lies the body of Job Charnock, or Channock, as Hamilton calls him. An inscription on a black slab informs us that he died January 10, 1693—three years before the original Fort William was erected.

Calcutta, when Hamilton visited it, consisted of a group of European buildings which clustered round the park— now Dalhousie Square—about the midst of which was the great tank called the " Lall Dighi." North of the park, and immediately fronting the fort, stood the old church, whose lofty spire formed a conspicuous object in the view. Hamilton writes :—" About fifty yards from Fort William stands the church, built by the pious charity of merchants residing there, and the Christian benevolence of sea-faring men whose affairs called them to trade there ; but ministers of the Gospel being subject to mortality, very often young merchants are obliged to officiate, and have a salary of £50 per annum, added to what the Company allows them for their pains in reading prayers and a sermon on Sundays."

Within the fort there was an official residence for the Governor, and convenient lodgings for factors and writers. On Sunday the Governor and Council and the civil servants and the military off duty walked in procession to the church. The Governor had applied for a state carriage for church-going, but his frugal masters at home informed him that " if he wanted a chaise and pair he must pay for them himself ! "

From Hamilton we get a glimpse of the social life of Calcutta in the days of old. He writes :

"Most gentlemen and ladies in Bengal live both splendidly and pleasantly, the forenoons being dedicated to business and after dinner to rest, and in the evening recreate themselves in chaises or palanquins in the fields, or to gardens, or by water in their budgeroes, which is a convenient boat that goes swiftly with the force of oars. On the river, sometimes, there is the diversion of fishing, or fowling, or both ; and before night they make friendly visits to one another, when pride or contention do not spoil society, which too often they do among the ladies as discord and faction do among men."

The old church was destroyed during the famous siege by Suraj-ud-Dowlah. The Portuguese church at the time being vacant, it was taken for English services ; but three years afterwards the Council, " taking into consideration the unwholesomeness and dampness of the church now in use, as well as the injustice of detaining it from the Portuguese," ordered their surveyor to examine the remains of the gateway in the old fort, " and report to us what it will cost to put it in tolerable repair and make it fit for a chapel, till such time as the chapel designed to be built in the new fort be erected." The new chapel was built inside the ruined fort immediately north of the great east gateway, and it is described as a ground floor. It soon proved too small for its purpose, and in 1768 the old or mission church was erected by the well-known Swedish missionary Kierander. He gave towards its building fifty thousand pounds, and the proceeds of the sale of his deceased wife's jewels. In *The Genuine Memoirs of Asiaticus*, published in London in 1785, we are told :

" It was not until the year 1782, under the auspices of the princely and munificent Hastings, that the inhabitants of Calcutta seriously determined to erect an edifice for the celebration of public worship suitable to the exercise of the ministerial functions, and to such a numerous auditory as might be expected in the capital of our Indian Empire." " On the eighteenth day of December, 1783, the new Church Committee first met, and the meeting was attended by Governor Hastings and his Council. As the sum of thirty-five thousand nine hundred and fifty rupees had been subscribed already, the Committee determined to commence the building."

The first stone of the new church was laid on Tuesday, April 6, 1784, " on the morning of which Mr. Wheler, Acting President, gave a public breakfast at the old Court-house, whence he proceeded, attended by the great officers of State and the principal inhabitants of Calcutta, to the ground upon which the sacred edifice was to be erected. The first stone was laid by Mr. Wheler with the usual ceremonies." Three years afterwards the church was opened with considerable pomp and state by the Earl of Cornwallis, who was at the time Governor-General.

The old Court-house, from which Mr. Wheler and his Council walked to lay the foundation of St. John's Church, occupied the site on which St. Andrew's Kirk is now erected. It was originally a charity school-house built by subscription. A portion was held by the Mayor's Court for their records, and when it ceased to be used as a school the portion not occupied by the Corporation was let for assemblies, lotteries, and balls. " Asiaticus " informs us that Anglo-Indian ladies were as fond of dancing in the beginning of the eighteenth century as they are at the present time, but he did not consider it a pastime suited to a hot climate. He writes :

CITIES OF INDIA

" For my own part I already begin to think the dazzling brightness of a copper-coloured face infinitely preferable to the pallid
and sickly hue which banishes the roses from the cheeks of the
European fair, and reminds me of the death-struck countenance
of Lazarus risen from the grave. The English ladies are im-
moderately fond of dancing, an exercise ill calculated for the
burning climate of Bengal; and, in my opinion, however ad-
missible in cooler latitudes, not a little indelicate in a country
where the inhabitants are covered with no more clothes than
what decency absolutely requires. Imagine to yourself the
lovely object of your affections ready to expire with heat, every
limb trembling, and every feature distorted with fatigue, and
her partner with a muslin handkerchief in each hand employed
in the delightful office of wiping down her face, while the tiny
drops stand impearled on her forehead ! "

In 1792 the old Court-house, being in a ruinous condition,
was pulled down by order of Government : and, as it had
been used as a town hall, a public meeting was held to raise
a building worthy of the city and its Corporation, which
had a quarter of a century previously—August 26, 1777—
been founded by Royal Charter. It consisted of a Mayor
and nine Aldermen, with power of holding a Court whose
jurisdiction extended to all causes—civil, criminal, and
ecclesiastical—in which an Englishman might be concerned
—high treason excepted. All purely native suits, however,
continued to be tried by an official called the Jemindar, who
was also responsible for collecting the local revenues from
fees, farms and ground rents. We find from a volume of records, which was one of those thrown into the boats when
the English abandoned Fort William, and which alone has
escaped the ravages of time and the white ants, that in
1748 Mr. Cruttenden was Jemindar. The following list of
officers enables us to realize the small beginning from
which the Indian Empire had arisen and its mercantile
origin :

CALCUTTA—VIEW FROM THE HIGH COURT.

Mr. FEAKE, *Accomptant.*

Mr. BELLAMY, *Export Warehouse-keeper, and to take charge of the books till Mr. Feake's arrival.*

Mr. FYTCHE, *Import Warehouse-keeper.*

Mr. DRAKE, *Buxey, and to continue Military Store-keeper till Mr. Blackford's arrival.*

Mr. CRUTTENDEN, *Jemindar.*

Mr. HOOPER, *Store-keeper.*

Mr. BLACKFORD, *Military Secretary.*

Mr. WATTS, *Collector of Consulage.*

Mr. BURROW, *to continue Sub-Treasurer till an employ is vacant.*

The Jemindar has become the Home Minister of a vast empire, and the Buxey holds the portfolio of Finance. The Mayor and nine Aldermen have long since vanished and their place is taken by a Chairman appointed by Government, and seventy-five Commissioners, the larger portion of whom are elected by the ratepayers. They hold their meetings in a substantial building of their own, and the Town Hall is now chiefly used for concerts, balls, and public meetings, held to further some noble work of charity like the Dufferin Fund, or to criticise some act of Government which has aroused public attention. The non-official European, to whose pluck and enterprise India owes her tea gardens, her jute industry, her coal mines, is not given to politics. Occupied much with his business, he is the most conservative and least revolutionary of the Queen's subjects ; but he is tenacious of his birthright. The Ilbert Bill or the Jury Question brings out the English character true to its old traditions, and at the Town Hall, with no uncertain voice, the Englishman declares his resolution to maintain his own.

In the old Court-house the Supreme Court, when it was first established by Royal Charter, held its sittings ; but when the buildings became unsafe, and had to be pulled down, another more substantial and handsome edifice was erected on the site of the present High Court. In the

Supreme Court Nuncomar was tried for forgery, not by Sir Elijah Impey, as Macaulay states, but by the Chief Justice, two of his colleagues and a jury, and after a long and patient trial was convicted and sentenced to be hanged. A full report of the trial was published at the time, and Macaulay might have ascertained the facts if he had referred to the Bar Library, where a copy exists. But he preferred rhetoric to accurate research.

When Impey's son, in an ill-constructed book full of interesting and instructive matter, pointed out how cruelly his father had been libelled, Macaulay refused to retract the slander. Sir James Fitzjames Stephen, in a book which is a model of sound workmanship and research, has cleared the character of Impey with regard to the foul charge of judicial murder brought against him by the Whig historian ; but sufficient credit has not been given to the first Chief Justice of Bengal for the independence he showed in maintaining the dignity and liberty of the Court over which he presided. Mrs. Fay mentions how her able but worthless husband was under an apprehension that, having come to India without the permission of the Honourable East India Company, obstacles might be raised as to his admission to the Local Bar. On expressing his doubts to the Chief Justice, Impey indignantly exclaimed, " No, sir ; had you dropped from the clouds with such documents we would admit you. The Supreme Court is independent, and will never endure to be dictated to by any body of men whose claims are not enforced by supreme authority. It is nothing to us whether you *had* or *had not* permission from the Court of Directors to proceed to this settlement. You came to us as an authenticated English barrister, and as such we shall on the first day of the next term admit you to *our* Bar." Thus was dealt the first great blow to the most valuable patronage which the East India Company possessed—the right of appointing its own lawyers, who were limited to twelve in number. A golden harvest must the twelve have reaped, for Calcutta has always been an El Dorado for lawyers and doctors. Mrs. Fay writes :—" A man of abilities and good address in this line, if he has the firmness to resist the fashionable contagion—gambling—need only pass one seven years of his life at Calcutta, to return home in affluent circumstances ; but the very nature of their profession leads them into gay connections, and, having for a time complied with the humour of their company from prudential motives, may become tainted and prosecute their bane from the impulses of inclination." The writer of *Hartley Hall*—a novel which under the thin guise of fiction describes the persons and social life of the day—states :— " Physic, as well as law, is a gold mine to its professors, to work it at will. The medical gentlemen at Calcutta make their visits in palanquins, and receive a gold mohur from each patient for every ordinary attendance—extras are enormous." The doctors, however, seem to have been considerate in not interfering with the profits of the undertakers, for a member of that fraternity about to sail for Europe asked twenty thousand rupees for the good-will of his business for the months of August and September.

When the Supreme Court of the East India Company (known as the Sudder Dewani Adalat) was amalgamated with the High Court, it was considered necessary that both should have a common habitation, and the present building was erected on the site of the old Supreme Court. It is designed after the model of the Town Hall at Ypres, but the architecture has suffered from transplantation. In the centre is a tower which the guide books call " massive," but which has cracked and begun to sink on account of the muddy foundation. From the top of the tower can be had a splendid birds'-eye view of the " City of Palaces." Below is a broad stretch of green sward covered with stately trees, and beyond are the lawn and walks of the Eden Gardens,

CALCUTTA—GOVERNMENT HOUSE.

winding among trees and shrubs of endless variety. In the far distance are the gleaming white barracks of Fort William, and the broad river with vessels of all sizes and descriptions gliding over its waters. Stately ships lie at anchor by the river bank, and their lofty spars tower up black into the air. On the left is the Town Hall ; beyond is a vast ugly square pile of buildings—the Imperial Secretariat —where the administration of the Empire is conducted during the winter months. At the end of the road is a lofty gateway which leads into the spacious gardens of Government House. The great Marquis, who first attempted to carry out the Imperial policy which the daring genius of Hastings commenced, pulled down the old small house in which the Governors used to reside, and erected the present building. He told his mercantile masters that " India should be governed from a palace, not from a counting-house ; with the ideas of a prince, not with those of a retail dealer in muslin and indigo." The palace cost a hundred and fifty thousand pounds, and the furniture fifty thousand pounds ; and the merchants of the East India Company expressed their strong disapproval—but the place was built. It was opened with considerable state and pomp to celebrate the Peace of Amiens. Lord Valentia, who was present, has given an interesting and graphic description of the ceremony.

" The State rooms," his lordship writes, " were for the first time lighted up. At the upper end of the largest was placed a very rich Persian carpet, and in the centre of that a musnud of crimson and gold—formerly composing part of the ornaments of Tippoo Sultan's throne. On this side was a rich chair and stool of state for Lord Wellesley : on each side three chairs for the members of Council and Judges. Down to the door, on both sides of the room, were seats for the ladies, in which they were placed according to the strict rules of precedency, which is here regulated by the seniority of the husband in the Company's service. About ten Lord Wellesley arrived, attended by a large body of aides-de-camp, etc., and, after receiving in the northern verandah the compliments of some of the native princes and the vakeels of the others, took his seat. The dancing then commenced, and continued till supper. The room was not sufficiently lighted up, yet still the effect was beautiful. The row of Chunam pillars, which supported each side, together with the rest of the room, were of a shining white, that gave a contrast to the different dresses of the company. Lord Wellesley wore the Orders of St. Patrick and the Crescent in diamonds. Many of the European ladies were also richly ornamented with jewels. The black dress of the male Armenians was pleasing from the variety, and the costly, though unbecoming, habits of their females, together with the appearance of officers, nabobs, Persians and natives, resembled a masquerade. It excelled it in one respect —the characters were well supported, and the costume violated by no one. About eight hundred people were present, who found sufficient room at supper in the marble hall below; thence they were summoned about one o'clock to the different verandahs to see the fireworks and illuminations. The side of the citadel facing the palace was covered with a blaze of light, and all the approaches were lined with lamps suspended from bamboos. The populace stole much of the oil, and, as it was impossible to light so great a range at one time, the effect was inferior to what it ought to have been. The fireworks were indifferent, except the rockets, which were superior to any I ever beheld. They were discharged from mortars on the ramparts of the citadel. The colours also of several of the pieces were excellent; and the merit of singularity at least might be attributed to a battle between two elephants of fire, which, by rollers, were driven against each other. The night was very damp, and gave very severe colds to many. We returned to our home much pleased with our evening's entertainment."

The Marquis of Hastings, a magnificent nobleman of the grand old school, who completed the Imperial work which Hastings conceived and Wellesley commenced, had even a more exalted notion of Viceregal magnificence than the great Marquis himself, and transplanted to India the state forms and ceremonies of an European Court. The minuteness of the Court regulations, and the etiquette to be observed, would do credit to some petty German State. " The first aide-de-camp and chamberlain "—-an old *Official Gazette* informs us—" had the management of all processions," and a Viceregal procession must then have been a very brave show.   At a Levée a procession formed in one of the corridors of Government House in the following order: " The Chamberlain with his wand ; Captain of the Body guard ; the Lieutenant of ditto ; Aides-de-camp, two and two ; the Governor-General ; Master of the Horse ; Aide-de-camp in Waiting ; Chaplain, Secretaries, etc., etc., and the rest of the suite."   " During the Levée," we are told, " a captain's guard of Grenadiers was on duty, and a lieutenant's guard or half-squadron of Dragoons."   The avenues to the Presence Chamber were lined with the Body Guard, dismounted ; servants, all in State liveries ; and State trumpets and kettle-drums.   A band of music, of course, attends the Grenadier Guards.

The programme for the Drawing Room was even more elaborate and minute than the programme for the Levée, and illustrates the extent to which State etiquette was carried in those days.

METHOD OF OPENING THE DRAWING ROOM.

" The Governor-General having taken his station—as at the Levée—the Countess follows in the procession, handed by the Lord Chamberlain, and her train borne by two pages.   She takes her place upon the left of the Governor-General, under the throne. The Chamberlain presents the person who requires that ceremony. The person presented makes a sliding bow of courtesy, and passes on, unless detained by the Countess addressing him or her. The presentation being over, their Excellencies converse, going round the circle.   They then retire to the card-room, where two commerce tables are placed.   Lady Loudon plays at one, His Excellency, the Governor-General, at the other : the Chamberlain and Masters of the Ceremonies selecting persons of the highest rank in the room to form the party.   They play at guinea pool. If their Excellencies are successful, it is the perquisite of the pages. When it is over they retire to their apartments, in the same order they came in ; and the suite observe the same conduct as at the close of the Levée."

The Lord Chamberlain with his wand, the Chaplain, and the Master of the Horse have disappeared in these prosaic and economic days. The Viceroy and his consort stand before Tippoo's throne, supported on either side by the leading officials, who have the right of private *entrée* ; and the Military Secretary to the Viceroy reads the name of the lady as she advances. The fair dame—the men are no longer presented at the Drawing Room—makes a " sliding bow of courtesy," and passes on to the ball-room upstairs, where she is received by her friends of the other sex. The vast room, with its double line of noble white pillars, lighted by innumerable wax candles, in rows of glittering chandeliers taken from a French ship in the good old times, presents a fine spectacle. Bright-coloured uniforms of every regiment in the army mingle with the rich dresses of stately, handsome women, who would adorn any Court in Europe. It is a representative party. Bengali ladies in graceful white robes mingle with their English sisters ; and, standing by an English warrior who has won his knighthood in frontier battle, is an Indian prince, one blaze of diamonds. As the band strikes up the National Anthem the many-coloured wave divides into two. The Viceregal procession—a mass of scarlet—enters and slowly proceeds down the room, their Excellencies stopping to be introduced to the strangers who are present—and every year the number of strangers who flock from all quarters of the globe to Calcutta for the winter season increases. A winter at Calcutta promises soon to become as popular as a winter at Cairo. The Drawing Room marks the opening of the winter season, and balls, picnics, dances, paper-chases, follow each other in rapid succession till the first day of Lent. Society at Calcutta is the only cosmopolitan society in India. To the stranger within the gates it is difficult to comprehend the different social sets—their laws of procedure, their jealousies, and their relations to each other. There is the Official set, consisting of military men and civilians who hold high office. As their position is by Royal enactment assured, their wives view from a slight eminence the Mercantile circle. Calcutta is, however, a great leveller—high officials become ordinary by mere force of numbers. It is a terrible revelation to the wife of a civilian, who has been a king in his own district, to find that at the capital he only counts as an ordinary citizen. The Mercantile circle consists of those who, thanks to tea, indigo and jute, are in a position to keep up a palace at Chowringhee. They are generous and hospitable in a degree not common in other lands. The third circle is the Lawyer set —and lawyers are good company all over the world. They have a larger experience of life than officials, and therefore, as a rule, take a wider view of affairs. If they are apt to be cynical, it must be borne in mind that their lives are mainly occupied with the worst side of Bengali human nature.

North-east of Government House runs Old Court-house Street—so called from the old Court-house which, as we have stated, stood at or near the site of St. Andrew's Church. The broad street, with its lofty row of houses and splendid shops, would do credit to any European capital. In fact, it is a Continental street transplanted to the East. Far different is the Burra Bazaar, with its old and shabby native houses, whose wooden verandahs face the street, and the marvellous dens on the ground floor filled with goods of every class and description. Here are to be found rich shawls from Cashmere, and piece goods of every vulgar colour from Manchester. Jewellers are sitting cross-legged before their charcoal pans, making silver bracelets and earrings, and loud is the din from the hammers of the workers in brass. There are stands for crockery, and there are stalls at which are sold drugs of every description. There are

CALCUTTA—THE BURRA BAZAAR.

293

dens filled with pulse and grain, and sweet-meat shops send forth a savoury smell. A strange tide of life ebbs through the street ; the sleek and calm money-lender from Marwar ; the mendicant who begs from door to door; the vendors of fruit and vegetables, with heavy basket-loads on their heads ; the bustling Bengali broker who fills the air with the voice of cheap bargains. It is a scene for a painter, but words can convey no accurate impression of an Oriental street.

Great is the transition from the Burra Bazaar to the Chowringhee Road, whose eastern side is bounded by a row of lofty white houses elaborately porticoed and colonnaded. Each stands in its own bright garden, trimly kept, and faces the Maidan, or wide plain, which is the characteristic feature of Calcutta. It is from these houses, designed by Italian architects in the days when the pagoda tree flourished, that Calcutta derives its popular name, " The City of Palaces." It was Lord Macaulay who gave currency to the flattering but somewhat inaccurate title ; but he stole the epithet from Lord Valentia, and, as was his wont, slightly disguised the theft. Lord Valentia wrote :—" On a line with this edifice (Government House) is a range of excellent houses, chunamed and ornamented with verandahs. Chowringhee, an entire village of palaces, runs for a considerable length at right angles with it, and altogether forms the finest view I ever beheld in my life."

When Lord Valentia wrote, Chowringhee had just begun to cease to be a village on the outskirts of Calcutta. Ten years before he visited the city there were only twenty-four houses in the locality. In 1792 was advertised for private sale at 1,500 Sicca rupees, " A neat, compact, and new built garden-house, pleasantly situated at Chowringhee, and from its contiguity to Fort William, peculiarly well calcu-lated for an officer. It would," continues the advertisement, " likewise be a handsome provision for a native lady or a child," which throws light on the morals of the day. English ladies were few in number, and men took unto themselves savage women to rear their dusky race.

Sir Elijah Impey was one of the first to erect a spacious garden-house at Chowringhee, and Park Street was so called because it bordered his wide domain. Here the Chief Justice—who besides being an able and learned lawyer was an accomplished scholar—devoted his leisure moments to the study of Persian, of which he acquired an extensive and accurate knowledge, and Bengali, which he soon learned to speak fluently. At Chowringhee also resided his accuser, Thomas Babington Macaulay. In one of his letters he writes—" I have a house almost as large as Lord Dudley's in Park Lane, or rather larger." The residence of the Whig historian now forms the main building of the Bengal Club, an institution known to all the dwellers of the East. Some of its past glory has departed, owing to the depreciated rupee, but it still remains one of the most comfortable and hospitable clubs in Asia. Travellers who bring proper credentials are freely elected as honorary members, and they can have a bedroom in the club if one be vacant. Besides the Bengal Club, Calcutta has the United Service Club, whose doors are closed to all who do not belong to the army or one of the civil departments of the State. Like the Bengal Club, the United Service Club is situated on Chowringhee Road and faces the Maidan. Next to it are the rooms of the Asiatic Society of Bengal, founded by Sir William Jones, aided by the sympathy and active co-operation of Warren Hastings. " As the first liberal promoter of useful knowledge in Bengal," to use the words of the address, " and especially as the great encourager of Persian and Sanscrit literature," Hastings was requested to accept the title of President ; but he refused the proffered honour, and William Jones was appointed President. The pages of the early volumes of *The Asiatic Journal* were enriched by his eloquent discourses, which even now, though almost a century has elapsed since they were delivered, are well worth reading, on account of their eloquence and the wide scholarship displayed in them. Sir William Jones may have been lacking in the accuracy of the German School of Oriental Scholarship, but he was undoubtedly a man of genius.

Nearly opposite the United Service Club rises the fine bronze statue of Outram : " faithful servant of England ; large-minded and kingly ruler of her subjects ; doing nought through vain-glory, but ever esteeming others better than himself ; valiant, uncorrupt, self-denying, magnanimous : in all the true knight." It was the poet-Viceroy who spoke of Calcutta as the " City of Statues " ; and few capitals in Europe contain finer examples of the sculptor's art. Facing the south entrance of Government House is a full-length bronze statue of John Lawrence, and it conveys the dignity and power of the saviour of the Punjab. Near him is the statue of Canning, who steered the Empire through the tempestuous waves of mutiny into the calm waters of material and moral progress. At the south-east of Government House is a splendid equestrian statue of the " young soldier with the eye of a general and the soul of a hero." An inscription on the pedestal informs us that " The statue was erected by the inhabitants of British India, of various races and creeds, to Henry Viscount Hardinge, in grateful commemoration of a Governor who, trained in war, sought by the acts of peace to elevate and improve the various nations committed to his charge." It was well said of him that he had crowded into one short administration all the services of the highest order, both civil and military. Not far from the statue raised to perpetuate his memory rises a lofty minaret, erected to commemorate the services of David Ochterlony : " for fifty years a soldier, he had served in every Indian war from the time of Hyder downwards." The monument is a bad imitation of the London Monument, and the future historian of the Empire will note

CALCUTTA

that the Moghuls erected the Kutub Minar at Delhi, and the English erected the Ochterlony monument. The gulf which separates the artistic instincts of the two races will be illustrated by these two structures.

From Lord Hardinge's statue to Kidderpore Bridge extends " the Course, the oldest road in the Maidan, so called from being two miles in length." It is described in 1768 as being " out of town in a sort of angle made to take the air in " ; though an old song states that those who frequented it " swallowed ten mouthfuls of dust for one of fresh air." On the east side of the road runs a broad gravelled walk known as the Secretary's walk, so called—a sarcastic pamphleteer informs us—from being the place where secretaries and their sycophants discuss the news of an evening. At the south end of the Secretary's Walk, standing in the centre of the spot where four roads meet, rises the statue of Frederick Temple, Marquis of Dufferin and Ava. It is meretricious, like much of Boehm's latter work ; but the sculptor has caught the striking air and manner which distinguished the statesman who, with conspicuous tact and energy, governed our Indian Empire.

Some little distance south of the Dufferin statue is the racecourse. At a very early period the English transplanted to the East their national sport. On January 2, 1794, there appeared in a Calcutta paper the following advertisement :

" The Stewards present their compliments to the subscribers to the races, and take this opportunity to inform them, that a breakfast with music will be provided in tents on the course after the races on Monday, Tuesday and Wednesday, the 16th, 17th and 18th of January, and a ball and supper at the theatre on Wednesday, the 18th, when they hope for the honour of their company."

The races run for were for (1) the Plate, (2) the Hunters' Plate, (3) the Ladies' Plate. " After the race of each morning," to use the words of the chronicler of the day, " the company of upwards of one hundred and fifty sat down to a public breakfast," and "after breakfast the company adjourned to an adjoining tent of very capacious dimensions, handsomely fitted up and boarded, for the purpose of dancing. Country dances commenced in two sets, and were kept up with the utmost gaiety till *two* in the afternoon."

A century elapses, and a very different spectacle presents itself at the Calcutta races. It is two in the afternoon, and the grand stand is filled with noble dames from England, from America, and all parts of the world, who have come with their spouses to visit the Indian Empire. In the paddock is a noble duke, a few lords, one or two millionaires from America, and some serious politicians, who have visited the land to study the Opium Question, and feel ashamed of being seen at a racecourse. The air resounds with the cries of the bookmaker, and an eager crowd surges around the totalisator—for on the Viceroy's Cup day even the most cautious bank manager feels bound to have one bet. Beyond the grand stand, on the other side of the course, the wide plain is covered with beings dressed in brilliant garments—crimson, blue and orange are mingled together. Men, women and children have walked many a mile to see the *tamasha*, or show. They are all so happy and good-tempered, and to purchase some bright piece of cloth for the ebony dot by their side is the sum of happiness. A few sweetmeats and a little handful of grain is to them a handsome lunch. All of a sudden the hum of voices ceases and all eyes are turned to a corner of the racecourse. A cavalcade approaches. At a fair trot come the troopers of the Body Guard in scarlet uniforms—magnificent men on splendid horses ; a carriage and four containing the Viceroy and the Vice-Queen follows. " Wah ! wah ! " exclaims the native crowd. Loud cheers burst forth as the carriage draws up opposite the grand stand, for no man is more respected than the Marquis of Lansdowne, and no woman more popu-

lar than the noble lady by his side. When the Viceregal
party are settled in their box, the horses about to run for the
Cup, given every year by the reigning Viceroy, are paraded
before them. Some have been victors at Melbourne, some
on an English course. After the preliminary canters they
are marshalled before the starter, and after one or two attempts the cry rises, " They are off ! " and they thunder by
the grand stand.

Leaving the racecourse and proceeding south, we come to
a bridge leading to the Zoological Gardens, which Calcutta
owes to the great energy of Sir Richard Temple, a strong
administrator and a man of genius. He found a swamp,
with a few native huts on it, and converted it into a
garden with lawns, flower-beds, and wide walks, lined
by the endless variety of shrubs and plants to be found
in the East. The waters of the swamp have been converted
into an artificial lake, by whose banks palms are growing in
the greatest luxuriance.

A short distance beyond the Zoo stands Belvedere, the
official residence of the Lieutenant-Governor of Bengal, in
large grounds of its own, with trees which, in shape and
foliage, would do credit to an English park. At the west
entrance of Belvedere was fought the famous duel between
Warren Hastings and Francis. On September 27, 1780,
Mrs. Fay writes :

" The bad news I hinted at some time ago is already avenged,
and a much more serious affair has happened since ; but for
the present I must relate what has occupied a good deal of
attention for some days past—no less than a duel between the
Governor-General and the first in Council, Mr. Francis. There
were two shots fired, and the Governor's second fire took effect.
He immediately ran up to his antagonist and expressed his
sorrow for what had happened, which I daresay was sincere,
for he is said to be a very amiable man. Happily the ball was soon
extracted, and if he escape fever, there is no doubt of his speedy
recovery. What gave occasion to the quarrel is said to have

been an offensive minute entered on the Council books by Mr. Francis, which he refused to rescind ; but being unacquainted with the particulars, I have as little right as inclination to make any comments on the subject. It always vexes me to hear of such things."

Not far from the spot where the duel took place stands Hastings' House. It is fast crumbling into ruin, but it should be purchased by Government, repaired and converted into a public institution. It was the favourite residence of the man whose far sight first saw, and whose brave and confident patience realized, the romantic idea of his country founding an empire in the East. When he returned to England he always remembered with fond affection the house at Alipore, the paddocks in which he bred his Arab horses, and the grounds which he planted with rare trees from all parts of Asia. On the bank of the Thames he erected a house after the model of his home at Alipore, and when he retired to Daylesford he laid out the grounds after the fashion of his Indian country seat.

Alipore was dear to him because there he spent the best years of his life, with the woman for whom he had an unbounded love and admiration. There was not such another being in the world. As long as she was by his side, nothing could come amiss to him : the cares and fatigues of the day made no impression on his spirits. When the state of her health had laid him under the stern necessity of sending her to England, he wrote : " I miss you in every instant and incident of my life, and everything seems to wear a dead stillness around me. I come home as to a solitude." After she had gone he cared not to dwell at Alipore, and he determined to sell the property.

Mrs. Fay thus describes the woman who won the great heart of Hastings :

" Mrs. H——— herself," she writes, " it is easy to perceive at the first glance, is far superior to the generality of her sex

though her appearance is rather eccentric, owing to the circumstance of her beautiful auburn hair being disposed in ringlets,
throwing an air of elegant, nay, almost infantine simplicity
over the countenance, most admirably adapted to heighten the
effect intended to be produced. Her whole dress, too, though
studiously becoming, is at variance with our present modes,
which are certainly not so : perhaps for that reason she has chosen
to depart from them—as a foreigner, you know, she may be
excused for not strictly conforming to our fashions ; besides,

A RUSTIC SCENE IN BENGAL.

her rank in the settlement sets her above the necessity of studying
anything but the whim of the moment. It is easy to perceive
how fully sensible she is of her own consequence. She is, indeed,
raised to a ' giddy height,' and expects to be treated with the
most profound respect and deference."

Driving through what Macaulay, with considerable
poetic latitude, calls " the rosy lanes of Alipore," we come
across a primitive cabin, little more than a roof of grass to
keep the sun and rain out, for this is all that is needed. At
the door is a woman grinding corn ; about her are a group

of scantily-clad men discussing the state of the crops and the hardness of the heart of the village money-lender. The carman, carrying a load of timber to the great town, leaves the bullocks by the roadside and joins in the conversation. A stalwart peasant who is walking with his son—whose graceful olive-brown figure is marred by no clothes—has also stopped for a few seconds to exchange greetings. It is a picturesque and peaceful scene. The people are both blithe and gentle. The passions of the Oriental, like those of children, are on the surface. But the combination of passion and softness in the Indian peasant has a great charm, when one has learned by the observation of twenty years that their lives are laborious and frugal, and that their vigour is hardly less than their kindness to the old and the young. Happy are they, and happy they will remain till their minds are poisoned against their rulers by a seditious press. Then athwart the mind of the Indian ryot may arise, as it arose in the mind of the French peasant, the idea that he is one of a multitude, starved and fleeced ; and then he may in his wrath do what the French peasant did. Let us never forget that when reverence for authority perishes among the masses, it will be an almost superhuman task to keep peace in India. " It is a noble empire," said that distinguished traveller and diplomat, Baron Hubner, to me the day he left India, " and it is well worth keeping : but do not lose it by introducing what you please to call Liberal ideas."

As we leave the hamlet the lane grows narrower, and lofty bamboos and tall palms line its sides, and great banian trees spread a green roof over all. By a graceful palm is a well. A bullock cart drawn by oxen with wide-spreading horns has halted by its side. The driver with his shaven head, and his spouse in her scarlet cotton robe, gaze at us with curiosity as we drive past. Waves of conquerors have swept by and been forgotten, but the bullock cart continues a symbol of the immortal East.

MADRAS, FROM THE SEA.

XIII

MADRAS

FROM the deck of a steamer in the grey dawn of the morning Madras rising from a long stretch of bright sandy beach beyond the dark green sea has the appearance of a continental city. Madras has, however, kept to a large extent an early individuality, and the past is a living presence in the old town. The fine storehouses which line the surf-beaten shore with colonnades to the upper stories, belong to a former generation, and the old roadstead of Fort St. George recalls to mind stirring events of a bygone age.

Madras is a town with a history, as all know who have read their Orme. There was a time when it ranked higher than Calcutta, and it was from Madras, then a flourishing settlement, that Job Charnock went to found on a swamp by the banks of the Hughly, the City of Palaces.

The foundation of Fort St. George was due to the struggle between the Portuguese, the Dutch and the English as to who should enjoy the trade between India and the Spice Islands. In 1611 (eleven years after Elizabeth had granted the first charter of "the Governor and Company of Merchants of London trading with the East Indies") Captain Heppon, of the *Globe*, touched at Pulicat, then the chief port on the Eastern or Coromandal Coast. The Dutch had established a factory and built a fort there, and the Dutch Governor, Van Wezik, refused to allow the English to trade. Taking with him two merchants who had been in

304

the Dutch Service, Heppon left Pulicat, and coasted up the Bay of Bengal until he reached Masulipatam, at the mouth of the Kistna, then the principal mart of that part of India. Here they managed to establish a small agency, which was put under a chief, and a council was chosen from the merchants. Twelve years later a factory was established and fortified at Armagon, a roadstead south of Masulipatam, and forty miles north of Pulicat. It was the first fortification erected by the English in India. In the year 1628–29 Armagon is described as being defended by twelve pieces of cannon mounted round the factory, and by a guard of twenty-three factors and soldiers. To it the same year, owing to the oppression of the native Governor, the factory at Masulipatam was transferred, but Armagon was not a good entrepôt for the supply of the " white cloths," and two years later the agency was again established at Masulipatam. But when the chief and merchants of Masulipatam were at Armagon they sent Francis Day, one of the Consuls, to examine the country in the vicinity of the station which the Portuguese who were then friendly to us had established at St. Thomas. Day "was ordered to go towards St. Thomay to see what paintings those parts doth afford ; as also to see whether any place were fit to fortify upon." In August 1639, three years before the outbreak of the Civil War, Day " having dispatched what he was sent about," returned to Masulipatam and told his colleagues what he had done.

" And first he makes it appear to us that, at a place called Madraspatam, near St. Thomay, the best paintings are made, or as good as anywhere on this coast ; likewise excellent Long cloth, *Morrees*, and *Percalla* ; of which we have seen Musters—and better, cheap by 20 per cent. than anywhere else. The Naque of that place is very desirous of our residence there ; for he hath made us very fair proffers to that effect ; for first he proffers to build a Fort, in what manner we please, upon a high plot of ground adjoining to the Sea, where a ship of any burthen may ride within musket shot close by a River, which is capable of a vessel of fifty tons ; and upon possession given us by him and not before, to pay what charges he shall have disbursed."

Day was sent back to Madraspatam, and so important was the new acquisition considered that the agency at Masulipatam directed him to begin building the fort without waiting for the orders of the Court of Directors. But the Native Governor was " as good as his word " in all things, except " the forte exactions (the main thing of all), but in that thing he excuseth himselfe." Day offered " to pay the interest of all the moneys that should be expended till the fort was finished," but their Worships at home refused " to allow of any charges at all neither in buildinge or payinge of garrisone." For in their first letter, dated 20th September, 1612, " The Agent and Factors on the Coast of Coromandel write :

" When wee doe (as that wee doe often) fall into Consideration how much your Worships are displeased with vs, for proceedinge on this 'worke, it euen breakes some of our hearts. 'Tis now to late to wish it vndone, and yett wee may not but tell you that if soe bee your Worships will follow this Coast Trade (or rather the Karnatt) this place may proove as good as the best, but all things must have its growth and tyme, but on the Contrary if your Worships will not Contineu it, you may doe it away to proffett, and not hazard the loss of a man, if you Resolve vpon the latter, after advice given once within 12 mo, it may with ease be effected, vnless the Moores Conquer the Country before."

Madras proved " as good as the best." A large number of natives seeking the protection of the English, a prosperous settlement arose outside the English bounds, which port was styled the Black Town. The original settlement where none but Europeans were allowed to reside being known as the White Town. Owing to the trade from England to the coast of Coromandel, to the great return it makes in calicoes and muslin, " to its considerable trade with China, Persia and Mocha," and to its " not being a great way from the diamond mines of Golconda," Madras rose " to a degree of opulence and reputation which rendered it inferior to none of the European establishments in India except Goa and Batavia."

The fort, as first erected, was but a small place, not a quarter of a mile long and only a hundred yards wide from east to west, and was situated at the north-east corner of the present fort. Five years after its first erection, its total cost had been only Rs. 23,000, and the highest estimate of a sufficient garrison was one hundred soldiers. In 1652, thirteen years after its foundation, it was considered safe with a garrison of twenty-six men. No great change was made in it for a century.

When La Bourdonnais laid siege to Fort St. George, it was surrounded with a slender wall, defended with four bastions, and as many batteries ; but these were very slight and defective in their construction, nor had they any outworks to defend them. The principal buildings inside were fifty good houses in which the chief Europeans resided, and an English and a Roman Catholic Church, the warehouse of the Company, and the factory in which their servants resided. On the morning of September 12, 1746, the French fleet having on board the troops, artillery, and stores intended for the siege of Madras, sailed from Pondicherry. A letter from Madras, dated October 27, states : " They came in sight the 2nd nine sail, and landed 800 Europeans at Covalong, marched to St. Thome, there landed more." The neighbourhood covered with country houses was given up to pillage, and the French Commissary-General states that La Bourdonnais and his brother La Villebague harassed the town of St. Thomas, for loot. On the 17th September the French " began to play their mortars, being fifteen in number, from behind the garden house, 10 and 5 from Cross the Bar ; the strength on shore I compute

2,000 Europeans, Seapiahs, and 3,000 Coffrees; they have when all on board about 3,000 Europeans, 600 of which were Pondicherry troops, their intent was to have stormed us by escalade, which we were in no condition to prevent, 1,000 bombs having prevented our sleeping for 3 days and nights. Yet we had more to dread from our own disorder within and want of Government and Council than from the enemy without." In the afternoon of September 21, La Bourdonnais, at the head of a large body of troops marched to the gates of the fort, where he received the keys from the Governor. The French flag was immediately hoisted, and the boats of the French squadron took possession of the Company's ships. Three years later (1749) the news of the peace of Aix-la-Chapelle restored Madras to the English in exchange for the restitution of Louisburg, in North America, to the French. The honourable Board, in their letter to the East India Court, complain of the condition in which it was given back to the English.

" Your Honours have been already informed in an address we made you overland, the 30th August, that your Settlement of Fort St. George was restored to us on the 21st of that month. We have, therefore, here only to acquaint you that the condition in which it was delivered was so extremely bad that we apprehend it will require to be entirely new fortified, all the walls and bastions being undermined in such a manner that they must, in all probability, fall down in the ensuing monsoon, and it is represented by His Majesty's Engineers and all the bricklayers that they are no ways to be repaired, neither are they in the least capable of bearing any cannon upon them, on which last circumstances we have been obliged, so far to deviate from your directions, as to permit a platform that was begun by the French to be finished, as we are informed it tends greatly to the present security of the place ; and we hope, your Honours will not be displeased thereat, as we conceived it to be absolutely necessary. As our engineer is gone, we cannot at this time send you a plan thereof, but will endeavour to get one prepared with an estimate of the expense in readiness to send by the January ship."

The Board then proceed to refer to the efforts they had made to improve the fortifications of the fort : " We have completed the stonework on the north side of the fort and about half finished the Lunette to the east and west, the latter of which is now proceeding on in a gradual manner, and we judge the completing of them and filling up the covered way will be sufficient to employ our workmen till we have the pleasure to receive your further commands on this head, and in the interim have only to assure you that the constant and sincere regard we have always had for your Honour's interest will oblige us still to continue our utmost care and industry to prevent putting you to the least unnecessary expense in all the progress we may make therein." The further commands on this head could not have been satisfactory, for Orme, who was in 1756 a member of the Madras Council, informs us that, " the English let the place remain in the state they received it from the French in 1751 until the beginning of the year 1756, when the expectation of another war with that nation, and the reports of the great preparations making in France against India, dictated the necessity of rendering it completely defensible." An addition had been projected many years before, the plan having been approved by Mr. Benjamin Robins, who had come to Madras as Engineer-General of all the Company's fortifications in India. Robins was a close friend of Orme, who described him as a man of great science and an honour to his country. Robins was the real narrator of Lord Anson's *Voyage Round the World*, though the title page carries another name, and he also wrote *A Discourse concerning the Nature and Certainty of Sir Isaac Newton's Method of Fluxions*. His works were edited by Nourse, who himself was a good mathematician and the friend of Newton. The new fortifications had only been erected a short time, when the fort was again attacked by the French under Lally, who, though a hot-headed martinet, was a soldier of great courage and rare unselfishness. We find from the old records that at a consultation held on December 12, 1758, present :

> GEORGE PIGOT, Esq., Governor, President.
> HENRY POWNEY.
> STRINGER LAWRENCE.
> WILLIAM PERCIVAL.
> JOHN SMITH.
> CHARLES BROUCHIER.
> JOHN PYLVES.
> HENRY VANSITTART.
> MR. NORRIS, indisposed.

" The enemy having marched this morning from the Mount, and appeared about daybreak upon Choultry Plain, our army, after about two hours' cannonading, returned into garrison, and the enemy encamped upon the spot where our troops were last night, about a mile and a half to the southward of the Fort. At the same time their advanced guards were seen at the Garden House and Chebauk, the village just on the other side of the Bar. From these motions it appeared to be the enemy's design to form immediately the siege of Madras, and the Board being of opinion that the necessary orders for conducting the defence cannot, without great inconvenience and delay, be debated on and issued by the whole Council, it is therefore unanimously agreed to leave the conduct of the defence to the Governor, who, with Colonel Lawrence, is desired to take the assistance of the other Field-officers and the Engineer as often as maybe requisite, and immediately to issue the necessary orders."

Among the ancient archives in the Record office at Madras there is a *Journal of Transactions during the Siege of Fort St. George, began 12th December*, 1758, that has never been printed. It gives a brief, but clear and precise account of a siege which the Gibbon of our Indian Empire describes as " being without doubt the most strenuous and regular that had ever been carried on in India ; and we have detailed it in hopes that it may remain an example or incitement."

" In order to dispose the garrison with spirits and as a Reward for the Bravery, it is resolved to publish to them in case the enemy shall be either defeated or compelled to raise the siege, the sum of fifty thousand rupees shall be divided amongst them five days after their defeat or retreat, following in this promise of reward the example of the Honourable Company, who have thought two thousand pounds not too large a recompence to the seamen of any of their ships who shall make a good defence when attacked, and repel the enemy."

Wednesday, the 20th.—" This being the day appointed by the Charter for Mayor and Sheriff annually elected to enter on their respective offices, the Council assembled as usual, and a message being brought that the Mayor elect and Sheriff are ready to take the oath, they are introduced with the other members and officers of the Mayor's Court, and the oaths of allegiance and office are first administered by the President to Charles Turner, Esq., who was chosen the 5th instant, and then to Mr. Henry Eustace Johnstone, who was the same day elected Sheriff, both for the year ensuing.

" It having been always usual upon this occasion to salute the new Mayor with nine guns, nine guns were shotted upon the Royal Bastion and pointed at the enemy's quarters and works, and discharged in honour of the new Mayor, and it is hoped with good effect on the enemy."

Thursday the 21st.—" By this sortie the enemy has been thrown into a general commotion, besides the good effects such sallys may have on our sepoys, by enduring them to danger ; the enemy's people are harassed and fatigued, and their works retarded."

Saturday, the 23rd.—" The firing was kept up last night very briskly, as for some nights past, upon the enemy's parallel, as well as upon the other parts where we were informed they are at work. Their parallel seems to be but little advanced, but the French dispersed.

" As it is reasonable to think that public demonstrations of joy upon occasion of victory gained by Colonel Ford might have a good effect by raising the spirits of our people and producing the contrary on the enemy, it was therefore resolved to put the whole garrison under arms and to march them into the covered way, which it was supposed would alarm the enemy and bring them to their front post, and so expose them the more to our shot, and then to fire twenty-one guns into different parts of their quarters and works, and give three running fires from the covered way of the whole garrison, which was executed accordingly."

Sunday, the 24th.—"Yesterday a soldier was tried by a general court martial for cocking his piece at his serjeant and threatening to kill him, and received sentence of death, which was executed this day. Severe examples being thought absolutely necessary at this time to prevent disorders at the garrison, which might prove fatal."

Tuesday, the 2nd.—"The French cannonading during the day. Most of the shells were directed at the houses, and a great many at the Governor's quarters in the Fort House; two fell in it and broke through the first terrace, and twelve or thirteen others fell in or upon the building of the Inner Fort."

Sunday, the 7th January.—"The enemy threw many shells in the night, and at daybreak began to batter with their cannon; their shells all this day continued, as before, to be directed chiefly at the houses, by which many are already in ruin. Their fire from Lally's Battery was from seven cannons and seven mortars, and from the Lorrain Battery from seven cannons and one howtz; as yesterday, they also opened another battery this morning to the left of the Burying Ground, from whence they fired with two pieces on the left face of the North Lunette. The damage done to our works by the enemy's fire is not very great. The embrazures and platforms are more impaired by our own cannon than by their shot or shells, the greater part of which flew into or over the Town. A working party of 100 men are ordered to repair in the night with sand-bags the damaged embrazures on the old North-East, the Demy, the Royal and Pigot Bastion, and 100 sepoys to get up two twenty-four pounders in the place of two which have had their muzzles knocked off on the North-East Bastion. The enemy's works appeared to be much disordered by our fire. They ceased firing about six this evening, and our working party in the covered way can plainly hear them repairing their embrazures and platforms. We have had one European, one Coffree, and one sepoy killed this day, and two Europeans and three sepoys wounded."

Monday, the 8th.—"The enemy ceased firing last night about sunset, and began to throw shells again between eleven and twelve, and continued so all night; they also began to fire from some cannon about two o'clock in the morning, and at daylight they began to play with the same guns and mortars and in the same direction as yesterday, with the addition of two guns more from the Burying Ground, so that their battery at that place now consists of four guns. The damage done to the works this day is much more considerable than yesterday ; the enemy have lowered their embrazures, having probably observed that many of their shots flew over. A working party of 100 Europeans and two companys of sepoys are ordered to repair the damage done to the works."

Friday, January 12th.—" Pursuant to the Resolution taken yesterday, a sortie was made this morning to the southward. Major Cholmondely Brereton, who commanded the sortie, reports that half an hour after four o'clock this morning he marched from the covered way with one company of Grenadiers and a detachment consisting of three officers, three serjeants and eighty-three privates with four hundred sepoys. When his advance party arrived near the Bar they were fired at by some sepoys the enemy had placed behind a trench, who then retired immediately. He then advanced through the topes into a lane which leads to the Governor's house, and there a trooper, who was advanced before the party, brought him word that the enemy were posted at the end of the lane, and had one gun pointed the way our party was marching up ; he thereupon gave orders for the advanced party of Grenadiers to move up briskly, which they did, and gave their fire at about thirty yards' distance from the enemy. The enemy then fired their gun, which was charged with grape, and then abandoned it, and we took possession ; the enemy being quite dispersed, our people were drawing off the gun when the Commandant of sepoys brought word that there was another gun pointed towards the bridge leading to the Island, and desired leave to draw it off, which they did. The number killed and wounded of the enemy's not known. We took prisoners one officer (the Chevalier de ———, a Lieutenant of Lally's Regiment) and four private men. Our loss will appear by the report hereunder."

January 13th.—" Lieutenant Charles Todd, Commandant of Sepoys, reports that the sepoys' arms and ammunition are in very bad order, and in general their officers so ignorant of anything relative to military affairs, and so totally unacquainted with discipline, that there is great difficulty in making them understand the most simple occasional orders."

January 19th.—" It being judged from this intelligence that

the enemy's design to make some attempt this night, the intended sally was countermanded, and all the garrison ordered to lay under arms at their several alarm posts."

February 14th.—" Before the moon rose the enemy advanced a galrionade about thirty feet in front of the stockade under cover of the bank of the glacis, and formed a traverse with a direct communication behind it to the stockade. This work was discovered by the light of the moon about 9 o'clock, and a constant fire of musketry, round and grape, was kept upon that part the whole night, and at daybreak the old guards of the demi-place of arms and facine Battery sallied out and entirely destroyed the work the enemy had done in the night without any other accident on our part than two men slightly wounded."

February 16th.—" As soon as it grew dark three lights were hoisted at the flag-staff as a mark for the ships to come in ; by about eight o'clock at night the six ships anchored in the road, and to the great joy of the garrison, proved to be His Majesty's Ship *Queenborough*, Captain Kemperfelt, and the Company's frigate *Revenge*, with the *Tilbury*, *Winchelsea*, *Prince of Wales*, and *Britannia*, having on board six companys of Colonel Draper's Regiment. Mr. Pybus, one of the Council, went off with a letter from the Governor to Captain Kemperfelt to compliment him on his arrival, and to desire him to land as many of the soldiers as he can to-night ; and Colonel Draper wrote off to Major Monson to the same effect, it being apprehended that if Mr. Lally does intend to make any rush, he will do it this night before our succours can come to our assistance. All the garrison, the Company's servants and inhabitants, were therefore ordered under arms, and continued so the whole night at their several alarm posts, and about two companys were landed from the ships in the night. A constant fire was kept upon the enemy's trenches, which they sometimes returned, and threw a few shells in the beginning of the night, but none after 11 o'clock. About midnight three deserters came in separately from St. Thome, and report that the French entirely abandoned that place, and left several mortars and some stores behind, which were sent there to be embarked in boats and sent to Pondicherry. That their outposts have been ordered to join at the powder mill, and that the enemy intend to raise the siege and march off before daybreak."

February 17th.—"About three in the morning the enemy set fire to several large piles of wood in the rear of their guard battery, and as soon as the day broke it appeared that the enemy had abandoned their trenches and batterys, and were retreating, and about nine o'clock in the morning they blew up the powder mill at Egmore.

"In the enemy's hospital were found 44 sick and wounded soldiers without one person to attend them. Mr. Lally's sudden march may account for his leaving these people behind, but nothing can justify abandoning them without leaving a line to recommend them to our care. They, however, found humanity in their enemy, which was denied them by their General; immediate orders were given that the same care should be taken of them as of our own people, and the greatest part have since recovered. The enemy's precipitate retreat prevented the destruction of the Black Town, which was fully intended, as appears by Mr. Lally's letter of the 14th February. The houses in general have suffered, notwithstanding, considerable damage, as well by the loss of doors, windows, etc., which were useful to the enemy, as by our shot and shells. The Company's garden house and the houses belonging to the European inhabitants in the environs and at the Mount have suffered a severe fate; all of them are greatly damaged; some have only the walls left, and nothing but want of time prevented the total demolition of every one."

So ended the memorable siege of Madras. Time has wrought but little change in the old fort. In *An Account of the War in India, between the English and French, on the Coast of Coromandel*, by Richard Owen Cambridge, 1761, we have *A view of Fort St. George as it appeared after the Siege in* 1759; and the old fort presents very much the same appearance at the present hour. The glacis, the ditch, the basement, all seem familiar to us. Threading a narrow passage, we come to a quaint, rude square, which takes the memory back a century. On one side of it is the statue of Lord Cornwallis, under a stone canopy. Murray informs us that the statue is by Chantrey. But in

Bacon's *First Impressions and Studies from Nature in Hindustan* we have the following :

" This figure was executed in London by the late Thomas Banks, R.A., whose genius won him just celebrity ; though he was peculiar in some of his sentiments, an example of which was exhibited in his design of this statue. Those who were acquainted personally with the late noble Marquis need not be told that he had a cast outwards of one eye. While the work in question was in the model, Banks received a visit from a brother Royal Academician, who expressed his astonishment on observing that Banks had thought proper to make the statue commemorate this obliquity of vision. Banks, however, contested the point on these grounds : ' If,' said he, ' the cast had been *inwards*, it would, I conceive, have conveyed the impression of a contracted character, and I would have corrected it ; but as eyes looking to the right and left at the same moment would impart the idea of an enlarged and comprehensive mind, I have thought it due to the illustrious Governor-General to convey to posterity this natural indication of mental greatness, which I am convinced all must be sensible of, on observing the peculiarity referred to.' Had I been in possession of this anecdote before I went out to India, I should have been particular in ascertaining if Banks really persisted in this notion, so far as to transfer the defect from the model to the marble ; but having been in ignorance of this story while at Madras, I must leave others who may hereafter visit the statue to make observation. Be this as it may, for the fact above stated I have excellent authority, since the artist who remonstrated with Banks was my grandfather, and he related the circumstance to my father on his return from Banks' studio."

The Editor of a charming little work called *Pickings from old Indian Books*, published at Madras some years ago, adds :

" The marble confirms that it was carved, but Banks laboured under a mistake in supposing the cast was a *natural one*. While at Eton, Cornwallis received, by a sad mischance, from a schoolfellow, such a severe blow on the eye from a hockey stick, that for a time his sight was considered in danger ; it, however, only produced 'a slight, but permanent obliquity of vision.' The boy who struck the blow was Shute Barrington, afterwards Bishop successively of Llandaff, Salisbury, and Durham."

From the Cornwallis statue we proceed to the small church which stands near, and is one of the oldest, if not the oldest, Protestant church in India. It was on Easter Monday, April 1, 1678, when Charles II was on the throne, and the madness of the Popish Plot was raging in England, that " the foundation of the English Church (to be built with the contributions of the English in these parts) was begun to be laid, and in respect that it was lined out, and the ground first broken up, upon Lady-day last—'tis intended to be called St. Mary's, and will be eighty feet long, fifty-six feet broad within the walls, and built with aisles arched with brick and stone." The church took a year to build, for it is entered in the Consultation of the 28th October, 1679 :

" The new Church was dedicated by virtue of Commissions directed to the Governor, and Mr. Richard Portman, the Minister, from his Lordship ye Bishop of London, the solemnity was performed in very good order, and concluded with volys of small shott fired by the whole Garrison drawne out and the cannon round the Fort, the Church named St. Mary's as first intended, and from this day forward all public divine service to be there performed."

The interior of the church is picturesque and full of interest to Englishmen, for it contains many memorials of the brave, wise and good, who have helped to make the Empire. One of the most striking of the sepulchral monuments is the statue of that fine soldier, Conway, " the father of the Madras army." Few men saw more active service than he did. On the pedestal are engraved these words : " The Soldier's Friend," and no nobler epitaph could a soldier desire. Not far from the statue of Conway is the bas-relief which represents the death-bed of one of

the noblest soldiers of the Cross—Christian Frederick
Schwartz. Schwartz is surrounded by his friends, and
an angel is seen in the clouds, holding up a cross to his
view. True-hearted, truly loving, devout, the poor loved
him and the powerful respected him. " Do not send me,"
said the warrior Hyder, " any of your agents, for I do not
trust their views or treaties ; but if you wish me to listen to
your proposals send to me the missionary of whose character
I hear so much from every one : him I will receive and trust."
Schwartz, at the earnest request of the Madras Government,
accepted the office of English Envoy. For three months
he lived with Hyder, won his confidence, and did his best to
promote peace. But war was inevitable. When it broke
out Hyder showed his respect for Schwartz by issuing an
order to his officers " to permit the venerable padre to
pass unmolested, and to show him respect and kindness ;
for he is a holy man, and means no harm to my Govern-
menf." The memory of that noble soul still dwells in the
heart of the heathen, and a crowd of primitive native
men and women comes yearly to visit his tomb.

There is a good deal to be seen in Madras. There is a
Government House with a detached banqueting hall,
which was built to commemorate the capture of Seringa-
patam. It contains the portrait of the great Marquess,
who crushed the power of Tippu, of Harris, the curate's
son, who took his capital, of Stringer Lawrence, who trained
Clive to be a soldier, and there is the famous picture of
Eyre Coote, which Wilks informs us the sepoys of old used
always to salute.

Madras has a cathedral which is built after the Italian
or " Jesuit " style of architecture, of which we have so
many examples in Rome, and was evidently designed by
some one who was familiar with the old churches at Goa.
The interior is striking on account of its fine proportions,
its handsome ceilings, and its noble pillars glistening as

if they were made of the purest marble. The chief object
of interest in the cathedral is the fine statue of Bishop
Heber. The face is refined, fastidious, and suggestive of
the finer insight which his Journal displays. In the figure
of the girl kneeling before him we have the unconscious
grace and sweetness of girlhood. The face of Sir James
Anderson by the same artist conveys the expression of
powerful thought, and the whole figure has the appearance
of calmness and repose. In the statue of Dr. Corrie the eye
is attracted and the grace of the composition destroyed
by the figure of a native with an obtrusive rope of hair.
The monument to Broadfoot, the gallant defender of Jella-
labad, is also marred by the figures of the two sepoys. An
inscription informs us that he was the last of three brothers
who died for their country in the battlefield of Asia. Of
him Lord Hardinge said, and it is no small praise coming
from the soldier that turned the tide in the battle at Albuera,
" He was as brave as he was able, and second to none in all
the great qualities of a soldier."

Madras has a Museum which has a name among scientific
men all over the world for its many unknown forms of
animal life. It has also a fine collection of coins. Among
them is the *Aureus* of Claudius, which was struck to commemorate the conquest of Britain, and found in the Madura
District. Strange that its last resting-place should be in a
museum in one of the capitals of an Empire greater than
the colossal dominion of Rome. Our Oriental Empire is only
a century old, and therefore young compared to the long
leadership of Rome. We seldom realize how thoroughly
the Romans had established themselves in Britain, and that
their occupation of it lasted for nearly four hundred years.
They had anticipated in many important features our administration of India. They had their collectors and their
judges and they, too, built magnificent roads and enjoyed
the expensive luxury of a Public Works Department. The

Forum was the cutchery and something more—it was the centre of business. The Roman magnate lived in his villa in the country, as the collector and judge live in their bungalows. But the villas were adorned with rare marble and mosaics. All was, peaceful and quiet. Then came the time when Rome needed all her soldiers at home, and the departure of the Roman legions left Britain defenceless. The Britons knew nothing of self-government. All authority had been centralised at Rome and all local vigour had been repressed and crushed. Patriotism had died by foreign conquest, and no one was ready to defend his country. The savage horde marched through the land and the grand buildings of the Romans were given to the flames. When the enemy arrives at our northern gate the stability of our Indian Empire will, let all men bear in mind, depend mainly on the loyalty and contentment of the people.

Madras has also another institution whose work has won it an European reputation—her Observatory. A century ago the East India Company, who were more generous patrons of literature, science and art than the Imperial Government which has succeeded them, resolved to establish an observatory at Madras " for promoting the knowledge of astronomy, geography, and navigation in India." Sir Charles Oakely, feeling certain that his liberal-minded masters would sanction the proposal, sent home to build an observatory, had it erected and supplied with instruments before the orders of the Court reached Madras. But he would not have been able to accomplish this good work except for the liberality of William Petrie, Member of Council. Two years previously William Petrie (1787) had built an observatory at his own expense, and collected in it the instruments which the Company had sent out from time to time, which were scattered over the country. At his own expense William Petrie added a small, but excellent transit instrument. When he went to Europe he presented this observatory and instruments to the public.

On the south wall of the observatory we find a slab bearing the following inscription :

Astronomiæ Consecratum
Sumptibus Societatis Anglicanæ
in India mercaturæ faciendæ
favente Carolo Oakeley Barto:
Præfecto Præsidii Sancti Georgi
A.D. MDCCXCII.

A translation in Tamil, Telugu, and Hindustani is carved on the granite pier that bore Petrie's transit instrument, in order that " Posterity may be informed a thousand years hence of the period when the mathematical sciences were first planted by British liberality in Asia." After noticing with profound respect the old astronomical clock, which for a century has proved " a most excellent timekeeper," we take our departure, wondering whether there were many things manufactured in the present day which would so rule and stand the test of time.

XIV

PONDICHERRY

I T was a fresh morning in September when we left Madras for Pondicherry. The recent rain had refreshed the atmosphere and made the trees green and fresh. For the first fifty miles we passed through stretches of land covered with scrub, dotted here and there with patches of cultivation. From the carriage window we saw scenes which Homer had seen and painted many centuries ago. The ploughman had turned his team of sleek oxen at the end of the furrow, and with his wife and children was enjoying his morning meal of cakes and corn. The bright scarlet dresses of the women and children contrasted well with the rich green of the shrubs. Then we went by patches of broad green rice fields, covered with water, in which men and women were reaping. In the distance were the blue Arcot hills, reminding us of the Deccan ; but the frequent groves of palm trees bore testimony to our being not far from the sea. The further we proceeded the richer grew the soil, and the country spread out into broad fields of red and yellow corn ripe for the sickle. As we neared a village we fled past many a lodge in a garden of cucumbers, and the daughter of Zion was standing at the door. At noon we arrived at Villupuram junction, where we had to change carriages for Pondicherry ; and after a run of a couple of hours the train drew up at a platform, where a band of dark savages addressed us in French. They took possession of us and

PONDICHERRY.

our luggage, and soon we found ourselves rolling rapidly down the main street of Pondicherry in a *pousse-pousse*. A *pousse-pousse* is an enlarged perambulator, and a man of mature years finds it a little incongruous to be wheeled down the street as in the days of childhood. But the place of the dainty nursemaid is taken by a stalwart, well-built, coal-black savage, whose dress has not troubled the sewing-machine. Another savage pushes the vehicle from behind. The *pousse-pousse* is, however, a decidedly comfortable conveyance, it makes no noise, and though the progress is rapid, is safe. The *pousse-pousse* man neither shies, nor kicks, nor jibs. Carriages and horses are almost unknown in Pondicherry, and the absence of noise is one of the charms of the French capital. After a drive of twenty minutes, we found ourselves at the entrance of the Hôtel de Londres et Paris, and a landlady from Paris received us. A room clean and neat, facing the sea, is secured at the modest cost of Rs. 4 a day. For this sum we are fed far better than at the majority of Indian hotels. Pondicherry is a paradise for a poor man. A large house built on the model of a mansion in a French country town costs Rs. 60 a month, and smaller villas can be had for Rs. 20 to Rs. 40. The balconies that project from the windows give a continental and picturesque aspect to the streets. There is not the slightest trace of the genius of ugliness, which our Public Works Department possess, and which is imparted by them with such considerable success to the buildings they erect. The cost of maintaining these houses is as moderate as the rent. It has to be small, because the incomes of those who occupy them are small. The pay of a High Court Judge is about Rs. 250 a month. He is a man who has been carefully taught the science of jurisprudence at a French university, and has had some practical experience of the law courts in France before appointment. The salaries of the other French officials are on the same modest scale

324

as those paid to the Judicial Department. The French,
when they founded their settlements, introduced into
them the habits of thrift, which are characteristic of the
nation. The Englishman unfortunately imitated the
luxurious splendour of the nobles of the Moghul Empire, and
a luxurious style of living came to be regarded as a necessity.
In the days of the pagoda tree the factor and merchant
considered it enhanced their importance if they took no
heed of what they paid for their ordinary articles of daily
consumption, and the natives have continued to charge
their unfortunate successors fifty per cent. more than the
market price for all they have. The day is, however, not
far distant when English officials and English merchants
will have to study economy, and there is no reason why the
sons of merchants, squires, and vicars should, in India,
live as luxuriously as English noblemen. But a truce to
digression. After a short rest, we leave the hotel, and a
walk of a few yards brings us to the Place de la République,
at the head of the pier, where, arranged in a semi-circle,
are the lofty carved monoliths, which tradition says Dupleix
had brought from Gingee, the great mountain fortress sixty
miles from Pondicherry. Of the many heroic deeds by
which the French attempted to found an empire in the East
few equal and none surpass the storming of Gingee. " This
place," writes Orme, " was formerly the residence of a race
of Morratoe Kings, whose dominion extended from hence
to the borders of the kingdom of Tangore: these princes
were the ancestors of the famous Sevajee, who became king
over all the Morratoe nations, and Sevajee himself, it is
said, was born at Gingee." When Orme wrote his great
work little was known regarding the history of the Mahrattas : Shivaji was born many hundred miles away
from Gingee, but the fortress was captured by him when
it was in the possession of the Bijapur kingdom, and it
remained in the possession of the Mahrattas for twenty-two

years, when it fell into the hands of the Moghuls. Orme, who gives a good plan of the town and surrounding mountain, writes :

"A strong wall, flanked with towers, and extending near three miles, incloses three mountains, which form nearly an equilateral triangle ; they are steep and craggy, and on the top of each are built large and strong forts : besides there are many other fortifications upon the declivities : On the plain between the three mountains is a large town. The Indians, who esteem no fortifications very strong unless placed upon high and difficult eminences, have always regarded Gingee as the strongest fortress in the Carnatic."

Dupleix thought the capture of Gingee would make him master of southern India, and he sent Bussy with a small detachment to take it by surprise. By petarding one of the gates the young French General gained possession of the town at sunset, and proceeded to erect a barricade of baggage waggons in the streets. But his position was one of great peril, for from the heights above the enemy poured down a deadly shower of shot and grape. The French returned their fire with the mortars and guns till the moon set, which was the signal to storm the fortifications. "None but the Europeans were destined to this hardy enterprize, who attacked all the three mountains at the same time, and found on each redoubts above redoubts, which they carried successively sword in hand, until they came to the summits, where the fortifications were stronger than those they had surmounted. They nevertheless pushed on and petarded the gates, and by daybreak were in possession of them all."

On a pedestal constructed from old fragments of temples brought from Gingee stands the statue of Dupleix. He is represented in Court dress, with long riding boots, and there is considerable originality and life in the attitude of the figure. The sculptor has also succeeded in giving the magnificent head, lofty and wide forehead, and the intellectual face full of energy and penetration of the great French administrator. After a century of neglect, France determined to erect this monument of one of the most famous of her sons. With much pomp and ceremony the statue was unveiled on July 16, 1870. The Pondicherry paper, which gave a glowing account of the fête that took place, that day also announced that the Prussians had crossed the French frontier and occupied the first French village.

A few yards from the statue of Dupleix is the Place du Gouvernement, on the right of which is Government House, or La Gouvernement—a fine substantial building. In the centre of the Place is a curious rectangular stone building, which, on approaching, we discovered to be a fountain. A quaint Latin inscription records that here, in olden times, stood a dancing girl's house. A King and his minister were passing in the dusk of the evening when they saw a light burning in it, and mistaking it for a shrine they worshipped at it. But when the mistake was discovered the king was so wroth that he ordered it to be levelled to the ground, and a fountain mysteriously sprung up at the spot. The King and his minister mistaking at night a dancing girl's house for a shrine might create a suspicion in a vulgar mind. The origin of the legend is, however, probably due to the fact that two miles from Pondicherry is a tank which was dug at the expense of a dancing girl, and from this tank comes the water of the fountain. Another inscription informs us that on this spot stood the original citadel built by François Martin, the founder of Pondicherry. François had lent the Governor of Gingee money which he could not repay, and in return he bestowed on him a village near the coast and gave him permission to fortify a strip of land by the sea. The fortification that Martin erected could not have been of any great extent, seeing that it cost only the modest sum of seven hundred crowns. Beneath the shelter of the slender walls, he however proceeded to lay out streets and to build houses for the native weavers, whom he wished to attract to his new settlement. The aim of his policy was to gather at Pondicherry a thrifty,

DUPLEIX' STATUE, PONDICHERRY.

loyal population, and he was wise enough to see that the best way of doing this was by respecting the manners, customs and religion of the people, and so winning their love and confidence. His policy proved eminently successful. However, just as Martin's little colony began to rise and flourish, a grave danger menaced it. Shivaji seized

Gingee and threatened an attack on the new settlement. But Martin pacified the great Freebooter by a present of 500 pagodas, and he obtained from him a grant for the French to reside at Pondicherry in perpetuity, on condition they did not interfere in the wars of the neighbouring States. Shivaji, however, insisted that the French should pay him a heavy tax on the imports and exports of the little colony which continued to grow in wealth and importance. To protect it still further Martin now threw around the town a wall which was flanked by four towers, each of which mounted six guns. Martin had hardly finished the new fortifications when war broke out between France and Holland, and in 1693 Pondicherry was attacked by a Dutch fleet consisting of nineteen ships of war. Martin, who had only forty European soldiers to defend the place, was compelled to surrender. The Dutch fully realised the value of their new possession and proceeded to improve the town and fortification to make it the capital of their Indian possessions. But five years after it had come into their hands, the treaty of Ryswick restored Pondicherry to the French. Martin hastened from France, again to take possession of the city which he had founded, but the Dutch refused to restore it until they had been handsomely compensated for the improvements they had made. A French writer, with patriotic indignation, states : " The sale, characteristic of a nation of traders, took place on the 17th September, 1699, when Martin paid 16,000 pagodas to the Director of the Dutch Company as the price of the improvements and fortifications they had made." Under the wise and vigorous administrations of Martin the town rapidly grew in prosperity. He mapped out new streets on the lines of an important European capital, erected substantial houses, warehouses and shops, and built a palace for the Governor. When the English had only a small factory at Calcutta, and Chowringee was a malarious swamp, Pondicherry was a flourishing town with fifty thousand inhabitants. For the greater protection of the city Martin proceeded to construct a citadel after the model of Tournay. When finished, the new fortress was consecrated with great pomp and ceremony. On the 25th August, 1706, a stately procession of laymen and priests, chanting the *Te Deum* and *Exaudiat*, wended its way around the town, and as it reached a bastion the cannons sent forth a roar of triumph and joy. This was the crowning day of François Martin's life. A few months later the patriot's manly heart ceased to beat. The priest who buried him wrote :

" Aujourd'hui, 31 Décembre, 1706, j'ai enterre dans la fortresse de Fort-Louis, M. François Martin, Chevalier, général et governeur de Pondichery, après avoir reçu les sacraments à l'église. Pondichery lui a obligation de ce qu'il est aujourd'hui. Signe Fr. Laurent de Angoulême, Capuc. Miss. Apostolique, et custode indigne."

Near the fountain, according to local tradition, lie buried the remains of François Martin, a man worthy to rank with Hastings, Munro, Elphinstone. Like all men who have been great and successful administrators in India, he possessed the intuitive knowledge that kindness and sympathy are potent factors in governing Orientals.

Leaving the fountain, we walk to the end of the square opposite to Government House, and take the street which leads by the cathedral called *Nôtre Dame des Anges*. It is built after the modern Italian style of architecture, which the Portuguese have so frequently employed at Goa, and which lends itself to the use of white chunam. From an architectural point of view there is nothing to admire, but there is nothing positively ugly or offensive, as is the case with the majority of churches built by the English in India. It has been said that the fanes for prayer erected by a people express in stone their highest aspirations. A cynic has remarked that the churches erected by Anglo-Indians at the beginning of last century are a striking example of the truth of the statement. The square body of the church represents a beer case, and the short ugly steeple the beer bottle.

Going from the Cathedral we enter a narrow street, and coming to a gateway with the door open we enter a court-yard which contains some old tombs. Among them we find a plain substantial one, on which is inscribed the name of Bussy. Here lies at rest, after a stormy career, the great French general, whose sagacity and address was equal to that of Warren Hastings, and whose courage and genius were hardly inferior to Clive's. It is strange that no French writer has given us a satisfactory memoir of Bussy. It is the English historian who, in stately prose, worthy of his theme, has given an account of the campaign in which Bussy played so prominent a part, that has paid the best tribute to his memory. When Orme, after the publication of the first volume of his history, visited France, Bussy asked him to visit him at his château because he considered himself under an obligation to the historian for the precision and impartiality with which he had recorded his actions. The French general presented his guest with several important documents, including a narrative of his career in India, which unfortunately was never printed. He also gave him a draft of the routes of his various marches. As Orme states : " Bussy was the only man of distinguished capacity who served under Dupleix, and Dupleix's conduct to this officer showed that he knew the value of merit, and was capable of employing it to the utmost advantage, for although M. Bussy had by his expedition to the northward acquired much reputation and a great fortune, he beheld his successor without the least envy, and implicitly followed his advice in all affairs of which M. Bussy by his situation might be a better judge than himself." Far different was the behaviour of Lally. Arrogant and vain, he was jealous of Bussy and dispensed with the Indian experience of the sepoy general. " The practice of European warfare," writes Colonel Wilkes, " was with him the bed of Procrustes to which all Indian habits and prejudices must be forcibly accommodated." If Lally had taken the advice of Bussy all hopes of French dominion in the East would not have perished at the fatal field of Wandewash. Bussy was among the prisoners, and Colonel Coote did homage to his character by immediately complying with his request for a passport to Pondicherry. The Madras Government were wroth when they heard that Eyre Coote had allowed Bussy to depart, for in those days paroles were frequently broken, and they requested that Coote should ask Bussy to return to camp, according to his promise to surrender himself when requested. Bussy was ill and some delay took place in complying with the request. Lally, when too late, realised the value of Bussy's experience and knowledge of war, and attempted to ransom him. The fiery Eyre Coote, ever ready to take offence, wrote to the Madras Government :

" Here is a letter come down from Mr. Lally to you with a bag of pagodas, which I suppose is for the ransom of Brigadier-General Bussy, and the other two who have broken their honour with me. I shall send the man to you the first opportunity who brought it. I have had the rope about his neck, and threatened to hang him, but shall do it in reality to pretended men of honour if I chance to meet with them. I beg, Sir, you will return the pagodas, and let Mr. Lally know that though he is General of the French Army, he has no pretentions to regulate the English town. I have hardly philosophy enough to have patience when I enter upon the subject."

But Eyre Coote did an injustice to Bussy, who wrote him an indignant manly letter, warmly repudiating the insinuation that he was capable of breaking his word, and stating that he would return to camp as soon as his health would permit. He kept his promise, and after staying a short time at Madras, he returned to France. After an absence of twenty-four years, Bussy returned to India, but standing by his grave we forget the Bussy, incompetent from age and disease, and think of the brave and gallant leader who led the storming party at Gingee.

Leaving the tomb of Bussy, we go to the State Library, which contains twelve thousand books, neatly arranged and catalogued. Amongst them are many rare histories, memoirs, and travels. When the old Brahman Librarian discovered we did not visit the library merely for the vulgar pleasure of reading books, but that we loved their sight, their touch, he brought forth from hidden recesses his treasures. The keen intellectual face of the old man lighted up with pride and joy as he showed us old folios of travels, and dainty classics in their original morocco. His special pride was a Polyglot Bible printed more than two centuries ago, and one enjoyed the exquisite pleasure which only the lover of books can feel in turning over its leaves of hand-made paper and in gazing on its clear-cut types. In a room adjoining the library are kept the ancient records. Among them are many memoirs written by French adventurers regarding the state of the country, when the death struggle was taking place between the English and the French dominion in the East. These memoirs, while they throw fresh light on the subject, also confirm the marvellous accuracy of the historian who wrote *A History of the Military Transactions of the British Nation in Hindustan.*

One evening, taking a volume of Orme with us, we walked into the country to see if we could discover any traces of the old fortification of the town, for in its great siege we had always taken the deepest interest. Thirty years have passed since we first discovered in a library Orme's History, three folio volumes, bound in leather, with mouldy backs. We remember the days we spent in reading about the battles and sieges, and the delight with which we used to look at the maps and plans. De Quincey tells us of the effect produced on his imagination by the study of Livy. At the sound of the words *Populus Romanus* old Rome was revealed to him, he saw the array of the lictors with their fasces, and he heard the tramp of the Legions and the shouting of the crowd that lined the Sacred Way. A feeling akin to this possessed our boyish imagination when we read in Orme's " pictured page " the closing scene of the siege of Pondicherry. We saw " the garrison drawn up under arms on the passage before the citadel and the English troops facing them." We looked with pity on the grenadiers of Lorrain and Lally, who " once the ablest-bodied men in the army, appeared the most impaired, having constantly put themselves forward to every service, and it was recollected that from their first landing throughout all the services of the field and all the distresses of the blockade, not a man of them had ever deserted to the English colours." We shared the " victor soldier's sigh to this solemn contemplation of the fate of war, which might have been his own," and deep was our sympathy for French troops, who " after they were reviewed, marched into the citadel, where they deposited their arms in heaps and were then conducted to their prisons." Sorrow was, however, tempered with patriotic pride when we read :

" The next morning the English flag was hoisted in the town and its display was received by the salute of a thousand pieces of cannons from every gun of every ship in the road, in all the English posts and batteries, the field artillery of the time, and on the ramparts and defences of Pondicherry."

The English treated Pondicherry as the French had treated Fort St. David and Madras : the fortifications were blown down, and in the *Madras Record* there is the following grim entry :

" That notice was given to the inhabitants of Pondicherry that they are permitted to pull down their houses, provided they carry materials to Madras, Cuddalore, or Fort St. David."

Orme in hand, we wander over the fields attempting to settle where was the bleaching town and the North Redoubt and follow in the theatre of its actions the great siege until the sun sets a golden ball beneath the ocean, the sky for a few seconds grows blood-red, and darkness falls on the land.

XV

CUDDALORE

TWELVE miles south of Pondicherry is situated Fort
St. David at Cuddalore, which, owing to its association
with the great names of Stringer Lawrence, and Clive, must
always be to Englishmen who take pride in the brave deeds
of their forefathers, one of the most memorable places in the
Empire.

One morning at dawn we manage to squeeze ourselves
into a jutka, which is to take us to Cuddalore. The
operation requires considerable skill and agility, for the
jutka is a small box on two wheels. A small pony drags the
box, and a large naked black savage drives it. At full gallop
we proceed through the streets of Pondicherry. Our
body sways to and fro, and our knees, being in our mouth,
threaten to dislocate our jaws. When we reach the suburb
we pray for mercy and implore the driver to stop. We
prefer to walk, and with some difficulty we extricate our
bruised and battered bodies. Delightful was it to enjoy
once more the use of our limbs. The morning was fresh and
the sea was golden with the rising sun. The peasants were
coming to market. The men looked fine robust fellows, and
many of the young women were handsome, and one was
struck with the free grace that distinguished their move-
ments as they went by, carrying huge baskets on their heads.
Men and women laughed and chatted, and the children
trotted by their side, looking solemn and grave, as only
Oriental children can. But they are always picturesque,

with their naked legs and their short bright jackets of orange and yellow. Large carts laden with vegetables rolled by, and we were struck with the size of the oxen, their delicate skins, and long stately horns. The road, lined with large trees, passes through a fertile country, dotted with populous villages. The ryots are working in the fields, and from a broad tank close by comes a creaking sound. It is due to the water buckets which the men are raising with their feet as they have done from time immemorial in the east. "The land whither thou goest in to possess it, is not as the land of Egypt, where thou sowest thy seed, *and wateredst* it with thy foot, as a garden of herbs ; but it is a land of hills and valleys, and drinketh water of the rain of heaven."

The sun now grows too powerful for us to continue our walk, and we have again to resort to the jutka. Deeply rejoiced are we when, after driving through a stately avenue, we reach the porch of a fine upper-storied house. It is the official residence of the Collector, and with the wide and generous hospitality, which is a special characteristic of the Madras Presidency, he had kindly placed it at our disposal, and sent servants to attend to our wants. The house has many historic associations, for it is the garden house so often mentioned in the old Madras records, and was built one hundred and sixty years ago. Orme writes :

" At the distance of a mile and a half to the north-west of Fort St. David was a country house, appointed for the residency of the Governor, behind which, to the north, was a large garden, inclosed with a brick wall, and, before the house to the south, a court with buildings on each side of it."

The garden, with its old trees, still exists, and the buildings on each side of the court have been converted into offices for the Collector. In two rooms are neatly arranged the old muniments. Turning over their leaves we realize more fully than we did before that the founders of the Empire were factors and merchants. It is the price of mulmuls and taftas which occupied their minds, and they devoted their days to drawing up charter-parties and bills of lading. They ask their masters to send them writers and workmen, and they are greatly pleased when they receive a letter from Madras advising that " they had sent us one John Dyer, a bricklayer, whom our honourable masters have entertained to serve for five years at the rate of ninety pounds sterling per annum, to commence from July 18, the day of his arrival." But these factors were not mere money-making merchants, for the old records bear witness that they were endowed with a strong sense of duty to God and their country, whose honour and interests they were always ready to defend, and many a street fight and many a signal deed of valour did the old fort witness.

It was in the year 1690 we purchased it from the Mahrattas, and Mr. Hatsell was ordered " to go to receive possession of the fort and pay the money," and with him were to be sent " some factors to be of council there, also a Lieutenant, two Ensigns, gunners, etc., officers, one hundred soldiers, twenty matrosses, twenty laskars, thirty great guns, one hundred barrels of powder, two hundred musquets, one hundred cartouches, one hundred swords, and ammunition, etc., necessary for such a garrison and settlement," and it was resolved " that the guns, stores, and household stuff be removed from Conimeer and the southern factories thither."

The cession included not only the fort but the adjacent towns and villages " within ye randome shott of a piece of ordnance." The best brass gun at Madras was sent with Hatsell, and he was informed that it " lyes in the gunners art to load and fire it to the best advantage." The gunner was evidently skilled in his art, for on September 23, 1690, at the time when Dutch William was busy establishing his power in Ireland, the " randome shott " was fired and it fell beyond Cuddalore. And to this day the villages included within the range of "that randome shott" are known as the "Gundu Gramam" or "Cannon Ball Villages."

The English proceeded at once to introduce law and order into their new possession. Mr. Haynes, Mr. Watts, and Macudum Nina were appointed justices of the Choultry "to try and determine causes Civill and Criminal, and to execute according to sentence, lyfe only excepted, which must be done by another court of judicature." "All tryalls of moment" were to be registered by "an English Clark of said coart," "and the differences amongst black merchants" be decided by "Arbitrators of their own cast." It was also proposed that a mint should be established, but the mint for coining silver and gold was not formed till the beginning of 1747, when the capture of Madras by the French made Fort St. David the chief settlement on the coast.

All, and their name is legion, who have read Macaulay's brilliant essay on Clive, know that he was one of the prisoners who escaped from Madras to Fort St. David. It was at Fort St. David he gained, by the daring courage which he displayed, his first commission. In a despatch to the court of Directors, dated May 2, 1747, we read :

"Mr. Robert Clive, writer in the service, being of martial disposition, and having acted as a volunteer in our late engagements, we have granted him an Ensign's commission, upon his application for the same."

An old writer, in English worthy of the great lexicographer, informs us :

"As Ensign he served under Admiral Boscawen at the siege of Pondicherry, September, 1748 ; his gallant conduct in the defence of the advanced breach gave the first prognostic of that high military spirit, which was the spring of his future actions and the principal source of the decisive intrepidity and elevation of mind which were his characteristical endowments."

Three years later, in the expedition against Devi-Cotah, Clive, then holding the rank of Lieutenant, volunteered to lead the attack at the breach. His small platoon of thirty-four Europeans became separated from the sepoys, and was attacked by a large body of the enemy's horse in the rear. They had no time to face about and defend themselves, and in an instant twenty-six of the platoon were cut to pieces. "A horseman had his sword uplifted to strike at Lieutenant Clive, who escaped the blow by stepping on one side whilst the horse passed him : he then ran towards the sepoys, whom he had the good fortune to join, being one of four who were all that escaped from the slaughter." Thus narrowly did England escape losing the man who by his courage and statesmanship laid the foundation of her Oriental Empire. Shortly after the capture of Devi-Cotah Clive resigned his commission and was appointed steward. But when prospects of active service again opened before him, he returned to the ranks, and in the old records we read :

"Mr. Robert Clive, who has lately been very serviceable in conducting several parties to camp, offering to go without any consideration to pay, provided we will give him a Brevet to entitle him to the rank of a Captain, as he was an officer at the siege of Pondicherry almost the whole time of the war, and distinguished himself on many occasions, it is conceived that this officer may be of some service, and, therefore, now ordered that a Brevet be drawn out and given him."

As a brevet Captain, Clive started from Fort St. David on the expedition for the relief of Arcot. He was then only twenty-five, and he returned to England at the age of twenty-seven, having earned the reputation of being one of the first soldiers of the age. Six years later he came back to Fort St. David as Governor, but had held the office only a few weeks when he was summoned to Madras, to command the troops which were being sent to Bengal to recover our lost possession, and to revenge a foul massacre.

CUDDALORE

Early in the afternoon we set forth from the garden house to visit the old fort. To reach it we had once again to submit to the tortures of a jutka, but our miseries were, to some degree, mitigated by the companionship of a retired native official. He had the good manners which distinguished the Indian gentlemen of the old school, and thirty years of Government service had not dulled his keen intellect. Vigorous in body and mind, it was difficult at first to determine to what race he belonged. However, after a few moments' conversation we asked him if he were not a Deccan Brahmin. Then he told us, with obvious pride, how his grandfather had commanded a squadron, under Shivaji, and for his services had been rewarded with a grant of land, and the family had been settled in these parts from that day. We became fast friends on our telling him that many happy years of our life had been spent in the capital of the Deccan, and that we took an interest in the tales of wild Mahratta battle. The old man grew eloquent as he discoursed about the brave deeds of his forefathers, for a lifetime spent in official harness had not destroyed the love and pride of race which the Mahratta has in common with the Celt. A staunch conservative, he did not seem to have much respect for the modern native official, the product of our higher education. He considered they wanted backbone. But what were you to expect if you destroyed the belief in the old gods, and sapped the force of customs which had existed for ages ? It required delicate handling, and the expression of tolerant views, to extract from him his opinion regarding the administration in which he had played a part. But it was the same tale we had heard in the Deccan and Bengal. He did not consider the people had grown more prosperous by our rule, and though, no doubt, the British Government was a very perfect and good Government, and meant well, it had not made the people happier. There was considerable distress amongst the poorer classes, and the old grain‾pits now lay empty. After having had to study for many years the optimistic opinions of official scribes, the pessimism of the old man was both interesting and instructive.

Time passed swiftly in discussing social, religious, and political problems with the old Mahratta, and we felt sad when the conversation was interrupted by the carriage halting at the gate of a small bungalow. Here we had to alight to see all that remains of the old ramparts of Fort St. David. Entering the garden we could trace, by means of a broken wall, the position of one of the old bastions facing the river. The view from it was noble. Below, the river spread itself out, full and broad, between low banks covered with palms. Large boats, furnished with brown sails, were dropping lazily to the sea, and in the far distance, beyond the wide expanse of waters, could be seen the red and white houses of the old city of Cuddalore. After enjoying the fair prospect for a little time, we proceeded to examine some of the subterranean " Roman ways," to which Orme alludes in his history. They seem to have gone completely round the Fort, under the glacis, and to have formed means of communication for the garrison. The greater part of the site of the old Fort is now covered with tall Casuarina trees and at the edge of the grove we found a bench where, deserting our companions, we sat for some time, and conjured up spirits of the past. We see the " writer " come forth after a busy day at the ledger, and the factor enjoying with his wife and children the freshness of the evening air. A stout, hale man, of about fifty, dressed in scarlet coat, with a rapier by his side and a three-cornered hat under his arm, is engaged in earnest conversation with a slim stripling. Major Stringer Lawrence, commandant of all the Company's troops in the East Indies, is relating his experiences with Clayton's own regiment, to Clive. He tells him about Gibraltar and its siege, in which he took part, when serving in the ranks, and he gives him an account of his adventures with Wager's fleet on the coast of Italy. He describes how the column, headed by the King's son, broke the heart of the French line at Fontenoy, and how they would have won the day if they had not been deserted by the Dutch. The lad's heart beats fast as Lawrence describes the gallant charge of the French guards, and how, with a wild yell, the Highlanders broke our ranks at Culloden, They eagerly discuss the news from Trichinopoly, which Lawrence considers, from all accounts, must be very like Gibraltar, and Clive with eagerness assures him that if he could get together a small force, he might, by a rapid dash on Arcot, save the rock from falling into the hands of the French. Time is precious. News has reached them of a large convoy of French ships having left Mauritius, and they scan the horizon with anxious eyes, to see if they can catch the first glimpse of the English fleet, which is expected from Madras. Their conversation is interrupted by a messenger, who comes in hot haste to inform them that the Mahratta horsemen have attacked " the Bounds," and two of their small band of officers have fallen, fighting gallantly to the last. Lawrence orders the call to arms to be sounded, and sends Clive to see that the gates are securely guarded. The evil tidings swiftly spread, and the men and women hasten away from the rampart. No sound breaks the stillness of the air, except the tramp of the sentry, and the roar of the ocean, as it breaks on the bar.

A voice interrupts our reverie. It is the old Mahratta, who has come to remind us that it is growing dark, and we must hasten home, for the road is not very good.

At break of dawn we start with our Mahratta friend to visit the city of Cuddalore. A more enjoyable drive it would be difficult to imagine. The air is fresh, the road is lined with noble trees, and the country is rich with maize, corn, and rice, spreading as far as the eye can scan. Before we reach the town, we skirt the broad river, lit with the scarlet shafts of sunrise, and here nature grows even more rich and lavish. But man has not been lavish in his bounties on the city of Cuddalore. The streets are extremely narrow and dirty, and with some difficult we thread our way through them, in order to reach the old factory. We pass through a lofty gateway and enter a wide courtyard, where a large number of women are busy in packing ground-nuts, which are exported in large quantities to Europe for the manu-facture of "olive oil." The rapid growth of this export has done much to increase the prosperity of Southern India, but my conservative friend refused to regard it as a blessing. Men, he stated, had begun to cease to grow corn and rice in order to cultivate the ground-nut, and when there was no corn grown the people would starve. In fact the good old man displayed as much ignorance of economics as a cabinet minister. Passing through the courtyard we come to a fine massive building which was once the old factory. For some years it had been used as a gaol. On the ground floor are spacious vaults, in which the factors stored the piece-goods, the cinnamon, the pepper, meant for Europe : above-is a spacious lofty room which used to be the common dining-room, and adjoining it is the chamber which, by order of their masters, was fitted up as a chapel, for the directors of the East India Company were as solicitous for the welfare of the souls of their servants as of their bodies. They not only sent arms and ammunition for the Fort, but also a supply of Bibles and catechisms for distribution, and " when any shall be able to repeat the catechism by heart, you may give to each of them two rupees for their encouragement." In the present day we fear there is not a single Member of Council or Secretary to Government who could earn two rupees by repeating the catechism. It was ordered that " whosoever shall be guilty of lying shall pay four fanams." " Whosoever shall profaine the name of God by swearing or cursing he shall pay twelve pence to the use of ye poore for every oath or curse, and in case of non-payment after demand, the said sume shall be levyed by distress, and in default of such distress the offender shall sett in the stocks three hours." The penalty for remaining out of the house all night (without license from the chief), or being found absent at the time of shutting the gates after nine at night (without reasonable excuse), was " ten rupees to the use of ye poore, or sett one whole day publikely in the stocks." But whosoever committed the offence of having "appeared to be drunk " had to pay five shillings for the use of the poor for every offence, and in case of non-payment after demand, " the said sume shall be levied by distress, and in defect of such distress, the offender shall sett in the stocks six hours." Every Protestant that lodged " within the house " who was absent from the publike prayers morning and evening on week days, " without lawful excuse," had to pay twelve pence for the poore, or be confined one whole weeke within the house for every such default ; but whatsoever Christian in the Hon'ble Company's service that was absent from the publike prayers morning and evening on the Lord's Day, without a lawful excuse, had also to pay twelve pence for the poore for every such offence, but in case of default the offender had to suffer imprisonment " until payment of said sume so forfeited by law." It was also commanded " that these orders shall be read publikely to the ffactory twice in the yeare, that is, upon the Sunday next after Christmas day, and upon the Sunday next after Midsummer day in the forenoone, after Divine service, that none may pretend ignorance thereof ; and all persons concerned therein are hereby strictly charged and commanded to give due observance and not contrary to the same, upon paine of undergoing the penaltys appointed, and suffiring further displeasure." These orders were made by " the Agents and Council for affairs of the Hon'ble the English East India Company upon the coast of Chormandell, and in the Bay of

Bengal (for advancing the Glory of God, upholding the honour of the English nation, and the preventing of disorders) to be observed by all persons imployed in the said Hon'ble Company's service in the Factorys in the Bay of Bengal." They were issued the 12th day of December, Anno Domini, 1679, and in the one and thirtieth yeare of the raigne of Our Soveraigne Lord Charles the Second, by the Grace of God, King of England, Scotland, France, and Ireland, Defender of the Faith, etc.," and they show that the wild orgy of the Restoration had not reached India, but that the factors were what Puritanism had made them, serious, earnest, sober in life and conduct.

After wandering over the old factory we proceeded to the church, a small neat building, which is believed to be the identical building taken from the Jesuit priests in 1749, on their expulsion from Cuddalore as French spies. In the churchyard there are some interesting old tombs. Here lies Agnes Macdonald, " who died on the 7th July, 1732, of a broken heart, aged 20 " ; her husband had been " murdered by an infuriated noble of Muslem " a fortnight before. Leaving the churchyard we found our way with some difficulty to the old cemetery. With proud and pensive thought we wander among the tombs and read the inscriptions carved upon them. It is only when we visit these old cemeteries scattered about the land, we realize the courage and self-devotion, the suffering and woe, by which England's Empire has been bought. These old tombs are sacred trusts, and it is gratifying that in future they are to be carefully preserved by the State. The cost of saving them from ruin ought not to be great, for, though the illustrious living are many, the illustrious dead are few.

Cities of India]

[Archibald Constable & Co., Ltd.

WORKS BY G. W. FORREST, C.I.E.

OPINIONS OF THE PRESS.

SELECTIONS FROM THE LETTERS, DESPATCHES, AND OTHER STATE PAPERS PRESERVED IN THE MILITARY DEPARTMENT OF THE GOVERNMENT OF INDIA, 1857–58.

"Mr. Forrest, the Director of Records to the Government of India, has issued a volume of Military Selections of great interest. It consists of the Mutiny papers preserved in the Military Department in Calcutta. We hope to notice adequately this carefully prepared work at an early date. Although Mr. Forrest travels over well-trodden ground, his patience and accuracy have succeeded in presenting, in a new light, several important facts connected with the Mutiny. His introductory chapter is, as usual with him, an admirable piece of impartial historical narrative. At present we have only space to welcome his work without attempting even to summarise its contents."—*Times' first notice.*

"Mr. Forrest has performed a public service, an important although a painful service, by the publication of the Mutiny papers preserved in the Military Department."—*Times' second notice.*

"Not only has Mr. Forrest, while indulging in no padding and no fireworks, clothed the skeleton of his abstract with the flesh and blood of a 'live' and interested as well as interesting story, but he has managed at the same time to articulate and display that skeleton so clearly, that the reader has no difficulty in recognizing the connection of all the proceedings recounted later under the legal and professional verbiage of courts-martial and despatches."—*Saturday Review.*

"Mr. Forrest's book consists mainly of a selection from the military archives of those papers which exhibit clearly the causes and circumstances of this extraordinary revolt ; showing how it began with premonitory symptoms of mutiny among the troops in Lower Bengal, seemed for the moment to have subsided under vigorous repression, but soon exploded into murderous insurrection at Meerut and Delhi. Then follow the official documents recording in detail the vicissitudes of that brief but fierce campaign, which broke the neck of rebellion by the storm of the Imperial city. To the student of Anglo-Indian history, to all who love graphic particulars of great transactions, to those who desire to know not only what was done but how it was done, these papers will be very welcome and very interesting. More :˜Mr. Forrest has given an introduction, wherein the whole story is told in clear and vivid style, accurately and comprehensively ; with the sympathetic animation of one who describes a sharp and stubborn contest, yet without the fervid exuberance, whether of praise or of pathos, that has been indulged in by certain (otherwise excellent) writers upon the event."—*The National Observer.*

"The narrative in this volume is one of profound and absorbing interest. We say the narrative, because, after all, it is the introductory chapter by Mr. Forrest, rather than the despatches and other documents which fill the greater part of the volume, that will be most attractive to the general reader. And what a narrative it is ! . . . It is this splendid story of which we have the full account in Mr. Forrest's volume, told not only in the graphic narrative of the editor, but in the contemporary despatches of the chief actors in the memorable drama. After reading the narrative, one turns with renewed admiration to the documents on which it is based, only to find ourselves called upon to admire afresh the stern simplicity of these records, the conspicuous absence of anything like self-praise or hysterical exaggeration. Clearly it was only the men who could do such deeds who were capable of writing of them with such studied calmness and self-restraint."—*The Speaker.*

" By a few words Mr. Forrest often illustrates the steady discipline and stern resolve of the British soldier."—*Pall Mall Gazette.*

" The papers now issued comprise all the military records from the first outbreak of disaffection to the siege and storming of Delhi by the English troops. The editor contributes an admirable introduction summarising the despatches."—*The Westminster Gazette.*

SELECTIONS FROM THE LETTERS, DESPATCHES, AND OTHER STATE PAPERS
    PRESERVED IN THE FOREIGN DEPARTMENT OF THE GOVERNMENT OF
    INDIA, 1772–85.

" It is impossible to exaggerate the historical value and importance of the three volumes of Selections."—*Times' first notice.*

" Mr. Forrest, by the publication of these three volumes of records, has, for the first time, converted the acquittal of Warren Hastings by the House of Lords into a complete historical discharge of the high crimes and misdemeanours of which he stood impeached."—*Times' second notice.*

" In publishing the Proceedings of the Secret Select Committee of the Bengal Council from 1772 to 1785, Mr. Forrest enables us to trace the whole course of Hastings' Indian Administration from the day when he took his seat as Governor of Bengal to the day when he resigned the office of Governor-General. . . . More light was needed to dispel the mist that still hung around a great man's memory. The light now turned upon it from Calcutta reveals the full extent of the injustice done to Hastings, both in his lifetime and since his death. These Bengal State Papers deal the death-blow to the group of legends invented by Philip Francis for the use of Burke, and brought into order, and more lasting currency, by Macaulay. . . . In a masterly introduction of a hundred pages, Mr. Forrest condenses the political history of the thirteen years during which Hastings governed Bengal. His narrative bristles with references, and with quotations, not only from the State Papers, but from every known authority of any weight."—*Athenæum.*

" A highly important work, giving for the first time the real history of the governorship of Warren Hastings from the official documents, which had previously been unavailable to refute Macaulay's caricature of the subject. Mr. Forrest has done what the accused statesman was unable to do, and has furnished a vindication, which, however tardy, is absolutely complete, so far at least as the scope of the Selections has extended. The Editor has included a vast number of State Papers extending from 1772, the year in which Hastings became Governor of Bengal, to 1785, when he left India. Together with the Editor's excellent introduction, the matter fills three large volumes, which will be found interesting alike to the Indian specialist and the general student of history."—*Academy.*

" Introduction and documents together form a most valuable addition to the store of learning on which the future historian of the period will have to draw. We rejoice that Mr. Forrest's skill and industry have rescued these invaluable records from the perilous interment of a public Record Room."—*Saturday Review.*

" The reader will, therefore, be grateful to Professor Forrest for the lucid and masterly introduction in which he relates the history of the period covered by the Selections. In performing this task it was impossible for him to avoid constant reference to the attacks made both at the time and afterwards on every act of Hastings' career. He is careful, however, not to allow the personality of that much-badgered ruler to overshadow the exciting incidents of his times. With rare skill and perfect fairness he reviews the whole period, and while showing the relation of the men to the events, it is to the events rather than to the men that he directs our attention. It is this attitude that constitutes the special value of the introduction, for after all, what concerns us moderns in these selections is not so much the character of the men as that of the measures by which the British Empire in India was established."—*Pioneer.*

" It is these proceedings that supply the vindication of the illustrious man who was so much maligned while these papers remained unpublished. He himself said that if these official documents were given to the world his defence would be strengthened. The Directors at that time did not think it fit to grant this request. But now the work has been done, and Hastings' vindication has been made complete. Every future historian will have to take account of these volumes ; and to them Professor Forrest has, as Editor, prefixed a valuable introduction, in which he clearly states the case, and refutes the charges with the aid of the documents published in the body of the work."—*Times of India.*

" Mr. G. W. Forrest has made another valuable and interesting contribution to the store of material of Indian history in the Hastings' papers, which have just been published at Calcutta by authority of the Government of India. The papers extend from 1772, the year in which Warren Hastings became Governor of Bengal, to the 1st of February, 1785, the day on which he resigned the office of Governor-General. They thus cover a momentous period in the history of British rule in India—a period abounding in wars and negotiations and intrigues, and in conflicts in Council more embittered even than those in the open field. Here the story of the Rohilla Campaign, which Macaulay has told with highly embellished vindictiveness, may be read in the dispassionate simplicity of original documents. More light—if more light were needed after Sir James Stephen's elaborate investigation of the whole affair—is thrown upon the story of Nundcomar and of Hastings' relation to that high-bred malefactor. Hastings' conflicts and misunderstandings with the Governments of Bombay and Madras are represented in the dry light of papers for the most part new even to the historical student. The story of the Benares rebellion, as well as that story of the Begums of Oudh, upon which Burke lavished all the resources of his brilliant but cruel rhetoric, are told at length, not as lucidly perhaps as Macaulay had told them, but in a way nevertheless which carries with it all the living interest of first-hand testimony, and which will mislead no one who knows how to weigh historical evidence. They are all official papers, it is true, but all of them relate to events by which modern India has been moulded and built up, and they are eminently readable. Of Mr. Forrest's performance of the duty entrusted to him by Government, nothing but praise need be said. So far as we have seen in a necessarily rapid survey of the three volumes, the selection has been made with great care and judgment, the whole of the papers printed having a direct and important bearing upon the leading events of Hastings' administration. And there are few of them which will not make themselves excellent reading apart from their value as *mémoires pour servir.* In an introduction of just one hundred pages Mr. Forrest surveys the whole of the field covered by his three volumes. The *Introduction* is all that it ought to be. It is a piece of clear, crisp, and concise writing, in which the Editor keeps closely to his subject, avoiding the temptation, which must often have been strong, to tell himself the story, which could properly be told only by the papers with which he was dealing."
—*Bombay Gazette.*

THE ADMINISTRATION OF THE MARQUIS OF LANSDOWNE, VICEROY AND GOVERNOR-GENERAL OF INDIA, 1888–94.

" Valuable and interesting."—*Times*.

" Into a thin octavo volume of fewer than seventy pages, Mr. G. W. Forrest has compressed a full, clear, and faithful summary of Lord Lansdowne's Indian Administration, from the close of 1888 to the beginning of 1894. As Director of Records to the Governor of India, Mr. Forrest adds to his many other qualifications the special knowledge and experience which such a task demands."—*Athenæum*.

ADMINISTRATION OF WARREN HASTINGS, 1772–85. REVIEWED AND ILLUSTRATED FROM ORIGINAL DOCUMENTS.

" Another work of capital importance to all students of the history of British India is the Administration of Warren Hastings, 1772–85, Reviewed and Illustrated from Original Documents by G. W. Forrest, B.A., (Calcutta, Office of the Superintendent of Government Printing, India.) This is a reprint in a single volume of the Introduction prefixed to the three folio volumes of ' Letters, Despatches, and other State Papers, preserved in the Foreign Department of the Government of India, 1771–85,' which were printed by official authority and edited by Mr. Forrest. This important publication has already been fully noticed in our columns, and its unrivalled value as a contribution to the authentic history of Warren Hastings and his administration has been universally recognized."—*Times*.

" A few words of special praise were reserved for the ' masterly ' Introduction in which Professor Forrest worked up his new materials into a full review of Hastings' political career as Governor of Bengal and Governor-General. This introduction he has now reprinted in a separate volume of 317 pages octavo, followed by an appendix of fifty pages and an index of thirty-six. In its present form we may heartily commend it to all those readers—and there must be many such—who, ' though they have not the leisure to study official writings, take an interest in the great ruler who, by his genius and courage, raised the Company from being a body of merchants and adventurers into the most powerful state in the politics of India.' "—*Athenæum*.

" Mr. Forrest has done well to reprint his Introduction to the State Papers bearing on the career of Warren Hastings. He has succeeded in showing conclusively that Macaulay was completely misled by Mill, and that the celebrated Essay on Hastings must be regarded as an eloquent piece of romance, so far as several of its main features are concerned."—*Manchester Guardian*.

SELECTIONS FROM THE STATE PAPERS PRESERVED IN THE BOMBAY SECRETARIAT (HOME SERIES).

" The two volumes now before us deal with the great Company's domestic affairs in India from 1630 to 1788, the year before Tippoo provoked the wrath of Cornwallis by his attack upon Travancore. ' In the letters and narratives of the chief actors we have here related,' says the able Editor, ' the earliest domestic history of our Indian Empire.' In these volumes we can trace the gradual change in the servants of the Company from factors to soldiers and rulers of men. They show us how the modest little factory founded at Surat in 1614 proved to be the germ of a dominion nearly as large and populous as all Europe.

" In an introduction of fifty-two pages Mr. Forrest provides an excellent historical summary of the period embraced in these two columns.

* * * * *

" The Editor's share in the production of these volumes cannot be too highly praised." . . .—*Athenæum*, June 9, 1888.

" The selection has been uniformly judicious. The editing is careful, and if there is a repetition here and there this will enable the student of manners and customs to be quite certain that he does not depend on an isolated fact and on a single row of figures for any adornments and illustrations of history."—*Saturday Review.*

" They contain an immense amount of curious and valuable information, not only about the commercial and political affairs of the East India Company, but also on the subjects of the mode of life followed by Englishmen resident in the country and of their relations with the natives. . . . . . . These volumes contain much new material towards the history of the East India Company which is sure to be written sooner or later, now that our latest investigations of the manuscript records, still happily existing both in London and in India, are establishing the incompleteness and frequent inaccuracy of the hitherto accepted standard work—' Bruce's Annals.' Among those who have brought this hidden wealth of knowledge to light, no one deserves more credit than Mr. Forrest."—*Asiatic Quarterly Review.*

" These extracts will show that Mr. Forrest's Selections are full of interest and historical value."—*Times.*

" The last volume dealt with the Mahrattas from the time of Shivaji to their defeat at Assaye. The two volumes we now receive belong to the ' Home Series,' and are even more interesting, for they comprise all the important documents regarding the internal administration of the Bombay Presidency, from the foundation of the Factory at Surat to Wellington's great victory, which made the English masters of India. In these documents, which have been transcribed and printed with the greatest care, we can, as the Editor says, trace the gradual change in the Company's servants from factors to soldiers and statesmen, while we have the domestic history of the Indian Empire in the very words and quaint spelling of the men who made it. It is quite impossible in one short article to present any real idea of a great book that fills a thousand large quarto pages. But the volumes are well indexed, and with the help of index and Professor Forrest's very admirable introduction, we will try to give a short account of the beginnings of Bombay."—*Times of India*, October 6, 1887.

" What is wanting in all such books, and especially for the comfort of the ordinary reader, a thread connecting and explaining the great variety of incident, is supplied by Professor Forrest in an introduction, where the events that happened are described in a style concise but picturesque, interesting but accurate."—*Pioneer*, December 5, 1887.

" The two most recent volumes which form the first and second in the Home series are, in their way, quite as important as the collection of papers relating to the Mahrattas which Mr. Forrest brought out a couple of years since."—*Bombay Gazette*, January 21, 1888.

SELECTIONS FROM THE STATE PAPERS PRESERVED IN THE BOMBAY SECRE-
TARIAT (MAHRATTA SERIES).

" In a quarto volume of more than seven hundred pages, Mr. Forrest, of the Deccan College and the Bombay University, has brought together the firstfruits of his researches among the mass of records preserved in the Bombay Secretariat. By means of these records he has traced anew ' the history of the Mahrattas from their founder Shivaji, who welded a few tribes into a great nation, to their defeat by the matchless genius of Wellington.' The documents which form the bulk of the volume record, in fact, our dealings with the Mahrattas from 1739 to 1803—that is, from the siege of Bassein to the battle of Assaye.

" So carefully has he discharged it to the smallest detail, that there is hardly a misprint noticeable in the whole volume.

" In his ' Short Historical Introduction ' of thirty-four quarto pages Professor Forrest has extracted the pith and essence of the raw material contained in the body of the book. This clear, lively and connected narrative of the Company's dealings with the Mahrattas during sixty eventful years shows how skilfully, with how much care and judgment, the Editor has discharged his difficult task. Only those who have waded through the original records can fully appreciate the skill and labour bestowed on a summary which may be read with interest and advantage by many who might not choose to explore further. Among the new matter reserved for this opening essay is the letter in which Lieutenant Pruen, of the Bombay Marine, describes in sober, official language an exploit rivalling that of Sir Richard Grenville on board the *Revenge*."— *Athenæum*.

" A considerable portion of these State Papers is rather the source of history than history itself. But Mr. Forrest has written a preliminary chapter in which he connects one event with another, and gives to the whole work something of unity, consistency, and design. . . . But arguments on this and other suggestive topics should be studied carefully in Mr. Forrest's valuable contribution by those who wish for something better than a mere superficial sketch of early empire in India and a spiteful caricature of the character and aims of its founders."—*Saturday Review*.

" Mr. Forrest has performed his part of the labour of producing these records in a readable form with great skill and equal success. The series promises to occupy an important position among the historical *pièces justificatives* of India, and we shall look forward with pleasant anticipations to the appearance of the successors of this volume."—*Asiatic Quarterly Review*.

" Here, in a handy form, we have all the original documents illustrating the Mahratta period in the conquest of India. Professor Forrest has done his work admirably. The documents are carefully edited, and the introduction is a model of concise, yet spirited writing."—*Times of India*.

" Professor Forrest's Selections from the State Papers in the Bombay Secretariat are so arranged that they form an excellent history of the Mahratta confederacy from its first consolidation under Shivaji to the battle of Assaye. The plan followed is similar to that chosen by Carlyle in his edition of *Cromwell's Letters and Speeches*. The story is told as much as possible by ' the letters and narratives of the chief actors.' But it is always difficult to give a perfectly intelligible and connected history out of original documents alone, and in the present case the difficulty of so doing would have been intensified by the fact that the Editor had to confine his selections for the most part to such documents as had never before been published. But from the circumstances of the case the documents selected for publication would, without a commentary, have been only partially intelligible to the ordinary reader. To supply this want the Editor has given in his introduction a graphic sketch of Mahratta history, by which the letters quoted in the body of the work are bound together into a connected whole, so that the work will not only be a storehouse of materials ready for future historians to use, but is itself an interesting and readable account of one of the most important periods of the history of Western India."—*Pioneer*.

" The substantial quarto which Mr. Forrest has just brought out under the auspices of the Government of Bombay represents painstaking and continuous work, which every future historian of the growth of British rule in Western India will heartily appreciate. Mr. Forrest, as a mere glance at his book will show, must have made courageous flights into the realm of ' Dryasdust ' before producing a collection of papers of such abiding historical interest as these. For in work of this kind the worker's merit is only half shown by what he puts in print : one must think of the ponderous files of manuscript which the careful Editor has rejected before one can quite appreciate the industry and selective judgment shown in the printed pages."—*Bombay Gazette*.

" . . . Professor Forrest's volume contains reprints of those clear and far-seeing State Papers which were compiled by Mr. Elphinstone to inform his superiors or to explain his methods of government. They are by no means prolix, and the style is most happy. An admirable mean between official exactness and simple unaffected narrative. The spirited little memoir which Professor Forrest has prefixed to his volume is highly appreciative of Mr. Elphinstone's character, and efficiently serves its purpose of placing an outline of his life before the reader."—*Quarterly Review.*

" . . . Mr. Forrest's Selections illustrate the life very well indeed."— *Pall Mall Gazette.*

" . . . The chief State Papers by Mountstuart Elphinstone which Mr. Forrest has collected and published are the well-known Minute on Education written in 1824, a narrative of the events which led to the equally well-known conflict with the Peishwah, while Elphinstone was at Poona, and a report on the territories conquered from him. . . . But these papers are still models of clear, unrhetorical statement. Elphinstone was in most respects, as we have already said, an example to Anglo-Indian officials. In none was he more so than in his attitude towards the native populations of Hindoostan, which these papers place in a pleasant light."— *Spectator.*

SEPOY GENERALS (William Blackwood and Sons).

" A writer who recalls in stirring language the deeds of the great men who won the Empire is deserving of a double welcome. . . . There are names amongst them which stir the blood of Anglo-Indians as the bugle stirs the war-horse turned out to grass. . . . They are all recalled to life in this admirable volume, by a master of all the enthralling mystery of the English Orient."—*Daily Telegraph.*

" Mr. G. W. Forrest was well inspired in revising and republishing these studies of Sepoy Generals. His lively style lends play to his erudition, and he has the one supreme merit in the narrative of stirring events— that of a keen eye for an effective quotation from contemporary records."— *Pall Mall Gazette.*

" Mr. Forrest, in his admirable *Sepoy Generals*, has sketched commanders of either kind. Wellington and Roberts belong to the history of the world. Herbert Edwardes and John Jacob did all their work and won all their glory in India itself. But Mr. Forrest has drawn them all with equal skill. . . . He knows the history of our great dependency as few living writers know it ; he is as familiar with the Indian records as most men are with the daily paper ; and it is impossible to read a page of his book without recognizing the grasp which he has of a subject peculiarly his own."—*Spectator.*

" Mr. Forrest, who displays a lively affection for the natives of India, is always careful to bring out every good point in their character, and to record their gallantry in action. . . . The descriptions of battles are spirited, which is a great thing, and, what is even less common, they are intelligible."—*Standard.*

" His work is altogether invigorating and delightful."—*St. James Budget.*

" The subject is intensely interesting ; it is dealt with in a bright an interesting way within managable bounds, and the author has kept the general reader steadily in view. On the other hand, these biographical studies are the result of long and careful original research carried on by the writer in circumstances peculiarly favourable to the acquisition of accurate information. For this reason the book is worthy the attention of the serious historical student, while at the same time it is put in a form

A A

which will attract the casual reader and provide him with entertainment as well as instruction in a period of our Imperial existence which is liable to be overlooked nowadays. The Scotsman, Mr. Forrest, has put together an interesting and valuable book comprising succinct sketches of those great British soldiers and administrators who have helped to give Great Britain her Empire of India."—*Irish Times.*

" A noteworthy feature of Mr. Forrest's book is that throughout it he makes an earnest endeavour not only to commemorate the heroism of the British soldier but also the gallantry of the Sepoy. He bids us remember that a handful of Englishmen could never have conquered India if we had not been assisted by the bravery and devotion of the native armies of Bengal, Bombay and Madras. *Sepoy Generals* is an excellent book and should be widely read."—*Sketch.*

" We heartily commend his admirable work to our readers, none of whom will rise from the perusal of it without gaining much information and an increased feeling of national pride that their country has produced such men as these."—*Broad Arrow.*

" All are well worth perusal, but probably the one to which most readers will turn in the first place is that of the present Commander-in-Chief of our Army. They will there find an admirable account of Lord Roberts' services in the Indian Mutiny, based on official records and contemporary literature ; a story of the Afghan Campaign mainly told from Lord Roberts' own despatches, which the author had occasion closely to examine as he was at one time asked to edit the official history of the war ; and finally an account of Lord Roberts' share in the South African campaign, mainly based on his own despatches."—*United Service Gazette.*

" It is written with equal spirit, knowledge and discretion."—*Navy and Army Illustrated.*

" An admirably planned and executed book of military biography."— *Military Mail.*

" Close reading as the volume is, the pages are brim full of interest from start to finish."—*Naval and Military Record.*

" Of the quality of Mr. Forrest's book nothing but good can be said. . . . We should be glad, for many reasons, if more currency could be given to Mr. Forrest's volume. It is essentially a work which is calculated to do good both in India and in England."—*Times of India.*

Butler & Tanner, The Selwood Printing Works, Frome, and London.

Books on India and the East

Love and Life Behind the Purdah

By CORNELIA SORABJI

Sketches and Stories of Indian Native Life, with an Introduction by the
MARCHIONESS OF DUFFERIN.   Crown 8vo.   3s. 6d.

" Miss Sorabji's work is calculated greatly to help forward the improvement in the condition of
Indian women, and this high purpose, added to the genuine merit of the writing, will cause the
volume to be read with very real interest."—*Bookman.*

An Autumn Tour in Western Persia

By LADY DURAND

Illustrated from Photographs.   Demy 8vo.   7s. 6d. net.

" Hill and valley, river and stream, houses and gardens, and the ways and appearances of the
inhabitants are brightly described in this agreeable book.   This happy and picturesque record
of travel is not only good to read. but is adorned with one of the best selections of photographs
we have yet seen."—*Morning Post.*

"Pleasantly written, well illustrated, and furnished with a good map."—*Field.*

"Excellent and animated description of a most interesting, but little known country."
—*Athenæum.*

Asia and Europe By MEREDITH TOWNSEND

Being Studies presenting the conclusions formed by the Author in a long life devoted
to the subject of the relations between Asia and Europe.   Demy 8vo.   Price 10s. 6d. net.

" If I could only afford to buy one book this summer I should certainly choose Mr. Meredith
Townsend's."—*British Weekly.*

" The public interested in that country (India) will do will to study the pages of this volume."
—*Athenæum.*

" It would be difficult to exaggerate the interest of this remarkable book.   In it Mr. Meredith
Townsend deals with some of the most poignant problems that confront the British people as
the ruler of the greatest and most Asiatic of the Empires of Asia."—*Spectator.*

Ancient India as Described in Classical Literature

By J. W. McCRINDLE, M.A., LL.D.

Demy 8vo.   7s. 6d. net.

" For Students of Indian History, Dr. McCrindle has performed a great service in bringing
together his collection.   To any one who has the leisure to examine it, such material for history
possesses a fascination that does not belong to a finished history.   It gives us the delight of being
our own historians.   Besides that, it transports us to the ancient world in a way that no modern
historian can possibly do."—*India.*

Burma Under British Rule

By JOHN NISBET, Author of " British Forest Trees," " Studies in Forestry," etc.

Two Volumes, demy 8vo, with frontispiece to each volume, Maps and Plans.
Price 32s. net.

Kalhana's Rajatarangini

By M. A. STEIN

A Chronicle of the Kings of Kashmir, with three Maps.   Translated, with an
Introduction, Commentary and Appendices.   Two Volumes.   £3 3s. net.

A. CONSTABLE & CO., LTD., WESTMINSTER

355

Books on India and the East

ASIA AND EUROPE

By MEREDITH TOWNSEND. Being Studies presenting the conclusions formed by the Author in a long life devoted to the subject of the relations between Asia and Europe. Demy 8vo. Price 10s. 6d. net.

BURMA UNDER BRITISH RULE

By JOHN NISBET. Author of "British Forest Trees," "Studies in Forestry," etc. Two Volumes, Demy 8vo, with frontispiece to each volume, Maps and Plans. Price 32s. net.

KALHANA'S RAJATARANGINI

By M. A. STEIN. A Chronicle of the Kings of Kashmir, with Three Maps. Translated, with an Introduction, Commentary and Appendices. Two Volumes. £3 3s. net.

ANCIENT INDIA AS DESCRIBED IN CLASSICAL LITERATURE

By J. W. McCRINDLE, M.A., LL.D. Demy 8vo, 7s. 6d. net.

NEW AND CHEAPER EDITION

AMONG THE HIMALAYAS

By MAJOR L. A. WADDELL, LL.D., Author of "The Buddhism of Tibet." With over 100 Illustrations. Large Crown 8vo, 6s.

BELOW THE SURFACE

Sketches of Life Among the Natives. By MAJOR-GENERAL FENDALL CURRIE, Late Commissioner of Oudh. Crown 8vo, 6s.

THE CHRONOLOGY OF INDIA : From the Earliest Times to the Beginning of the Sixteenth Century

By C. MABEL DUFF (Mrs. W. R. Rickmers). Demy 8vo, 15s. net.

THE RISE OF PORTUGUESE POWER IN INDIA

(1497–1550). By R. S. WHITEWAY (Bengal Civil Service), retired. Demy 8vo, 15s. net.

2 IMPERIAL RULE IN INDIA

By THEODORE MORISON, M.A., of the Muhamadan College, Aligarh, V.W.P., India. Crown 8vo, 3s. 6d.

TWO NATIVE NARRATIVES OF THE MUTINY IN DELHI

Translated from the Originals by the late CHARLES THEOPHILUS METCALFE, C.S.I. (Bengal Civil Service). Demy 8vo, with large Map. 12s.

GOLD, SPORT, AND COFFEE PLANTING IN MYSORE

Being the thirty-eight years' experience of a Mysore Planter. By ROBERT H. ELLIOTT. Crown 8vo, 7s. 6d.

PROBLEMS OF THE FAR EAST : Japan, Corea, China

By LORD CURZON OF KEDLESTON, Viceroy of India. With numerous Illustrations and Maps. Extra Crown 8vo, 7s. 6d.

LOVE AND LIFE BEHIND THE PURDAH

An Insight into the Hidden Life of Indian Women. By CORNELIA SORABJI. With Photogravure Portrait. Cloth gilt, gilt top, 3s. 6d.

A. CONSTABLE & Co., Ltd., WESTMINSTER